SUPPLEMENTAL REPORT OF JOINT COMMITTEE

OF THE

GENERAL ASSEMBLY OF LOUISIANA

ON THE

Conduct of the Late Elections,

AND THE

CONDITION OF PEACE AND GOOD ORDER

IN THE STATE.

NEW ORLEANS:
A. L. LEE, STATE PRINTER.
1869.

REPORT.

NEW ORLEANS, January 5, 1869.

To the Honorable the President and Members of the Senate, and the Honorable the Speaker and Members of the House of Representatives of the State of Louisiana, in General Assembly convened:

Since the submission of our former report, of date of September 24, 1868, the General Assembly passed the following joint resolution entitled,

A Joint Resolution relating to the sitting of the Joint Committee on the late election and the condition of peace and good order of the State during the recess or adjournment of the General Assembly.

Be it resolved by the Senate and House of Representatives of the State of Louisiana, in General Assembly convened, That the Joint Committee upon the conduct of the late election and the present condition of peace and order in the State, be and they are hereby authorized to continue in session during the interval between the recess or adjournment of the session of the General Assembly and its next session, with all the powers hitherto conferred upon them; *provided,* that its members shall only receive their per diem for the number of days they are actually in session and shall not be entitled to any mileage.

(Signed) CHAS. W. LOWELL,
Speaker of the House of Representatives.

(Signed) OSCAR J. DUNN,
Lieutenant Governor and President of the Senate.

Approved October 21, 1868.

(Signed) H. C. WARMOTH,
Governor of the State of Louisiana.

In compliance therewith your Committee continued their investigations into the present condition of peace and order in the State during the interval between the last and the present sessions. They have the honor to submit the following report of the result of their labors:

Your Committee would earnestly ask the attention of the good people of the State to the following statement, praying a dispassionate judgment thereon, and not deprecating any just criticism, but to the contrary inviting it. If they have erred either in the credence which they have attached to the evidence which appears hereafter, or in the conclusions at which they have arrived they welcome any scrutiny of the former, however rigid, or any refutation of the latter. It is to the uncontroverted facts about which there is no dispute, to which with all good feeling they invite the candid attention of every good citizen without regard to party, and upon which they ask a disinterested and honest verdict.

The history of the last twelve months presents a frightful record, such as has never been furnished before in the history of nations without leaving an indelible blot upon the character of the generation of which it was written.

The facts elicited by this report rival in atrocity and in the exhibition of the basest of human passions any thing that can be found in the annals of the darkest age of the Christian era, and the day will come when the relation of their horrors will curdle the blood of whole generations, and men will wonder that monsters who committed such crimes were permitted to live among mankind.

The total number of murders reported by this committee in their first report was two hundred and four (204). The number included in the present report is five hundred and eighty (580). The number of murders as taken from Brevet Major General Hatch's record for the months of September, October and November, 1868, is two hundred and ninety-seven (297). Some of the latter are probably repetitions of those included in the committee's reports. On the other hand neither the committee nor General Hatch have been able to obtain full reports of all the murders committed in the State. In some of the most violent parishes, the terrorism has been so great that no testimony has been received from them at all.

The total number of the murders committed in the State within the last twelve months reported, is over one thousand (1000).

The total number of killed, wounded, robbed and otherwise outraged during the same period of which we have accounts is one thousand eight hundred and eighty-seven (1887). Is the continuance of such a state of affairs compatible with the maintenance of law and order, with the interest of the people of this State or of any class of people among us, or with the dignity, self respect and Christian character of any community.

GENERAL REVIEW OF EVENTS SINCE SEPTEMBER 24, 1868.

After the adjournment of the General Assembly the excitement on the part of a portion of our population which first broke out into mob violence, in the riots and massacre of September 22, 1868, rapidly increased. Large mobs occurred and great numbers of colored men and white Republicans were slaughtered successively in the parish of Orleans on September 22, and October 24, 1868; of St. Landry, on September 28th, 1868; of Bossier, on September 30, 1868; of Caddo, on or about October 12, 1868; of Jefferson, on October 23, 1868, and of St. Bernard, on October 25, 1868. On the night of the 28th of October, 1868, Lafayette Square in front of the City Hall, was, a little after dark, quietly filled by bands of armed men who noiselessly filed into its inclosures; these were soon reinforced by large crowds of unorganized men until one immense mob filled the square and adjacent streets. A delegation waited upon the Superintendent of Metropolitan Police, and informed him that they had come to take forcible possession of the police station. This mob was addressed in friendly words by General Steedman, Colonel R. N. Ogden, a member of the Senate, and others. The burden of their speeches was not the unlawfulness or criminality of these proceedings, but expressions of hope and assurance that all their ends would speedily be attained by the election of Seymour and Blair.

Democratic processions marched through the streets in open defiance of General Rousseau's orders. The gun stores, during these disturbances, were thronged with streams of men, who, with or without money, were furnished with arms and ammunition.

In most parts of the State a systematic series of outrages, robberies and murders were committed on the loyal people with the avowed intention of intimidating, and thus forcing, them to abstain from voting, and of driving out of the country the Republican leaders. Organized efforts were set on foot to compel the laborers of the State to vote the Democratic ticket, under penalty of not obtaining employment, and even of being discharged from work in violation of existing contracts. Colored men were threatened with death unless they would accept of what were termed "protection papers" setting forth that they were members of some Democratic club, and would wear Seymour and Blair badges. Boards of Registration and Supervisors of Election were threatened repeatedly, in a large number of parishes, with death, shot at, and by various lawless proceedings either driven from their parishes or prevented from making a complete and fair registration. The advice of prominent and influential newspapers was inflammatory, and insidious, and calculated to aggravate, rather than assuage, the passions of the bad and tumult uous portions of the people. The civil authorities in many parishes seem to have been used only as additional machinery for the commission of further and worse outrages upon those whom it was their duty to protect. The committee are informed that in some parishes a man could not live twenty four hours, who would attempt to prosecute parties guilty of these murders; that in others an affidavit would no sooner be made out against the guilty parties, than the officer himself, before whom it was made would send information of the facts to the accused parties, that they might escape. These outrages were not the work of rowdies and roughs; their influential movers and backers were men called respectable and influential.

There was a fixed predetermination on the part of a portion of the white people of this State, to resist, by all means, fair or foul, the continuance of the State Government, based upon impartial suffrage.

Many property owners and business men encouraged them in this design.

The brutality of the outrages which attended the carrying of these purposes into effect and the disposition to conceal and apologize for them, are only to be accounted for on the ground of barbarism. The patience and forbearance of the colored people under these outrages is remarkable; that they did not spring from cowardice is shown by the devotion which they have manifested towards their friends, and the readiness with which they have exposed themselves in their defence. They manifested no desire to provoke disturbances, or to encroach upon the rights of others. A war of races is an impossibility. There has been slaughter of the negroes by the whites, but there has been nothing like war, simply because there must always be two parties to a fight. The heroism of this people as illustrated by many incidents recorded in this report, vindicates their claim to stand alongside of any free people. It must be observed however, that by reason of continued outrages without protection, the colored people are beginning to lose confidence in the government.

The charge of "negro riots" was hypocritical; it was intended solely to arouse the passions of the base and turbulent, so as to make them ready instruments of designing political leaders. There never existed a more peaceable and inoffensive population in any State than the colored people of this State. A negro uprising or riot, for a general onslaught upon the whites, was, to use the language of Macaulay, "no more to be apprehended than a rising of the women and children against the men." Leading Democrats pledged themselves to proscribe socially and in all business relations white and colored Republicans. In this connection it will be apposite to notice a circular issued by the Democratic Central Committee. The following is an extract from this extraordinary political document:

CIRCULAR OF THE DEMOCRATIC CENTRAL COMMITTEE.

DEAR SIR— * * * * * * * * *
and we would earnestly declare to our fellow citizens our opinion that even the most implacable and ill-disposed of the negro population, those who show the worst spirit towards the white people, are not half so much deserving our aversion and non-intercourse with them as the debased whites who encourage and aid them, and who become through their votes the office-holding oppressors of the people. Whatever of resentment you have, should be felt toward the latter and not against the colored men. But in no case should you permit this resentment to go further than to withdraw from them all countenance, association and patronage, and thwart every effort they may make to maintain a business and social foothold among you.

(Signed) THOS. L. MACON,
President State Central Committee.

(Signed) J. E. AUSTIN,
A. B. BACON,
THEO. F. THIENAMAN,
J. H. HALSEY,
Committee.

The planters in East Feliciana parish formed an association whose objects and workings will be seen by the following copy of their regulations:

Resolved, That we will not employ for the future any freedman who shall hereafter vote the Radical ticket, nor will we rent lands, advance supplies, or assist in any manner any such persons. A certificate from the employers will be necessary to show that any freedman has voted the Democratic ticket, or has not voted at all. We will always give our preference to those who voted the Democratic ticket and are members of the Democratic clubs.

Resolved, That we will not patronize any professional man or trade with any merchant who does not bind himself to be governed by the above regulations.

The planters in Rapides parish also resolved "hereafter not to rent, lease or give any portion of their lands to freedmen, reserving, however, the right to settle known conservative freedmen, who are to be under the eye and direction of the planters or landholders; also, that any planter or landholder among us who is so unmindful of what is due to himself and the society in which he lives as to let out lands in opposition to the will of a large majority of our people as above expressed, deserves to be and will be branded as a *public enemy and treated accordingly.*"*

In the parish of Pointe Coupée, certain citizens addressed the following letter to C. Kohn, Esq., of this city, the owner of a plantation in that parish, who proposed to rent it to certain parties. It smacks so strongly of the old slave customs, that even Democratic papers of this city have felt constrained to condemn it:

WILLIAMSPORT, POINT COUPEE, LA.
December 1, 1868.

MR. C. KOHN, Esq.,
New Orleans, La.

The citizens at large have had a meeting for the purpose of considering the condition of the labor of the country. We, therefore, as a committee of three, have been appointed to notify you, that you are about to rent your land known as the "White Place," situated on Bayou Latanache, to parties who are obnoxious to the community at large, viz: Tounoir & Co. We, therefore, as a committee appointed for the purpose above mentioned, request that the land in question should not be so rented. We find, from sad experience, that it is bad policy to rent land to the colored people where no white persons are on the place. It is, therefore, the wish of the community that no land should be so rented. *You will, therefore, take due notice and govern yourself accordingly.*

Yours with respect,

(Signed) F. M. YOIST,
H. W. COYLE,
JAMES DENNIS.

In some of the less enlightened portions of this State, political speeches to the negroes, provided they were on the Republican side, were and are to this day termed "incendiary."

The only thing that has prevented us from experiencing more than the horrors of St. Bartholomew, has been the righteous fear which the leaders of these mobs and appeals to violence, have had of the impending judgment of the North and the length of the arm of Congress.

THE MURDERS OF COLONEL POPE AND JUDGE CHASE.

On October 17, 1868, Colonel Pope, sheriff of St. Mary parish, and an ex-United States officer, of high character, and Valentine Chase, parish Judge, were publicly assassinated in the town of Franklin by an armed body of men. The particulars are given so far as they can now safely be published under the head of that parish.

These were purely political murders. Their perpetrators roam at large, though well known to the officers and citizens of that parish. In this connection it is pertinent to state that the names of several parties who are acquainted with the names of the murderers, and the details of the murders are known to the committee. But under the solemn assurances of these gentlemen, that if they should disclose the facts, their lives would not be safe even in this city, and in compliance with their earnest appeals not to be compelled to jeopardize their safety, and that of their dependent families, the committee have not deemed it proper to insist at this time upon their testimony. Their names however will be given to the proper authorities at any time that a judicial investigation becomes possible.

Your committee are informed that a Mr. John Hunt, of St. Mary parish, has been heard to boast that he knows all about these murders. It is proper here to state, that it is believed from the declarations of many parties, that the immediate cause of Colonel Pope's murder, was the rage of certain parties of that parish against him for his courage in replying to the circular of your committee which was issued to all parish and judicial officers, in accordance with your orders. That the public may judge of the amount of provocation deemed sufficient in St. Mary parish to justify murder, we here insert Colonel Popes entire letter:

FRANKLIN, PARISH OF ST. MARY. LA.
September 3, 1868.

Committee on the late election and condition of order in the State.

"GENTLEMEN—In reply to your request in a circular dated September 1, which is just received, I have the honor to submit the following:

"No murders in this parish have come to my knowledge, and but one case of personal violence being made, although threats have often been made.

"One Arnbrime, a claim agent, and his servant, colored, were taken from their boarding house in Jeanerett's by a band of armed men, at midnight in June last, blindfolded and carried to the timber where they were threatened with instant death unless they would promise to never step their foot into the town again.

"This I received from the parties, and both are probably now in the city and will testify to the same.

"The present condition of the parish is bad; there appears to be a settled determination on the part of the leaders of the Democratic party in the parish to draw out by every means in their power all white persons who differ with them in politics.

"This is not only expressed by their bearing, by the gross insults one receives daily on the streets, the misrepresentations and scurrulous abuse by the parish paper, but by threats that come to our ears.

"One way of carrying out their designs is to break up the club organizations, so as to control the colored vote. This, so far, has not been a success, although the most strenuous efforts have been made. The gentleman that has furnished the room in which the club in Franklin has met the last few months, has received warning that his life and that of his wife, were placed in peril by persisting in that course, and if he did not desist, his property also would be burned to the ground.

"The gentleman in telling me that he could not furnish the room longer, said he would not care for their threats if he could only get justice, but he knew under the present condition of things that would be an impossibility, as he already had experience.

"In the meantime affairs are getting worse, the abuse that at first only received from a few is now getting general, so that it is impossible for myself, or any one known to sympathize with me, to stir out without being insulted."

Your committee are informed that there are parties, now in Franklin, Parish St. Mary, who publicly justify the murders of Colonel Pope and Judge Chase, on the ground that they had vilified the people of that parish.

We call especial attention to the following atrocious paragraph, referring to these murders, which appeared in the New Orleans *Times* of the 24th October, 1868:

"The homicide of certain persons who have been installed exclusively by the votes of the negroes and a few white strangers and outcasts, in highly responsible judicial offices in the country are due to the exasperation produced by a system of oppression, wrong, insult and spoliation, which were never exercised towards a brave and spirited people without producing like results."

THE MASSACRE IN THE PARISH OF ORLEANS IN SEPTEMBER AND OCTOBER, 1868.

The excitement in the city of New Orleans first broke out into violence and bloodshed on the night of September 22, 1868.

The testimony of A. P. Dumas, a respected and honored citizen and old resident, shows the spirit that was abroad, and the momentary danger in which all prominent Republicans stood.

From this time until the last of October there was a continuous and high excitement.

Republican processions were continually assaulted and fired into.

The streets at night were patrolled by armed men who marauded, plundered and killed at will.

Of the numbers thus clandestinely murdered no account can be obtained.

Policemen were ambushed and shot while on duty.

Private citizens were stabbed and assassinated.

The gun shops were emptied of their arms and ammunition by crowds of men.

Armed bands of desperadoes paraded in front of the residence of the General commanding the United States troops, and fired at defenseless men and women.

Flags bearing the words "No Quarter" were borne at the head of these bands.

Although during these disturbances it is incontestably established that the attacks were exclusively by white Democrats upon Republicans, yet an attempt was made by a prominent citizen to ring a general alarm on the bells of the city, upon the hollow pretext of a "negro riot." It is now clear that such an act would have precipitated a general massacre of colored and white Republicans. It was only prevented by the coolness and firmness of the Superintendent of the Metropolitan police, Major Williamson.

On October 24, another preconcerted and unprovoked assault was made upon a Grant and Colfax procession, in which a number were killed and wounded.

After this the excitement was greatly intensified; Grant club rooms were broken open and sacked.

The houses of prominent Republicans were visited and searched, with the intention of killing them.

The nightly murders and robberies increased; numbers were compelled to flee from their residences and remain concealed for weeks.

Threats were openly made against the lives of citizens.

The General commanding informed those coming to him for protection that he could not afford it, and another United States General gave it as his opinion that the officer in command would be justified in "withdrawing his troops, as he would do in the face of a superior force." The rioters seemed to share in this opinion.

The secret organization of the Knights of the White Camelia met and drilled with arms nightly, and it was their boast that at the looked for signal they could demolish the United States troops in fifteen minutes.

An armed mob besieged the office of the Superintendent of the Metropolitan Police and demanded its surrender.

A colored man was tied up and shot at as a target till he was killed.

Many of the Boards of Registration were attacked, their offices sacked and the registrars themselves compelled to suspend their work and to fly for their lives. Colored men were fired at from the street cars.

A Senator speaking in the midst of these tumults and riots to their authors, termed them "the brink of a volcano—one of the greatest political convulsions that the world has ever witnessed," evincing a comprehension of the true objects and extent of the disturbances which coincides remarkably with the views of your committee.

The dead bodies of the murdered were shot and otherwise mangled.

General Rousseau having received ample orders from Washington to preserve the peace, issued an order, dated October 28, forbidding all political processions. In defiance of this order Democratic clubs continued to march through the streets, and that very evening an armed mob filled one of the principal squares of the city and adjacent streets.

During this time, about the thirty-first of October, General Rousseau paid a visit to the "Innocent" club and made there an address, which will be found in another part of this report.

The total number known to be killed during these massacres is sixty-three (63); a much larger number is estimated.

Under this condition of things it is not strange that the Republicans in a mass refused to attend or to acknowledge the election as legal or binding, notwithstanding the assurances of the Democrats that they would be permitted so to do peaceably.

A permission which depended upon the promise of the men who had scarcely left off slaughtering them was not reassuring; especially was this the case, when the commanding General of the United States troops could give them no higher guarantee of safety than the promise of their persecutors.

They had been robbed of their registration certificates, and almost two-thirds of them had been prevented by violence from registering. The fraud was complete; all that its perpetrators desired was, that now their plot having been successful, Republicans should appear to sanction it by accepting the protection promised. That their distrust of this promise was not ill-founded appears from the testimony of over fifty-three persons who presented themselves to vote on the day of election and were driven off by threats and violence.

The result of the massacre was, that out of the thirty-six thousand registered Republican voters of the parish, only two hundred and seventy-six votes were polled. The work intended appears to have been well done.

THE MASSACRE IN ST. LANDRY PARISH ON THE 28TH OF SEPTEMBER, 1868.

This massacre originated in a brutal assault, on account of political differences, upon the person of the editor of a Republican newspaper and school teacher, by a company of three men. The colored people came promptly to the rescue of their friend but were advised by him and others to disperse peaceably, which they did. The cry of "negro riot" was then suddenly raised, and circulated with the greatest industry and rapidity, until the whole parish seemed to have been in a flame of excitement. It is to be carefully noted that this cry was raised as the result of the acts of the very parties who began the trouble, and before any acts of violence had been committed by the colored people. The rioters convened from different parts of the parish, armed and mounted, and began by disarming the colored people ; and then the work of murder seems to have commenced. The printing office of the Republican newspaper was sacked, men were arrested, imprisoned and then taken from the jail and shot down in cold blood. The sheriff himself heads a gang and takes a black man to the woods to kill him. The murdered men were half buried, leaving their feet and arms exposed as a prey to the buzzards. Bands of armed men traversed the parish from plantation to plantation, shooting the colored men. Some men were murdered to get possession of their small crops of cotton. One witness states that more than thirty colored men were taken at one time from under the guard of citizens who had captured them, and were then shot ; people were called out of their houses at night and killed.

During this time colored men were led in droves to the registration office, by white men, and after having registered, their certificates of registration were taken from them by these white men. At the ensuing election these same colored men were driven to the polls and compelled to vote the democratic ticket at the peril of their lives. The result of this species of electioneering was that the Democrats polled an almost unanimous vote in this parish where the Republican registered vote was over 3,000. This massacre lasted from three to six days ; the total number killed was over two hundred. It is to be noted that during its whole progress, the only instance of the use of force by colored men was the firing by a party of them upon a band of armed white men, who had commanded them to lay down their arms and surrender. There is no evidence that the blood of a single white man on the side of the murderers was shed during the whole time.

It will throw much light upon this terrible slaughter, to read the avowed purposes and plans of the men who perpetrated it, as disclosed six months before to General H. N. Frisbie, an ex-United States officer; we here reprint that portion of his testimony which reveals the existence of a preconcerted plot to accomplish the control of the colored vote by these very means.

"In the spring of 1868, I was speaking in the parishes of St. Mary, St. Landry and Lafayette, in behalf of the ticket headed by Judge Taliaferro and Dumas, but for the Constitution also. In my intercourse with the citizens of these parishes, I was informed by parties of their plans and purposes, in the conduct of this and future elections. Among other things, I was told of their contemplated frauds upon the ballot box in the then coming election, and the particular manner in which said frauds were to be perpetrated, but what surprised me most was the general intention, as openly expressed to me by various parties in all of these parishes, to secure political control and predominance by any means and at any cost, even to the sacrificing of all the leaders of the Republican party in those parishes; the only reason for not doing it then was the effect it might have upon the public mind of the North, endangering the success they so ardently desired in the coming Presidential election, but that after that they would have control of the negroes at any cost, placing great emphasis upon these words, and looking very wise and knowing while speaking."

THE MASSACRE IN BOSSIER PARISH, SEPTEMBER 21, 1868.

This wholesale murder originated by the act of a strange white man at Shady Grove firing without provocation at an old colored man who was sitting peaceably in his house. The colored men arrested the criminal, and were proceeding to deliver him over for trial to the civil authorities, when he was rescued by a band of white men.

This man went off and brought back with him an armed crowd of one hundred white men who commenced an indiscriminate slaughter of the colored people, women were killed while pleading for their husbands, men were butchered in their houses, and while quietly at work in the fields, a man was hung to a tree and left there for three days, ministers of the gospel were dragged out and beaten, and forced to promise not to preach again. A colored man was butchered in cold blood for the crime of being "too much of a radical" for his butchers; a bowie knife was plunged through his shoulder to his heart, till the blood spurted about his head, and he fell dead on his back. The colored men were then forced to kneel and look into his eyes, and he was left on the side of the road as a prey for buzzards. Two women were hung by the roadside with lariat ropes.

As the rage for blood grow more intense, hundreds of white men, inflamed with liquor, assembled to prosecute the foul work still further. A United States Marshal came with some troops from Shreveport, and begged them to desist, offering to arrest all colored men against whom there might be charges, and turn them over to the parish authorities; but in the words of this officer, "*the white citizens of Bossier seemed determined to hunt the colored people in the swamps themselves*," and as the officer "well knew that they would shoot every colored man they found with arms," he withdrew and left them, to prosecute their "negro hunt," at will. This massacre lasted for three or four days. The total killed was one hundred and sixty-two (162). Total otherwise outraged, seven (7). At the ensuing election the parish of Bossier gave one vote for "Grant and Colfax," out of nearly two thousand (2000) registered Republican voters. Their work was well done.

THE MASSACRE IN CADDO PARISH, ABOUT OCTOBER 12, 1868.

Particular attention is called to the cold-blooded and unprovoked murder of Robert Gray, and the non-action of the authorities in allowing the murderer to go unpunished; also to the fact that Republicans, white or black, live in Caddo only at the risk of their lives. The advice of Dr. Moore of Shreveport to the crowd, "Whenever they met a Radical nigger that would not give in, to shoot him down," may in law-abiding communities seem strange. Notice will also be taken of the terrible murder of five colored men, October 12, 1868, by Wm. Wright, Sam Wright and others, and of the fact that twenty-five or thirty dead bodies of colored people have floated down the river, past Shreveport, in the space of one month.

The murders and outrages practised for some weeks previous to the late presidential election "fully established the supremacy of the white race in this parish," as is shown by the fact that on the day of election colored men were forced to vote the Democratic ticket, with pistols pointed at their heads; and only in one single instance did a colored man vote the Republican ticket, and he—James Watson—was shot dead "simply because he voted for Grant and Colfax."

Our report of forty-two killed and four maltreated in this parish during the month of October, 1868, probably falls short of the actual number.

We append the vote of this parish in the last Presidential election:

For Seymour and Blair.................. 1385 votes.
For Grant and Colfax.................. 1 vote.

The Republican registered vote in this parish is about three thousand.

THE MASSACRE IN JEFFERSON PARISH OCTOBER 23, 1868.

The evidence sets forth the details of the horrible outrages perpetrated in this parish from the twenty-third of October, 1868, to the close of that month, during which time five (5) persons were killed, nine (9) were shot and thirty-three (33) otherwise maltreated. No provocation can be named as an excuse for such conduct. Bands of armed white men traversed portions of the parish and under pretence of searching among the colored people for arms, committed murders and innumerable other outrages upon defenseless men, women and children.

Men claimed to be authorized by the military to patrol the town of Gretna in that parish, and under color of this authority, numbers of them roamed from house to house, breaking open houses, robbing men, women and children of money, clothing, household wares, arms, registration papers and other property, and maltreating, shooting and killing them, and threatening the colored people with wholesale massacre if they should vote the Republican ticket.

In their robberies nothing seemed small enough to merit the disdain of these chivalric gentlemen. To steal fifty cent pieces and old women's spectacles from "niggers," was not beneath the dignity of these champions of "a white man's government."

THE MASSACRE IN ST. BERNARD PARISH, OCTOBER 25, 1868.

The details of this massacre, which lasted for three days, are presented in the evidence. They show that it originated from an unprovoked attack upon the colored men by a Democratic procession; that respectable white men, planters and old citizens, were hunted, captured and exiled from the parish; and that bands of armed desperadoes patrolled the roads, shooting down colored men and committing monstrous outrages; an ex-United States soldier, who was a policeman, was killed without provocation. It was dangerous for a colored or white Republican to walk the street by day or night. The marauders, (white men), thirty in number, sacked houses, robbed the people of money, moveables, arms and registration papers; killed men and hacked them to pieces with bowie knives, and prevented the civil officers from performing their functions.

These outrages were accompanied with threats, that "after the soldiers leave we will kill every d—d Republican, white and black, in the parish." Large quantities of prepared cartridges with from nine to eighteen buck shot in each, were collected in and at the Millaudon Plantation. The colored men were generally informed beforehand, that on the day on which the massacre commenced "they would have a chance to join the Democratic party; if they did they would be protected; if they did not they would be killed." Fillieu, the baker who was killed by the colored men, had first fired at them from his house and had previously been one of the most violent and lawless oppressors of that people.

The total number of killed during this massacre which were counted was thirty-eight (38).

The number killed of whom reliable information was received was sixty-eight (68).

It is probable that many men were killed in swamps and other secret places, whose number is known only to the murderers and to God.

LETTER OF THE HON. A. R. FRANCOIS.

This letter, found upon page 134, gives an interesting and detailed statement of the abuses practiced upon colored men in St.

Martin parish, and of the entire absence of protection by the laws. The committee call especial attention to the state of affairs in this parish, and particularly to the sufferings of the colored people.

THE PRESIDENTIAL ELECTION.

In the parishes of Orleans, Avoyelles, East Baton Rouge, Bienville, Bossier, Caddo, Calcasieu, Caldwell, Catahoula, Claiborne, DeSoto, East Feliciana, Franklin, Jackson, Jefferson, Lafayette Morehouse, Sabine, St. Bernard. St. Helena, St. Landry, St. Martin, St. Tammany, Union, Vermillion and Washington, the election was simply a sham, and a nullity.

No single essential of an election, except certain forms, was complied with. A so-called election, which is accompanied by general fraud, bribery, violence, intimidation and coercion, that cannot be prevented or punished by the civil law, is no election.

The registration, under our recent law, is a preliminary part of the election. It is as essential to a real election that the registration should be free, fair and easy of access in order that it may be a full record of all the legally qualified electors who wish to register, as that the polls and ballot boxes on the day of election should be free from the pernicious influences above referred to.

The spirit evinced at this election has only been a continuation of that manifested at the spring elections.

In all the parishes above named, during registration, fraud bribery, intimidation, mobs, and murders were perpetrated with the avowed object of either forcing Republicans to vote the Democratic ticket, or to refrain from voting at all. In portions of them these outrages were suspended a few days before the election; but in most of them they continued up to, and after the election, and in many of them have not ceased to this day. Even in New Orleans the pretence of quiet on the day of election was not successfully kept up. In the parish of Orleans, particular attention is called to the evidence with regard to the riots during registration, and especially to a statement of an United States officer, who was an eye witness of some of them.

In this parish fraudulent naturalization papers were issued by thousands. It is even said that some judges so far forgot the law as to allow their clerks to issue them when not in open court. There is no doubt that a large majority of the legally qualified voters of this State at the late election were in favor of Grant and Colfax and the Republican ticket, and that if all those who were legally entitled to register and vote had been permitted to do so, the actual vote polled would have been Republican by a greater majority than at the spring election. In this estimate the committee have had regard to the notorious fact that thousands of whites in this State who voted for Seymour and Blair, secretly desired the election of Grant and Colfax. These voters if no proscription or intimidation had been used would have voted in accordance with their sympathies.

The studied design of that portion of the Southern Democrats who counselled and aided these outrages, as shown by concurrent testimony from widely separated parts of the State, was to frighten and starve the colored people into voting with them, or to prevent them from voting at all, and to banish or murder such white men, and intelligent leading colored men, as had dared to actively advocate Republican principles.

The recognized leaders of the Democrats could at any time have caused the murders and mobs to cease. The proof of this is, that at a word from these men, and from the public press that peace was desirable on the day of election, the mobs, murdering, sacking and violence in the city of New Orleans suddenly ceased.

We also quote General Rousseau's opinion on this point from his report to General Grant: "The Democratic clubs pledged themselves to aid in securing to every registered voter the right to cast his vote; and then *I had no fear that any man would be molested in voting on the day of election.*."

Members of the State senate indulged in threats, that the people would not submit to certain laws. In the senate, Monday, August 24, Mr. Jewell made use of the following language in debate on senate bill number one hundred and forty-two, which was an act intended to prevent laborers from being discharged in violation of existing contracts, for political reasons: "Are we to be governed and controlled in our domestic affairs? Is the sanctity of homes to be infringed upon? Sir, if senators will persist in the passage of a bill of this kind, and others of a kindred nature which I have heard proposed, I, sir, as a senator, as a citizen of Louisiana, will take the stump, and I will advise the people to resist all such laws even at the point of the bayonet."

The Democrats at first invited the colored men to join their clubs, assuring them that they were their natural protectors, and would guarantee them all their rights more effectually than the Republicans. Their attempt to inveigle the colored men to vote against Grant and Colfax signally failed. Then they turned back to their original programme, and the bloody history of September and October followed. Many parishes were in a state of anarchy; no civil law was, or could be enforced within their limits, and their so-called elections were but the proceedings of vigilance committees.

The degree of violence and intimidation which prevailed in certain parishes cannot be better illustrated than by the fact that in some Republicans were entirely, and in others almost entirely prevented from voting. It has been incorrectly asserted that this was "because leading Republicans advised them not to vote," whereas, it was notorious that the Republican State Campaign Committee, the only body in session and authorized to speak for the Republican party, published on October 31st, and every day thereafter, until after the election, an address to voters, in which occurs the following paragraph, "Therefore the committee calls upon all Republicans to do their duty manfully, it urges them not to be intimidated, not to yield to threats of violence, but to go peaceably to the polls on election day, and vote as their consciences shall dictate. This committee is satisfied that with a peaceable and fair election, our majority in this State will be more than twenty thousand." Terrorism prevented voting; not a preconcerted policy.

In this connection your committee ask attention to the following correspondence. It will be seen that the Governor of the State evinced a prompt and thorough comprehension of the real state of affairs; that he made use of all the means in his power for the preservation of peace, and that these means were very limited. Deprived by law of the sword of the State, he was driven for a brief period during the prevailing anarchy and defiance of the civil law, to a dependence upon the sword of the United States, to repress the turbulent, to prevent imminent revolution, and to stop wholesale massacre. Had that sword been in hands more friendly to the existing government and less in sympathy with the malcontents, we believe much bloodshed and mischief might have been prevented.

That the Chief Executive of the State discharged his whole duty, during these perilous times, with eminent courage, fidelity and wisdom, will not be denied.

State of Louisiana, Executive Department,
New Orleans, December 20, 1868.

Hon. William P. Kellogg,
United States Senate, Washington, D. C.:

My Dear Sir—In reply to your letter of recent date, I have to say, that the personal relations between myself and General Rousseau have been pleasant and courteous. He consulted with me freely, and sought my advice as to the best means of preserving the peace during the late troubles. We differed widely as to many of the means employed for that purpose. In my first interview with him, I directed his attention to the fact that Congress had by the act of March 2, 1867, stripped the State Government of the power to organize militia, its reserve force in the event of forcible resistance to its authority. I informed him of the existence of secret armed societies; the object of which was to overturn the State Government and disfranchise the colored people, and that I should rely upon him as the representative of the forces of the United States, whose laws he was here to maintain, and through which the government I administered was established, to repress violence and insure peace and tranquillity. He replied that he would, as far as it lay in his power, use every effort to accomplish the objects indicated. I did not find General Buchanan, General Rousseau's subordinate, and in the immediate command of the troops in this State, apparently as cordial or so much disposed to act in harmony with the civil authorities.

At an interview between General Rousseau, General Buchanan, General Hatch and myself, I became satisfied that the State had no friend in General Buchanan, and that but little reliance was to be placed in his active co-operation. He was severe in his criticisms, and seemed to sympathize with the hostility entertained by the enemies of the Government, to the Metropolitan Police department, and suggested as a necessity that the old rebel force be restored. Our interview terminated without any satisfactory understanding. Subsequently General Rousseau ordered all the troops into the city, with the exception of General Mower's regiment, the 39th Infantry. I urged him to bring this regiment from Ship Island and station it also in the city and adjoining parishes. I told him that the turbulent elements boasted that the troops about the city (all white) would not fire upon them, and that the moral effect of a black regiment in the city, would be worth a brigade of white troops. To this request General Rousseau at first assented, but afterwards, to my surprise, replied that the effect of such a movement would be to incense the people all the more, and that a collision could not be avoided, and that when once begun the colored troops could not be relied on, and even if they could, the whole force would not be sufficient to withstand the onslaught of the armed citizens. To these views I entirely dissented. I informed General Rousseau on the eighteenth day of October, that I had some days previously written a private letter to the Secretary of War, on the subject of the impending troubles, and predicting that unless more troops were sent to the State there could be no hope of a peaceable election, but upon the contrary, I feared bloodshed. To prevent which I had requested that two (2) additional regiments be sent to the State. General Rousseau said he was glad I had done so, and that he would telegraph immediately to the Secretary himself, and afterwards showed me the Secretary's reply, which was to the effect that General Gillem, of Mississippi, had been instructed to forward all of his available troops at once, and that it was the best that the Government could do.

After four days of intense excitement, resulting from the troubles in Jefferson parish, where armed bands of men were shooting negroes or driving them to the swamps, having driven the police force away from Gretna, in the face of a company of United States Infantry, sent to aid them in maintaining order; when the people of St. Bernard parish were in a state of civil war; and when the streets of New Orleans were filled with armed bands of white men, also killing negroes and bidding defiance to the police and laws of the State, I determined to throw the responsibility of preserving order upon the representative of the General Government, which had stripped me, by the act of March 2, of the power to organize a force for that purpose. On the twenty-sixth October, I addressed the following letter to General Rousseau:

Major General L. H. Rousseau,
Commanding Department of Louisiana:

General—The evidence is conclusive that the civil authorities in the parishes of Orleans, Jefferson and St. Bernard are unable to preserve order and protect the lives and property of the people.

The act of Congress prohibiting the organization of militia in this State, strips me of all power to sustain them in the discharge of their duties, and I am compelled to appeal to you to take charge of the peace of these parishes and use your forces to that end.

If you respond favorably to my request, I will at once order the sheriffs and police forces to report to you for orders.

Very respectfully, your obedient servant,

(Signed) H. C. WARMOTH,
Governor of Louisiana.

In doing this, I had no purpose of avoiding responsibility, but I was determined that no question of authority should be raised by the military commandant. General Rousseau telegraphed my letter to the Secretary of War, endorsing what I stated, and received the following reply:

WAR DEPARTMENT,
WASHINGTON, October 26, 1868.

Brevet Major General L. H. ROUSSEAU,
Commanding Department of Louisiana, New Orleans:

Your dispatch of the 26th, forwarding a message from the Governor of Louisiana and asking instructions, has been received. You are authorized and expected to take such action as may be necessary to preserve the peace and good order, and to protect the lives and property of citizens.

(Signed) J. M. SCHOFIELD.
Secretary of War.

It was then the duty of General Rousseau to have issued his proclamation, enjoining such regulations as might have been necessary to have preserved the peace and enforced it with his troops. This was my advice to him, but he believed he could accomplish more by diplomacy than by force, and did not issue any proclamation until the night of the twenty-eighth October. In the meantime armed white men patrolled the streets night and day, sacking Republican club rooms, the residences of Union citizens, churches and school houses. During the week preceding the election over sixteen persons were killed in New Orleans. On the night of the twenty-eighth of October General Rousseau issued the following:

HEADQUARTERS DEPARTMENT OF LOUISIANA,
(States of Louisiana and Arkansas)
NEW ORLEANS, LA., October 28, 1868.

To the People of New Orleans:

FELLOW-CITIZENS—I have received instructions from the authorities at Washington to take such action as may be necessary to preserve peace and good order and to protect the lives and property of citizens. As the city is quiet to-day, I think it a proper time to make the above announcement, and to call upon all law-abiding citizens to aid me hereafter in carrying out these instructions, and to that end they are earnestly *requested* to refrain from assembling in large bodies on the streets, to avoid exciting conversation and other causes of irritation and excitement, and to pursue their ordinary vocations as usual. The police force of the city has been reorganized and inefficient members have been dropped from the rolls and others appointed in their places; and General J. B. Steedman is appointed Chief of Police, *pro tempore*, by the Board of Police Commissioners. General Steedman and his police force will be supported by the military, and assurance is given alike to the peaceful and the lawless that everything at my command and to the utmost of my ability will be used in the endeavor to obey these instructions.

For the present, political processions and patrolling the streets by armed men are prohibited.

(Signed) LOVELL H. ROUSSEAU,
Brevet Major General U. S. A., Commanding Department.

In the face of this order, Democratic clubs did have processions, and armed bands continued their violence up to the day of election. The week preceding the election was one of intense excitement—the whole city was filled with alarm. My parlor was contantly filled with men who brought reports of outrages upon their persons and property. A constant stream of men ran from the gun stores of the city with arms and ammunition, and every evidence of general tumult and rioting was apparent. During this time I was in daily communication with the commanding General, who expressed great concern, and lamented the meagre force at his disposal. It was so small that General Buchanan stated, in General Rousseau's presence, that he (General R.) would be as much justified in retiring with his troops as he would before an enemy of superior force. Such was the condition of affairs in the adjoining parishes of St. Bernard, Orleans and Jefferson for the six days preceding the election; while for *weeks* previous a state of lawlessness existed in more than half the parishes of this State, affecting the security of every citizen.

You ask me the cause of all this trouble. The answer is to be found in the deep-seated animosity of the rebel element of this State, unwhipt of justice and turned loose by Andrew Johnson upon the country without a rebuke, and allowed to resist by force the government established through Congressional law by the people of this State; in the contumacy of the old ruling aristocracy who believe they were born to govern, without question, not only their slaves, but the masses of the white people; in the lack of sufficient physical force to punish rioters and protect the honest citizen in his life and property, and in the wanton neglect of duty by the President in not furnishing, upon the application of the Legislature, made on the first of August, even if he had been compelled to call out the militia of the several States, with sufficient force to preserve the peace. You ask me if I advised Republicans not to go to the polls and vote? To this I reply that I had no authority whatever to act for the party; I was constantly engaged in my official duties, and left to the respective executive committees the conduct of the campaign. I was, however, consulted by the chairman of the Republican State Committee, who showed me a circular imploring the Republicans to stand firm and go to the polls on the day of the election and vote. This circular I approved, acted upon the advice contained in it, and voted for Grant and Colfax, although I felt assured that the election would be throughout the State a farce or tragedy.

Such, indeed, was the fact, as the following figures are uncontrovertible evidence. The election for the ratification of the Constitution took place not quite six months prior to the Presidential election. As you know there were forty-eight parishes in the State, seven of which, De Soto, Lafayette, St. Landry, Vermillion, Franklin, Jackson and Washington, gave four thousand seven hundred and four (4704) votes for the Constitution, but did not cast a single vote for General Grant. Eight other parishes, to wit—Bienville, Bossier, Claiborne, Caddo, Morehouse, Union, St. Bernard and Sabine, gave five thousand five hundred and twenty (5520) votes for the Constitution, but cast only ten votes for General Grant. Twenty-one parishes, casting for the ratification of the new Constitution twenty-six thousand eight hundred and fourteen (26,814) gave General Grant only five hundred and one (501) votes, and the whole State polling for the Constitution in April, sixty-one thousand one hundred and fifty-two (61,152) votes, or a majority of seventeen thousand four hundred and thirteen (17,413) gave General Grant in November only thirty-four thousand eight hundred and fifty-nine (34,859) votes.

It is impossible for me to give in the limits of a letter all of the facts in relation to the late election in this State. A committee should be appointed by Congress to investigate the whole affair, upon whose report should depend the count of this State in the Electoral College and the admission of the Representatives elect to seats in Congress.

In conclusion, I assert that the late election did not elicit the honest will of the people, and that the result was attained by the most shameless resort to murder, assassination, tumult and intimidation, not to speak of proscription, that was ever known in this country, and that to allow it to go as the expressed will of the people would be an outrage upon republican institutions and ruinous to good government here for years to come.

Very Respectfully,

H. C. WARMOTH,
Governor of Louisiana.

Our conclusion, therefore, is that the so-called election in parishes which were in a state of anarchy was no election, and that the so-called returns from those parishes are null and void, and should not be counted; they do not express the free, unrestrained choice of the people, but are merely the registry of the dictates of armed mobs and brute force.

In three parishes a degree of order was maintained, and in twenty parishes the election was held according to the letter and spirit of the law. It is our opinion that the vote in these parishes should be considered, and should decide the vote of the State. Any other course would be virtually disfranchising the good and law-abiding citizens, not for any acts of their own, but because of the acts of their lawless and guilty persecutors. It is a recognized principle of law that the wrong-doer shall not, under cover of the law, derive benefit from his own wicked acts; and next to a successful result of the late election, the greatest triumph of the bad men who have disgraced our State will be to profit by the fruits of their own lawlessness, and to be allowed future opportunities to repeat their intimidations, violence and murders. The franchise of suffrage is the dearest privilege of American citizens, and surely the good citizens of a peaceable locality cannot justly be deprived of the legitimate effects of the proper exercise of this power because they chance to be in the same neighborhood or State with localities controlled by desperadoes or highwaymen. The case is analogous to what it would have been if the election had been wholly ignored in about one-half of the parishes of the State, and held fairly in due form in the remaining parishes, and if citizens and localities can voluntarily disfranchise themselves temporarily by staying away from the polls without malice *prepense*, how much more justly may they do so by infraction of the whole letter and spirit of the law by which the election was ordered and under which it was held. As in the former case the vote cast in localities where the election was lawfully held, would unquestionably have been legal and binding; so it is evident that the same rule should be followed in estimating the result of the late election.

In the opinion of your committee the General Assembly should memorialize Congress of the facts respecting the last election, and in the name of the State of Louisiana protest against the counting of the pretended electoral vote of the State, cast by those persons who assumed to act as the Presidential electors of the State, and request that it be excluded from the canvass as fraudulent and null.

Your committee recommend that the General Assembly request those electors, who received the highest number of votes in the parishes where a peaceable and fair election was held, to assemble and cast the electoral vote of the State and transmit the same in the manner prescribed by law.

Congress should also be requested to admit the Representatives to Congress who were duly elected by the votes of the peaceable parishes, excluding the votes of those in which there was no peaceable or lawful election.

Through the courtesy of William Baker, Esq., Chairman of the Board of Registration, the committee have been furnished in advance with the following tabular statement of the registry and the actual vote in the before mentioned parishes. The examination of this statement will confirm most strongly the other evidence in regard to the nullity of the election in these parishes;

PARISHES.	Total Registered in November, 1868.	Voting November 3, 1868.	Republican Votes November 3, 1868.	Democratic Votes November 3, 1868.	Number of Republicans registered in 1867.
Orleans	41,733	.....	......	......	......
Avoyelles	2,287	1,865	520	1,345	1,249
East Baton Rouge	2,099	2,598	1,247	1,350	2,835
Bienville	1,571	1,386	1	1,385	955
Bossier	1,898	1,636	1	1,635	1,908
Caddo	3,586	2,896	1	2,895	2,987
Calcasieu	970	823	9	814	200
Caldwell	768	536	28	503	437
Catahoula	1,196	959	150	809	881
Claiborne	3,157	2,954	2	2,952	1,682
DeSoto	2,361	1,260	......	1,260	1,700
East Feliciana	2,417	2,055	644	1,411	1,635
Franklin	1,186	......	......	......	606
Jackson	1,508	1,398	......	1,398	659
Jefferson	5,999	3,130	672	2,222	3,677
Lafayette	1,586	1,422	......	1,422	766
Morehouse	1,745	1,526	1	1,525	1,318
Sabine	1,063	936	2	934	.....
St. Bernard	1,187	474	1	473	679
St. Helena	1,528	1,230	136	1,094	681
St. Landry	5,113	4,787	......	4,616	2,102
St. Martin	1,981	1,481	25	1,456	1,618
St. Tammany	1,465	1,174	470	704	556
Union	1,572	1,417	1	1,416	664
Vermillion	999	958	......	958	246
Washington	851	656	......	656	363
Total	91,826	39,557	3,911	25,233	30,544

Deduct Republican, colored, (30,544) from number registered the remainder will show about the number of Democratic votes when there is a full registration and a free election, which would give the Republicans in those parishes a majority of not less than 13,000.

GENERAL ROUSSEAU.

The committee invite especial attention to the evidence with regard to the administration of this officer. That which appears in this report has been obtained incidentally. They have not sought to find any matter of criticism upon his official conduct, but the duty assigned to them cannot be faithfully performed without referring to such parts of it as are connected with the history of the past two months. They do this by simply stating facts of record, leaving the conclusions that may be justly drawn therefrom to your honorable body.

Elections have been held in this State under the protection of three successive military commanders, Generals Sheridan, Buchanan and Rousseau; under the first there was no disturbance or violence at the elections worthy of notice; under the second there was much more, the record of which will be found in the former reports of your committee; under the third there were more murders committed than during all the preceding administrations since the surrender. This statement, we believe, the reports of Major General Hatch, of the Freedmen's Bureau, and the evidence given before this committee, will fully establish.

We have no knowledge of the number of troops under the command of each of these Generals in this State, but we believe that from the time of the general withdrawal of all troops, except such as were needed for police purposes, the difference in the number of troops under the control of each was not great. It is due to candor and truth to state that the powers of General Rousseau were, in theory, more limited than those of his predecessors, before the inauguration of the State government; but we believe it is also true, that the executive of the State was at any time ready and willing to confer the most ample authority, from the State, upon General Rousseau, for the preservation of peace and order, and that, therefore, practically, his powers were, or might have been, had he desired it, as extensive as those of former commanders. But General Rousseau's own evidence is the most satisfactory upon this point. We quote as follows from his last report to General Grant:

"Officers of the army generally, and my staff especially, always found their uniform ample protection against either violence or the slightest disrespect, and a simple request from them was sufficient to disperse large and excited crowds of people."

This being true, as your committee believe it is, there was not a mob, nor a massacre, which occurred during this dark period, that he could not, by timely precaution, have prevented.

The committee also here call attention to the evidence on pages 194 and 195, by which it appears that certain gentlemen who were members of the State Government, and called upon General Rousseau for protection during the riots were recommended by him "to resign their positions and they would not be molested," the General at the same time, alleging as a reason for this strange advice, that "the State government was obnoxious to the people." The General did not specify to what portion of the people the government was obnoxious, nor for what reasons. This report will, perhaps, still further elucidate his ideas upon this point.

We also call attention to the testimony of Dr. Mackay, on page 186.

During the riots the efficient regiment of Brevet Major General Mower was lying idle at Ship Island. The committee are at a loss to comprehend why, in the alleged scarcity of troops, the aid of this regiment was not brought into requisition to preserve the peace. They are informed that General Rousseau was repeatedly requested to take such action by Governor Warmoth and many prominent citizens.

The committee believe that General Sheridan, with one regiment of men, would have preserved the peace throughout the State.

In the midst of the riot and bloodshed, General Rousseau visited the headquarters of a Democratic club called the "Innocents," and addressed them in words which were reported in the morning papers. This report appears on page 205.

SECRET POLITICAL AND SEMI-MILITARY ORGANIZATIONS.

Your committee are in possession of detailed, trustworthy and sworn information of the existence of a secret political and semi-military organization, in this State, styled, "The Knights of the White Camelia." The signs, ritual, and most of the operations of this society throughout the parish of Orleans and portions of the State have been made known to the committee by the same testimony.

They call particular attention to the evidence on this subject. They are of the opinion that it is a society most dangerous to the public welfare, and that its exposure, and its condemnation by all good citizens is greatly to be desired. The evidence shows that it exists throughout all the Southern States, and has branch organizations in many of the Northern States.

The concurrent testimony of General Thomas, General Reynolds, and Governor Clayton, of Arkansas, proves the existence of an armed secret organization in Tennessee, Texas and Arkansas, which is known as the "Ku Klux," and which is in reality a conspiracy against the present State Governments in the South.

The testimony before the committee shows that the order exposed in this report is the real organization which is known to the public as the "Ku Klux," and that the signs and ritual which we append are those of that mischievous and unlawful society.

It is the same society of which the lamented Judge Chase spoke in his letter to the Honorable L. D. Campbell, of Ohio, which is published in this report.

The committee state that the evidence shows that large numbers of respectable Southern law abiding citizens were in the political excitement preceding the late election drawn into this society. Most of such men we believe to have been ignorant of its real character and designs. Such men are rapidly withdrawing from its folds. The time is not far distant when it will be abandoned to the reckless and lawless portion of society, who have everything to gain, and nothing to lose, by tumult, violence, and anarchy. The dangers through which we have passed from this conspiracy, however, and which may arise again from it or similar organizations, lead your committee to commend the subject to your special attention.

It is to be noticed that this order drilled secretly with arms.

Your committee believe that the confidence and numbers and concert of action displayed during the events herein narrated, by the violators of law, and the perpetrators of these crimes were strengthened, increased, and caused by the existence and influence of this secret order.

It was boasted on the streets that it was able to defy, and, if needs be, to annihilate the military. It is in evidence that it is the custom of this organization, when any desperate deed is to be accomplished in any locality, to send members of the order from other localities to perform it.

Your committee are at a loss to know how any people, possessing the intelligence, the wealth, the land, and the arms of the country, can find it necessary to band together in secret armed organizations on any valid plea of self defence, against an equal number of poor, ignorant, landless, inoffensive and unarmed people. How can such action be reconciled with any sense of chivalry or manly courage? What reasoning can justify such oaths, and purposes, under the existing constitution, and the laws of the land?

So far as such societies are simply secret political organizations, no legislation can properly be recommended against them. Such societies, while they are immoral and pernicious in all their tendencies, are most dangerous to their inventors. But every government has a right, and it is its sacred duty to see that no secret military or armed organization shall exist, especially when their sole purpose is opposition to existing laws, and the destruction to the Government itself. Such societies are conspiracies, dangerous alike to public and individual safety.

Stringent penal laws should be placed upon our statute books against them, and should be rigidly enforced.

THREATS OF VIOLENCE TOWARD THE GENERAL ASSEMBLY AND STATE GOVERNMENT.

It is well known to all the State authorities and to the citizens at large that threats of violence toward the General Assembly, upon its re-convening, and toward the different departments of the State government, have been rife among a certain class of our population who are opposed, politically, to the present State government. It is also in evidence before your Committee that such threats were not only confidently used by large numbers of the populace during the prevalence of mobs, before the Presidential election, but also that they are, up to the time of the writing of this report, very current upon our streets; even members of the General Assembly have been heard to offer wagers that it would never again assemble.

Your Committee call attention to this fact merely as an incident of the times worthy of record, showing the dangerous and lawless tendency of the teachings of a school of politicians which happily must become extinct before the progress of wiser and more beneficent principles.

The class of men who utter these threats are not formidable of themselves, but only as they may be countenanced and encouraged by leaders of a higher class.

For this reason we think that their threats may be regarded as very harmless.

We would suggest, however, the passage of some stringent law for the punishment of persons found guilty of aiding, abetting or inciting to disturbance of the peace or resistance to the laws in this particular manner.

THE FREEDMEN'S BUREAU.

The Committee deem it proper to call the attention of the General Assembly to the faithful and efficient administration of this Bureau by Brevet Major General Hatch. Without this distinguished officer's energetic and persistent interposition in behalf of the freedmen, their sufferings and oppression would have been much greater than they have been. The Committee also acknowledge his kindness in furnishing them with valuable records from his office.

CONCLUSIONS.

Your Committee respectfully submit for the consideration of your honorable body the following conclusions and recommendations:

The one instance in English history of a political massacre, which is so deeply shaded with horror upon the pages of Macaulay, is known throughout the civilized world. At this day the perusal of its story chills the blood; its infamy shrouded the reign and the generation, and blotted the fame of the whole nation in which it occurred, and remorse and madness on account of their share in its commission blasted and prematurely ended the lives of nearly all its perpetrators, so that the name of "Glencoe" stands in blackness on the record of the world's crimes along with that of St. Bartholomew. The victims of Glencoe did not exceed one hundred (100). They were a band of robbers and outlaws, and their depredations were so numerous and great that their extinction was regarded by many of their own countrymen as a public blessing. Yet three years afterward the indignation of the public mind against the murderers was so great that it shook the throne of William, and in the language of Macaulay, "the cruelty and baseness of the murderers excites, even after the lapse of a hundred and sixty years, emotions which make it difficult to reason calmly."

The massacre of Glencoe fades into utter whiteness before the massacres of the last twelve months in this State, whether you regard the numbers of the murdered, the absence of all justification, the demon-like atrocities attending their commission, the character of the sufferers and their murderers, or the motives which prompted, and the spirit which accompanied their actions.

The effects of these occurrences upon the prosperity of our State have been serious, and cannot soon be remedied. Capital has been prevented from coming, commerce has been diverted to other ports, trade has been injured, emigration has been checked, and the fair name of our good State has been deeply tarnished.

The vice of invoking violence to accomplish political ends is deeply imbedded in the customs of a part of our population; it is probably one of the lingering relics of the times of slavery, when political opposition to that practice was deemed incendiary, and held to justify what were termed in the vernacular of those days, "extreme measures." However logical this reasoning may then have been, the cause of this vice having disappeared, the vice should cease with it. There can be no peace or prosperity until the community recognize practically the maxim that no citizen shall be allowed to take the law in his own hands, and that the law must be obeyed. Lawless men must be taught that the time for persuading men with clubs, knives and pistols, is past. At the close of the rebellion, by the supreme will of the American people expressed in the solemn forms of law, that large class of our people who have been freed from slavery, were incorporated into the body politic and clothed with the power of the ballot. This was to enable them to defend and maintain the civil and political rights into the possession of which they had so recently come, and of which they would otherwise have been speedily dispossessed. These people naturally joined the ranks of the political party which had freed and elevated them. They have sent us to these places, having confidence that while we shall legislate for the good of the whole people, we shall also as their agents lend the powers of the State government to protect and not to oppress them, and to secure them in the peaceable possession of all the rights which are lawfully theirs. Through persecution, want, robbery and murder, they have held fast their faith in the national government, and in their principles. This they have done under the frightful pressure of such trials and sufferings as have caused many prouder, and more boastful people to succumb. We owe it as the first and most sacred duty of the hour to see that their long tried, long suffering trust, be not disappointed ; and that the arm of justice, though slow, shall be sure, and shall reach the perpetrators of the horrid crimes of the past twelve months. Notwithstanding the long reign of passion and violence under which our State has suffered, there is hope in the returning sense of justice and of self interest of the people at large, and in the moral influence of the incoming national administration.

The cry of "Negro supremacy" is a bug-bear, in which its authors themselves do not believe. It is used merely for political effect upon the low and ignorant. The hostility to "negro suffrage" is not because it is "negro," but because it is Republican.

Nothing shows the preversion of moral sentiment so strongly as the complaint made by certain parties, that investigations like this stir up ill feeling, and are acts of enmity towards the people of the State. No parties have a more vital interest in the exposure of such crimes than all the good people of the State ; and not many months will elapse before an overwhelming majority of the people of this State will hail with delight all proceedings calculated to bring the guilty parties in these outrages to justice, and to prevent similar outrages in the future. It is not only the blacks who are living under a reign of terrorism. Thousands of honest white men will rejoice over the riddance of their parishes, from the dangerous characters, who have sought to rule white and black alike by brute force and a daring defiance of law.

The election of General Grant as President has already had a quieting and subduing effect upon the restless, lawless and revolutionary spirit that was rife and rampant throughout the State. He is respected by the good and feared by the bad. The firm hand of the National Government will need to be held sternly for months to come upon the shoulders of the refractory and evil-disposed men who have, with such impunity, defied its authority for months past, to save the State from anarchy, and the innocent persons, who have had the courage to deliver the testimony on these pages, from vengeance and destruction.

Not the least of the beneficial effects of this report will be the collection of facts and names, which will render the eventual punishment of the criminals more sure and speedy.

When the dream of a natural, inborn right to supremacy shall be abandoned and the higher race will content themselves with that superiority which their proud descent, their inherited virtues and abilities, their education, wealth, and social influence, their habits of political control, their command of all the avenues to commerce, art, science, and the learned professions, and last, but not least, which the natural desire for protection that the weak feel toward the strong, will perforce give them; perchance all will then see that a genuine chivalry and sense of superiority are not incompatible with a generous guarantee to the lowest and humblest class of men of every right, which any other men enjoy. Surely the time will come when the people of this State will dwell together no longer as Northerners and Southerners, as Union men and Confederates, as loyal and disloyal, but as citizens of a common country, entitled to equal rights, before the law, to a fair chance in the race of life, and to such meed of social and political distinction as each one's merits, and the favor of his countrymen may confer upon him.

RECOMMENDATIONS.

Your Committee recommend that the General Assembly memorialize Congress, setting forth the condition of affairs in this State, and requesting such Congressional legislation as may be proper and expedient in the premises.

If any one of the outrages recorded in this report had been committed upon the person of an American citizen abroad, the whole country would have been in a flame, and all the powers of the Government, even to the last and expensive resort of arms, would have been brought to bear, to redress his wrong and secure protection in the future. No cost of blood or treasure in such cases is deemed disproportionate to the object to be attained, namely, the making of the American flag and of the proud title of an American citizen, a perfect shield and protection about him against all wrong, wherever the sun shines.

Is the Government of the United States less powerful to enforce such protection upon its own than upon foreign territory?

It is notorious that under the administration of most of our State courts juries cannot be found who will convict men guilty of outrages during these political tumults.

If a State neglects, or is powerless to protect its citizens, must the United States remain a passive spectator of outrages upon its own citizens, or is its power not competent to provide for their protection?

Our Constitution declares that the allegiance which the citizen owes to the United States is paramount to the allegiance which he owes to the State. Protection is the correlative of allegiance.

If this state of things continues, your committee submit as a question worthy of grave consideration, whether Congress may not establish additional courts, with the necessary jurisdiction, over this class of offenses. Such protection would be far more ample and less obnoxious to the spirit of our institutions, as well as less costly than that of troops, whether National or State.

The committee also recommend that Congress should be requested to send a committee to this State to make a thorough investigation into the condition of affairs here, to the end that they may be better enabled to judge of the legislation necessary to enforce the execution of the laws and of the amendments to the Constitution of the United States.

It is impossible for any body of men at such a distance, even from the most accurate statements of others, to form an adequate conception of the evils to be remedied.

The committee recommend, with reference to cases of murder herein reported in which criminal prosecutions have not been commenced, that the Governor be authorized and required to offer a suitable reward for the apprehension of the criminals, and to employ competent counsel on the part of the State, to assist the district attorneys, which counsel shall also be authorized to prosecute every civil officer who shall refuse or neglect to perform his duty in bringing such criminals to justice. Laws should be made providing for the punishment by adequate penalties of district and parish judges, district attorneys, sheriffs and other civil officers who refuse or neglect to arrest, prosecute or punish parties guilty of murder, and disturbances of the peace.

We recommend that the General Assembly require an annual report from all district and parish judges, sheriffs, district attorneys, and police juries, of all the crimes committed in their respective parishes, and of the disposition made of the criminals.

We recommend, also, the passage of severe penal laws upon the subject of masked or armed bands of men traversing the country, for purposes of disturbing the peace.

A well regulated militia is the sword of the State, to be used when the civil officers fail to compel obedience. While it should be cautiously and prudently used, it should always be in readiness for emergencies like those of the last six months. It may be well to inquire whether a small body of mounted militia, which can be moved to any part of the State where it is needed, upon short notice, should not at once be organized.

If other means should fail to restore law and order in refractory parishes, we recommend that Congress be asked to enlist into the United States service, in such parishes as will not preserve the peace and execute the laws, a sufficient number of loyal men, to be stationed in these parishes—the cost of the same to be reimbursed to the United States government by the State, which shall then apportion it among such parishes by a special levy, to be collected as all other taxes.

Your Committee recommend that each House of the General Assembly appoint a standing committee upon the Peace and Order of the State.

We invite attention to a minority report from one of the members of the Committee. Presenting as it does, in the strongest light, whatever can be urged in extenuation of the course pursued by a portion of our people, we commit the widely differing conclusions of ourselves and our respected colleague to the calm and dispassionate judgment of the people of this State. All of which, together with the evidence appended, is respectfully submitted.

HUGH J. CAMPBELL,
of the Senate.
PETER HARPER,
EDWARD S. WILSON,
WM. MURRELL,
of the House of Representatives.

Joint Committee.

MINORITY REPORT ON THE CONDUCT OF THE ELECTIONS AND PEACE AND ORDER OF THE STATE.

The undersigned member of the committee, differing honestly from the report made herein by the majority of his co-laborers in the work assigned them, submits the following statement for consideration:

There have been many outrages committed in this State during the last year, and many frauds perpetrated at the recent elections.

Both political parties should bear its responsibilities.

The negroes have in many instances committed brutal outrages, sparing neither age nor sex, having been taught to believe by their white leaders that they were better than the white people of the State, and entitled to more consideration by the Government. In support of this statement I quote from a speech of Governor H. C. Warmoth, delivered at Mechanic's Institute, February 22d, 1868. He said: "The rebels (meaning the white people of the State) are prisoners, enemies captured in war, with no rights, no privileges, no anything, but what the Government in its magnanimity sees proper to give them. Rebels are traitors and treason under the Constitution is punishable by death."

Such teachings as these and the attempts to place the white men of the State under the domination of the negro, is the real cause of all the disturbances, disquietude and agitation, the violence and disorders in the State.

The white people have had reasonable grounds for fear of an insurrection, and they no doubt prepared themselves the best they could to protect themselves and innocents from violence and harm.

The undersigned deems it unnecessary to say anything further upon this matter as the official report of Major General Rousseau on the subject is full, complete, and substantially correct.

RECOMMENDATIONS.

The undersigned would respectfully recommend that the white people of the State be left alone to manage their own internal affairs, and that all political disabilities be removed from them and for "*God's sake let us have peace.*"

WILLIAM L. THOMPSON.

SUPPLEMENTAL REPORT.

PARISH OF JEFFERSON.

A. J. Kemp states, on oath, that he resides in Gretna, parish of Jefferson. That on Friday morning, October 23, 1868, just after leaving his house, he was shot at without provocation by a white man named Henry Kern, but escaped and remained concealed until 5 P. M. He was then advised by a man named Frank (a Democrat), to remain secreted, as he would be killed if he ventured out. When the military force arrived he did venture to look out of the door, and was seen by a crowd of white men, one of whom remarked, that is the d—n son of a b—h we were looking for.

About 10 o'clock that evening about sixteen men came to the house and demanded and obtained admittance; they came in and took Mr. Clark and then searched the house. One of them said to witness: "Come down you d—n son of a b—h, you are the very one we are looking for."

They asked witness his name, and when told, one of them said, "you are the very one we have been looking for." They took said Clark and witness to the house of the Hook and Ladder Fire Company, and asked witness where the arms of the Grand Army and Loyal League were kept, and added that if he did not let them know by 12 o'clock they would hang him, they having erected a gallows in the house of the Fire Company.

Witness answered that he knew nothing of any such organization. One of the party said: "You are a d—n liar, you are one of the Commanders." The leader of this party acted as judge; witness was arraigned before him three (3) times, each time telling the same story. They then wanted witness to take an oath to support the Democratic party, and use his influence among his colored friends in order to secure Democratic success at the coming election. Soon after, the military forces arrived and interrupted their further proceedings. The man who acted as judge told the commanding officer of the military to take charge of us, which he did, and placed a guard over us. About 9 o'clock A. M., on Saturday, the President of the

Democratic Club, of the town of Gretna, went to the commanding officer and told him to release witness, as he had not been seen in the riot, nor had any arms been found on his person, which was accordingly done. Members of the Democratic party searched the houses of the colored people, taking from them their registration papers, watches, money and many articles of value. They also took the banner belonging to the Gretna Republican Club. The house where witness resided was broken open and his clothing and shoes were stolen, and his books and papers destroyed.

Robert Miller states on oath that on Friday, October 23, 1868, a party of men whose names he does not know, but who can be identified, came to his house in Gretna, during the absence of himself and family (who had been compelled to leave to save their lives), and broke open the door with axes, cut open two trunks, and took therefrom property, money, and his registration papers. They also took two guns.

Robert Sparks states, on oath, that as he was walking along quietly through the streets of Gretna, on Friday, October 23, 1868, he was stopped and searched by four white men, who drew their pistols, and took from him his pocket book containing a ten dollar gold piece, and a fifty cent piece. They then made him take them to his house, under the pretence of searching for arms, and made his wife open her bureau drawers, and searched through the house, and stole about sixty or eighty dollars in money. One of them snapped a pistol at witness, but it appears it was not loaded. They also beat his wife brutally because she protested against their infamous proceeding.

Upon leaving they stopped at Gasper's grocery and divided the money between them. Witness and wife then appealed to some policemen to arrest these men, when said men again assaulted himself and wife in the presence of the policemen, who then arrested them, but turned them over to the citizens of Gretna, who allowed them to go free.

These same men shot at witness three times, but did not hit him. Witness went to the judge of the court at Gretna, and stated the case to him. The judge said he could do nothing in the matter, as the parties were residents of New Orleans.

Samuel Perkins states on oath, that on Friday, October 23, 1868, about five o'clock, A. M., he was walking from the ferry into town, he saw Mr. Worley, with a gun in his hand. A Mr. Lenton said to Worley, that "Sam was the cause of the thief getting away." Mr. Worley said "that's him" (meaning witness). "I will shoot him." Witness turned around, when Worley said, "I will shoot you." Witness said, "Don't shoot me, for I tried to stop the disturbance;" but he would have shot him if he had not gone close to him with another man.

Some eight or ten white men now came up and wanted to know who it was that set fire to the buildings. Witness answered that he could not tell them; that he was in Gretna when the fire commenced, whereupon Worley struck him on the head and neck. Witness then ran toward the ferry, but meeting some white men, who told him not to go across to New Orleans, that they would protect him. He went home.

At ten o'clock that night some unknown white men came to witness' house and knocked, and obtained admittance. They took him to the Engine House, and said, "Now we have the chief of the Republican party—he won't lead the party any more." They then told witness that he was to be hung at twelve o'clock, and actually erected a scaffold in the building. Soon after some United States troops arrived and took charge of the Engine House, when these men all left. The next morning a United States officer came and told witness there was no charge against him, and released him.

Mrs. Polly Gill states on oath, that she is a citizen of the State of Louisiana, and resides in Gretna, Jefferson parish, and is fifty years of age; that on the 23d day of October, 1868, about four o'clock, A. M., she was on the levee, where there was a fire, and assisted in carrying out the goods and furniture from the burning buildings. When the buildings were burned down, a riot commenced. Witness saw about twenty white men armed with guns, pistols, etc., who were citizens of the town. Among their number was Henry Carr, Fred. Carr, John Linton, Mr. Lambert, Fred. Strailey, B. Whitten and Jeff. Sutten. Witness saw a white man named Lambert shoot a colored man named Scott. She also saw John Linton, Henry Carr and Fred, Carr, white men, shoot Scott after Lambert had shot him.

Witness went up to Scott, who was then lying on the ground,

vomiting blood, from the effects of the shot wounds received at the hands of these men, Lambert, Linton, Henry Carr and Fred. Carr, who, after shooting him, went up and took hold of and straightened him out, saying at the same time, "You, God d——d son of a b——h, we wish we had ten thousand more killed!" A white man then took up an axe to strike him (Scott) on the head. Witness said, "Men, for God's sake, don't knock in his head, for he is dead!" They laid the axe down, saying, "We will kill some more God d——d black ones!" These men then turned around, and, seeing a colored man by the name of Raymo standing close by, one of them struck him on the head with an axe, knocking him down and causing the blood to flow from the wound. This colored man in a few moments raised his head, when another of these white men shot him through the shoulder. Some colored men put him in a wagon and carried him to his house, where he now lies, in bed, in a critical condition. While witness was watching some furniture, a young white man came to her and whispered in her ear, telling her that some white men had broken open her house and shot a colored man and child. The name of the colored man is Reuben Lindsey, and the child's name is E. Wilkins. The man was shot in the neck and the child in the face and breast. They are dangerously wounded and are not expected to live. The colored man did not have any weapons, or use any bad language to the men who shot him. When witness arrived at her house she found this colored man and child lying on the ground, but the white men had left. At night, about 12 o'clock, some white men came to her house and knocked at her door; she asked them what they wanted; they said they wanted the prisoner, Robert Mabey. Witness told them he was not in, and told them to come in and search, which they did. While doing so they stole two revolvers, which were in her drawer, and a musket. They then went away; in half an hour they returned again, came in and stole a banner, which belonged to the Third Ward Republican Club of Gretna, and broke the door down, and all the windows in the house.

Richard Hill states, on oath, that he is a citizen of the State of Louisiana, residing in Gretna, parish of Jefferson; that on the morning of the 23d of October, 1868, a party of five armed white men came to his house and took away two revolvers, and at night the same party returned and searched his house again. They overhauled his press and found his pocket book which contained twenty ($20) dollars in greenbacks, which they took possession of and left. Witness does not know who these men were; they were all strangers to him.

Witness further states that the colored people in Gretna are living in great fear of the white Democrats.

William Shingleton states on oath, that he is a citizen of the State of Louisiana, and resides in Gretna, Jefferson parish; that on the 23d day of October, 1868, about twelve o'clock M., a squad of white men—among whom he recognized a Mr. Doul, (a moss picker)—came to his house, armed with guns, pistols and bowie knives, and asked witness' wife for his gun. She replied that he did not have any. They then turned everything in the house upside down, taking witness' pocket book, containing $5 50 in greenbacks, which they found in the press. Then going out into the yard they took witness' axe and went away.

Colan Cesar states on oath that he is a citizen of the State of Louisiana, residing in Gretna, Jefferson parish; that on the 23d day of October, 1868, about 12 M., some white men came to his house, armed with pistols, guns and knives, opened his trunk and took from it his pocket-book, containing twenty ($20) dollars in greenbacks and his certificate of registration. They also took his order for pay that he had received from the railroad office, and his pistol. These men told witness' wife that if she said anything they would kill him and her. She then ran out of the house, and afterwards the men went away.

Rebecca Scott states, on oath, that she is a resident of the State of Louisiana, and lives on Main street, in Gretna, Jefferson parish. That on the 23d day of October, 1868, a squad of armed white men came to her house just after dinner, entered, and said they wanted her firearms; witness replied that she had none, when one of the men picked up a knife and told her if she did not give up her arms he would stab her with it. Witness had none in the house; they then took her spectacles, a black silk dress, three dollars and fifty cents in greenbacks, and five dollars in silver, and destroyed her cups and dishes, stating as a reason therefor, that "the d—d niggers had no business to live in Gretna; let them go back to their masters' plantations and hoe corn and cotton." These men were all strangers to witness.

Hypolite Williams states, on oath, that he is a citizen of the State of Louisiana, and resides in Gretna, Jefferson parish. That on the 23d day of October, 1868, at 12½ o'clock in the day time, one Thompson and Frederick Carroll, a hunter, with a squad of white men came to his home armed. Thompson asked if witness had any firearms, to which he answered, "No." Thompson then said, "I must search your trunk," as he supposed there was a revolver there. He (Thompson) then searched the trunk, but finding none, said he thought witness had no revolver, but finding witness' pocket-book, he said, "Let me see what is in here," but witness took it from him. Thompson finally went away with the rest of his squad, saying he did not believe there were any arms there. These men then went to John Lightfit's house and entered it throngh a window, the doors being locked, and searched for arms, but found none, but took a tin box containing fifteen dollars in greenbacks.

Elijah Hogans states, on oath, that he is a resident of the State of Louisiana, and resides in Gretna, Jefferson parish. That on the night of October 23, 1868, a party of white men, John Savan, Frank Hatch, and others, came to his house and ordered him to come out, saying they "wanted that powder that he had in his house," there being none there to witness' knowledge; he told them to go in and get it, but they did not go in, but said, "You need not think yourself so d—d smart, for as soon as we get you to our head-quarters we'll find were all that powder is." They then took witness to the Hook and Ladder House, and there asked him where the powder was. Witness replied, "You were there, and I told you to go in and get it," they answered, "Never mind, we will find it," and went back to the house and searched it for arms and the powder, but found neither. They took away witness' mare, clothing and other articles of value. When they returned to the Hook and Ladder House, they asked witness what he meant by mixing in politics, to which he replied that he did not understand them. They answered, "Oh, yes you do; haven't they told you, you should have lands and a mule, and a horse, if you would vote the Republican ticket? We know all about it, and we are going to kill you unless you tell us the whole truth," adding, "You are the very one we wanted; you have been the head one in this business, and we are going to shoot you all to pieces." Witness answered that he couldn't tell them any more. They said, "You shall not be hurt if you will vote the Democratic ticket," to which witness answered, "that he would die first." At this time the the troops came up and he was released.

Stephen Robbins states on oath, that he is a citizen of the State of Louisiana, resides in Gretna, Jefferson parish; that on the 23d day of October, 1868, about 10 o'clock, A. M., about fifteen unknown white men came to his house, broke open the door and took a half dozen knives and forks and two dollars and fifty cents ($2.50) in money. They opened all the trunks in his house, also his armoir and bureau. They took the sum of seventy-five ($75) dollars in greenbacks from one of his trunks. Witness had used no bad language to any white man or gave them any cause to treat him in such a manner.

Philip Brandon states on oath, that he resides in Freetown, parish of Jefferson, right bank; that on Friday, October 23, 1868, at about 11 o'clock, A. M., a gang of white men came to his house and took his gun and fifteen ($15) dollars in legal tender notes. They made witness fall into line and took him about a mile from home. They were met by a white man named Sawyer, who told them to release witness, as he had done nothing.

This party shot and wounded three colored men whose names witness did not know. After he was released he went home and remained there.

Mary Antoine states, on oath, that she resides in Gretna, Jefferson parish; that on the 23d of October, 1868, a squad of white men, armed with guns, pistols, hatchets and bowie-knives, came to her house about 12 o'clock, M., while she was absent. She had left her brother-in-law in charge of the house. Seeing so many armed white men roaming about the streets, and learning they were robbing and abusing colored people, witness started for home to try and protect her property. When she arrived there she found two white men in her house, and her trunk broken open, and her pocket book carried off, containing forty-four ($44) dollars in greenbacks. These men told her brother-in-law that they had "orders from headquarters" to search colored peoples' houses for arms. Witness had no fire-arms in her house, and was so badly frightened that she was afraid to speak to them about her money.

Telisphore Baptiste states, on oath, that he is a resident of Freetown, parish of Jefferson; that on the 23d of October, 1868, at 3 o'clock A. M., a squad of about twelve white men, armed with guns and pistols, came to his house, representing themselves to be police officers; three of them came inside and took three guns, one belonging to him, one to his son, and the other to his nephew; they then told him to go to the station and that the Captain of Police would talk to him. When he saw the Captain of Police he said he did not know anything about his guns. A German in Freetown says he knows where they are but he will not give the names of the parties. They did not take anything else out of his house. They took all the guns and fire-arms away from the colored people.

Delia Bethel states, on oath, that she is a resident of Gretna, parish of Jefferson; that on the 23d of October, 1868, four or five armed white men came to her house and ordered her to show them all the fire-arms and ammunition she had; she told them that she had nothiug of the kind in the house; that her husband had a pistol but had it with him. They said that they would wait for him, and when he came they would kill him; that they were going to kill all the d—d niggers that they met because they went with the Radical party, and turned against *them*. On the same day witness saw the body of a colored man who had been killed on the levee. The colored people in Gretna are afraid of their lives in consequence of the threats the Democrats are making against them.

Louise Brown states on oath, that she resides in Gretna, parish of Jefferson; that on the morning of October 23, 1868, she was standing on the levee with her husband, when a white man approached her husband with a large butcher-knife in his hand and asked him if he had any arms about him. He made no reply. At this time three other white men approached armed with pistols, and one had also an axe handle. One of them, named Toney Myers, and one Henry Carroll commenced beating her husband over the head in a brutal manner with the axe handle. He started to run down the levee, when one of the band named Fred. Carroll, fired a pistol at him, the ball entering his back. They then left him to die like a dog, offering no assistance whatever. Deponent further states that although it is well known to the civil authorities of Gretna that said Fred. Carroll shot her husband, and that the others beat him, yet they have made no effort to arrest said parties. On the day following, four or five men came to her house and searched for arms, but finding none, they left. Her husband is still confined to his bed in a critical condition.

Charles Green states on oath, that he is a resident of Freetown, parish of Jefferson; that on Friday, October 23, 1868, he went to the Gretna Ferry with his wife, and seeing some excitement there, he hurried home and commenced working in his garden. At about 11, A. M., a party of about fifteen white men (among whom was one Fred Carroll), led by a milkman named Pierre, came to witness' house, when some one of said party remarked, "there is an old nigger, let's kill him." Another said, "No! don't kill that old man, he is a good old man. I have known him for some time." One of them then drew his gun on witness and told him to open his door, and asked if he had any arms. Witness told them that he had none. They then searched the house and tumbled things about, but found nothing. They then told witness that if he staid at home they would not harm him this time, but if they caught him out they would kill him. Witness further says, that while he was at the Ferry in Gretna, he saw a fire burning and went to look at it, and saw there Henry Carroll and Frederick Carroll with a company of young men, and heard them say as a colored man passed along, "Come, let's kill him." They then ran towards him, and some one threw a brickbat at him, whereupon he started to run. Some said "catch him," and some said "kill him," and commenced shooting at him, several of the shots hitting him, but he continued running. Some one, however, headed him off, and as he ran upon the levee a man shot him dead. A colored man named Ramo seeing this deed, remarked, "What a pity that they have shot that poor man down for nothing," whereupon a white man fired at said Ramo and shot him down. His wife ran to him with her child in her arms, exclaiming "Lord! they have killed my husband." At this they fired at her, but missing her, hit the child (who has since died of its wounds). Witness believing it to be very unsafe to be there, then left for home.

Alexander Green states, on oath, that he resides in Freetown, in the parish of Jefferson. That on the 23d day of October, 1868, some fifteen white men came to his house, led by one Bob Milton; these men told him not to move, or they would kill him. They were all armed with shot-guns, revolvers, knives, etc. They inquired if he had any arms; he told them he had a gun. They then searched through the house, breaking open trunks, armoirs and bureaus; they found his gun and took it; they found his pocket-book, which contained $110, and took it, telling him if he said anything they would kill him, and when he remonstrated, they told him "hush your mouth, you d—d son of b—h, or we will blow your brains out."

Robert Maybury states on oath, that he is a citizen of the State of Louisiana, and a resident of Gretna, parish of Jefferson.

That on the morning of the 23d of October, 1868, while yet in bed he heard the bells ringing, and jumped up and went to the door, but not seeing any fire, he went down to the levee near the ferry landing, and then saw a great many buildings on fire. One Samuel Perkins, colored, told witness to guard some goods that had been taken from the burning buildings, but soon hearing the bells sound the alarm for that portion of the town where his house was situated he left and went to his house, but finding no fire very near, started to go back, but was stopped by a white man named Jake Woolly, captain of the steamboat Champion No. 3, who asked him "what that fuss was on the levee." Witness replied "he did not know." Woolly said "yes, there was a d—n big fuss;" and he had his gun there to stop it, and repeated the remark the second time, and because witness said he knew nothing about it Woolly gave him a severe punch under his ear with the muzzle of his gun. A catholic school teacher passing by stepped up and told Woolly he must not do that, at the same time taking hold of his arms, told witness to run, which he did. While he was running he was joined by a colored man named Albert Kemp, who was fired at by a white man of bad character named Henry Carr, who is always troubling colored people. Witness hid himself that night and until 8 A. M. next day, in an out of the way lot, when seeing the catholic teacher at a distance he went to him. The teacher said, "well! it was lucky I was passing by you at the time that man Woolly was attacking you, as I saved your life," and told witness to go home and hide any arms that he might have in his house. As he arrived there a band of white men, armed with shot guns, bowie knives, and revolvers, came and broke down the door of his house and entered. As they did so witness ran out the back door, leaving a colored friend, Reuben Lindsey, holding his nephew's baby; the baby's mother, Mary Wilkins, was also in the house. The party, thinking it was witness holding the baby, fired several shots, taking effect in the head of said Lindsey, and in the face of the baby. Lindsey was not killed but is now lying in a very critical condition.

Witness further states that the white men are particularly down on him, Samuel Perkins and A. J. Kemp, and say if they could only get them out of the way, they could control the colored vote for the Democratic party.

That during the riot these white men killed a colored man and would have split his head open with an axe, if a colored woman named Polly Gill had not prevailed upon them not to do it.

James Voorhies (colored) states, on oath, that he resides in Freetown, parish of Jefferson; that on or about Friday, the 23d day of October, 1868, a party of about fifteen armed white men came to his house and ordered his mother to open the door, which was done; they then entered and searched the house and compelled his wife, who was very sick in bed, to get up, whereupon they searched the bed, they took from witness five dollars in money, his gun and his watch, valued at twenty-five dollars.

Ruffan Wilkins states, on oath, that on Friday, October 23, 1868, as he was walking quietly along in one of the streets of Gretna, a white man came up and, putting a revolver to his head, said: "If you do not enter the Engine House, I will blow your d——d brains out!" Witness went into the house with the man, who threatened to shoot him if he attempted to escape.

On Saturday, 24th, a white man named Henry Carroll came to witness' house, broke open the door and took from him a shot gun and a musket, and then drew a revolver and fired at him; the ball missed him and struck another man in the neck. Witness' child was also wounded by shots in the cheek and stomach. Witness spoke to Carroll about having shot his child. He said, "If you say another word, I will blow your d——d brains out!" On the night of the 23d said Carroll came to witness' house and demanded his money and a Republican club banner then in his possession, which he took. Carroll also took witness' Registration certificate, and was about to tear it up; but he took it away from him.

On the same day a colored man was shot and killed by a white man named Bob Barracks, and no attempt was made by the authorities to arrest him, and he is now walking about the streets of Gretna. Another colored man named Ramo was shot and wounded by a white man named Lampouse. No attempt has been made to arrest him.

The white people are parading the streets armed with revolvers, and claiming to have authority from military headquarters to disarm all the colored people. Albert Kemp and Sam. Perkins (colored) are now hand-cuffed and marched through the streets. The military stationed there seem to pay no attention to these outrages.

Susan Williams states, on oath, that on the 23d October, 1868, as she was going out to work she was stopped at the ferry by a squad of white men, armed with guns and pistols, who asked her where she was going; she said she was going over to New Orleans to get work; they said, "go back, you damned nigger, you think you are going to take Gretna;" she then left to go home, but before reaching her house she saw so many armed white men surrounding it that she was afraid and went to a friend's house and stayed until they went away; she then went to her house and found that they had broken into her armoir, and had taken her pocket-book, containing $2 in greenbacks, house receipts, marriage certificate, and other minor papers; there was no one in her house at the time; she had locked the doors and windows when she left.

Barney Allen, states on oath, that he resides in Gretna, parish of Jefferson; that on the 24th day of October 1868, six white men came to his house and took his double barrelled gun, powder flask and shot bag; also, a silver watch, which cost him twenty-nine dollars and a half ($29.50), one razor, and also private papers, consisting of receipts, &c., out of his pocket book. Witness is now living in New Orleans, having left Gretna in consequence of threats having been made against his life. He has also heard that the Democrats were going to kill him the first chance they could get before the election.

William Green, states on oath, that he resides in Freetown, parish of Jefferson, that on the 26th day of October 1868, about one hundred armed white men came to his house in broad day light, and completely gutted it, taking his gun, axe, hatchet, wearing apparel, and every thing of value that they could find; they also took his Registration certificate, which they found in his pocket-book, in his pants pocket. Witness and his wife are afraid to remain in his house, as the Democrats have threatened to kill him when they get a chance.

Paul Hubeau, states on oath, that on Friday, October 30, 1868, a party of armed white men, (among whom were Milton and Carpel), went to his brother Ernest's house, in Freetown, and demanded all the arms that were in the house, and searched the house thoroughly, but found nothing. They found a gun in the potato patch, which a friend had left there for safety, this they took and promised to return after the election, but they have failed to do so.

[Ernest Hubeau,) whose house was thus searched a) is Justice of the Peace in the parish of Jefferson, and was absent at the time of the search. Witness was present in the house at the time.]

William White states on oath, that on Tuesday, October 27, 1868, at 10 o'clock, he went to the court house in Gretna for the purpose of paying the fine, and releasing his brother, who had been arrested on Saturday the 24th, but was refused permission by the Judge to see his brother, and started to leave, when a white man named Capt. Wirley, wanted to know his business; he told him he wanted to assist his brother. Wirley said he had no business there, and added, "G—d d—n you, get away from here quick." Witness did not move, whereupon Wirley struck him on the head with a large stick and drove him to the ferry landing and searched him, to see if he had any weapons about him, and said if he had found any he would have killed him.

Mima Hughes states, on oath, that she is a resident of the State of Louisiana, and is residing in Gretna, and is twenty (20) years old; that on the morning of October 30, 1868, between the hours of 8 and 10 o'clock, she saw a gang of fifteen or twenty (15 or 20) white men running after a colored man named Harry Scott. These men were armed with pistols, spades and axes, and they were crying out, "Head him off," "kill him," etc. Witness then saw Henry Carroll, a resident of Gretna, shoot Scott in the back; she also saw a son of John Linton, a keepeer of a coffee-house, in Gretna, and a Jew named Albert Lamben, both shoot him in the back. On the same day, a body of white men came to the house of a colored woman named Polly Gill—where witness was visiting—and after destroying most everything in the room, one of the white men raised his gun and shot a colored man named Reuben Lindsey in the face, and a baby four months old, which he was holding in his arms. These men took all the arms they could find in the possession of the colored men; witness further states that Henry Scott was killed by the men mentioned above; Scott, so far as witness knows, was a quiet and peaceable man. The men mentioned above, also took and destroyed a "Grant and Colfax" banner that was in the house of Polly Gill.

Henry Taylor states, on oath, that he resides in the City of New Orleans, La., and is employed as a messenger on the Committee on the Conduct of the Late Election and the Condition of Peace and Order in the State." That on Friday morning the 30th of October, 1868, he received from the chief clerk of the above committee, five (5) summons, with orders to deliver them to parties living in the town of Gretna, right bank, parish of Jefferson; that he crossed to the town of Gretna on the 4th district ferry, and inquired for the parties to whom these summons were to be delivered, but could get no information from the white men of whom he made inquiries, and who reside in the town of Gretna. Witness then went as far as the railroad inquiring for these parties; he asked some colored people who were living on the railroad; they told him they were acquainted with the parties, but could give him no information as to their residences. While there, witness met two colored men going up the railroad and asked them if they knew the parties; they said they did, and advised him not to go near them, as they were armed and were the leaders of the riot. Witness passed by the white men, who remarked that they "would like to kill a nigger." Witness then went to the ferry landing and looked for a policeman, but could find none. He remained at the landing an hour; while there two white men came down, accompanied by two soldiers, and got into a skiff; these men asked the soldiers to loan them their revolvers, which the soldiers did, and then they crossed over to the city. They afterwards returned, went into a grocery store with the same soldiers and there returned to them their revolvers.

JEFFERSON—SUMMARY.

Number killed positively sworn to........................... 5
Number shot positively sworn to............................. 9
Number maltreated positively sworn to......................33

PARISH OF EAST BATON ROUGE

J. T. Von Tromp states on oath, that he is a registered voter of the State of Louisiana; that he was a member of the Board of Supervisors for the parish of East Baton Rouge during the election of Nov. 3, 1868.

The board commenced registering in the city of Baton Rouge on the 8th of October, 1868, but was considerably interfered with—by G. W. Huested (Parish Judge) issuing writs of mandamus against it, whereby 150 white men and 1050 colored men were prevented from registering. While witness was in the performance of his duty James Cooper, Deputy Clerk, entered the room and said: "Mr. Von Tromp, I believe there will be a disturbance down stairs; in that case I will commence it in the registration room by shooting you the first one." Witness believes that those writs of mandamus were issued solely for the purpose of preventing the colored men from registering.

Our board was No. 1. Board No. 2 was prohibited from registering by writ of injunction after eight or ten days work, thereby throwing double duties upon us. Mr. H. J. Puckett, the chairman of our board, also did everything in his power to register the white citizens and to hinder the colored from exercising the same privilege. The board was so much interfered with during the day that witness told lawyer Avery that if the court did not stop issuing these writs that in order that the colored men and others should not be debarred from their rights to register, the registration should be carried on at night. He replied that if we would not do that, no more mandamus writs would be issued, but if we did, that lawyer Fuqua and others would have fifty writs of mandamus issued against us. This was said in presence of H. J. Puckett chairman of said board, and L. Francois, a member of the same.

On election day, Nov. 3, 1868, between the hours of 3 and 4 P. M., witness was standing in the courtyard, opposite the north door; several policemen were also standing there, keeping the people back. About this time one of said policemen raised a pistol. Witness, thinking it was pointed at him, ran behind a mule. Great excitement was created by policemen running to and fro; every white man seemed armed, and many of them wore badges.

Witness is certain that 200 colored men left the polls without voting, as they were thoroughly intimidated and feared the whites would kill them if they should attempt to vote the Republican ticket.

L. H. Burdick states on oath that he resides in Baton Rouge, La.; that he was appointed by the Board of Registration as supervisor of registration for the parish of East Baton Rouge, La., on Oct. 1, 1868; he was a member of the second board, traveling through the parish. The board opened their office Oct. 8, 1868, at Port Hudson, and went through the parish without being molested until they arrived at Baton Rouge, on the 19th of Oct.; at 3 o'clock of said day, the Deputy Sheriff served an injunction on the board of registrars, stopping further registration. When they went to Manchac precinct to open an office they found it impossible to obtain board or lodging; they returned to Baton Rouge, and according to orders opened their office in the City Hall. An injunction was then served on them by the deputy sheriff, and the office closed, preventing further registration. They filed their answer and went to trial before the parish courts, the case being called up and postponed from time to time until Oct. 23, 1868. The Judge then postponed decision until the 24th of October, thus preventing them from opening their books. They received written instructions from Wm. Baker, Chairman of the Board of Registrars, for the two boards, in joint session, to make up their books and appoint commissioners of election. Mr. O. H. Hackett came into the office and ordered them (the second board) not to appoint any commissioners of election, that the first board were to appoint them. Mr. Puckett, chairman of the first board, agreed with Mr. Hackett in this regard, and used abusive language toward the members of the second board, which caused a crowd to collect in and around the office; the men who composed the crowd were friends of Mr. Puckett, and were armed. Mr. Hackett then said that if the board did not appoint such commissioners as he wished there would be a big row. "We have got to have it and we may as well have it now as any time." Witness asked Mr. Hackett if *he* was chairman of the board of supervisors. He answered no. Witness told him he thought *he* was taking too much authority upon himself in appointing commissioners of election. He said he did not care a d— n for the second board. There was such an excitement, a member of the first board moved that the joint session of the two boards should be dissolved, which was done under protest by the second board. Mr. Puckett told witness if he opened his mouth he would send for the sheriff and have him put in jail. Witness answered that what he (Puckett) had done was contrary to instructions received from Mr. Baker, Chairman Board of Registration, and called for the reading of the written instructions, which Mr. Puckett refused to do. Witness then left the office; he was ruled out, and had nothing to do with the appointment of commissioners for that parish. On the 3d day of November, 1868, colored voters went to the polls to vote. The policemen requested them to show their tickets. The colored men gave these officers their tickets to examine, when these policemen would return to them a Democratic ticket in its place. The colored people who were unable to read, went and voted said Democratic ticket, being deceived by said policemen. Witness then wrote a note to the chairman of the board of commissioners, Mr. L. Gasta, informing him of this outrage, and requesting him to have it stopped immediately. The commissioner went to the policemen and gave them orders not to interfere with the colored voters, but this had no effect. Deponent then informed the voters on the outside of what the policemen were doing, and told them to put their tickets in their pockets and allow no one to see them, which they did. Then the policemen in the hall commenced searching their pockets, and if they found Republican tickets in their possession they passed them through the hall without permitting them to vote. In several instances deponent gave republican tickets to colored men to vote, and the policemen took them from them and tore them up, and offered to them Democratic tickets, which they refused to take, and came out without voting. Witness gave them another ticket, and they went a second time to vote, and met with the same treatment, and were prevented from voting. Witness saw a large number of colored men leaving the polls and was informed that they had been driven away by armed white men. J. O. Fuqua, A. S. Herron, and Mr. Stafford sued out the injunction writ, and Judge Husted issued the injunction, on the ground that the second board was registering in the city without legal authority.

George W. Eagan states, on oath, that he is a resident of East Baton Rouge parish, State of Louisiana; that he was a member of the Constitutional Convention of this State in 1867–8 and the Republican candidate for State Senator for the 13th Senatorial district at the election of the 17th and 18th of April, 1868, and contestant of the seat of the Hon. R. H. Day, at the present time; that he, witness, left New Orleans on the 23d day of October, 1868, and arrived at East Baton Rouge on the following day and found said town quiet and peaceable, a large number of the inhabitants being away at the time, a portion of them attending a Democratic barbecue at Pointe Coupee, others in the suburbs attending a horse race; also a large number of Republicans were attending a barbecue on the opposite side of the river. About dark on the day of witness' arrival, a cannon was fired, the report of which seemed to be the signal for the assembling of the Democracy, as about five or six hundred immediately gathered in front of the house where he had put up, kept by J. L. LeBlanc, a prominent Republican. This crowd remained sometime, making violent demonstrations, especially at every report of the cannon, and calling witness in the most insulting manner to come out, "and let them ride him on a rail." Some said "let's throw him into the river;" others said "lets drive him off." Some said "this is the last night you can stay in this town." During this time a Democratic procession was moving through town and passed several times before witness' residence, insulting him in a gross manner. Witness did not show himself at all, as he and his friends did not consider it safe to do so, either during that night or the following day. It was currently rumored about the city on the 25th, that witness had better leave, as an attempt would be made to assassinate him, and it was apprehended that a riot would be produced by an attempt to kill him. Apprehending this, witness decided to leave as soon as possible for New Orleans. Accompanied, therefore, by some friends he went down to the steamboat landing, and soon the steamboat R. E. Lee, bound for that city, came along, and going on board witness secured a stateroom, and carefully avoided any political conversation while on board. Knowing that he was surrounded by his political enemies, and fearing there might be a continuance of the violence manifested against him during his short stay in Baton Rouge he was determined not to give any offense, so that if he should receive any injury it should be unprovoked on his part. There was an apparent courtesy manifested toward him, but he thought they were trying to put him off his guard, in order that they might the more easily carry out their villainous designs.

He was frequently invited to the bar to drink by his political opponents, but declined every invitation to do so. Repeated attempts were also make to get him upon the hurricane deck, but he refused, believing that it was their intention to do him violence. While he was sitting in the cabin quietly conversing with a Mississippian, in regard to planting interests, a stranger came in and calling him by name informed him that a colored Republican was outside the cabin and desired to speak to him a moment, that the colored man had sent for him, as he was not allowed to enter the cabin. Believing it to be his duty to respond to this request, he went to the door, which he had scarcely closed behind him when he found himself surrounded by a dozen or more white men, a portion of whom had fire-arms. He was immediately attacked, as he believes, by three men, who struck him with brass knuckles and the muzzle of a large sized revolver, and was immediately felled to the floor senseless. When he recovered his senses, he found himself in the barber-shop under the care of a physician, the captain and two barbers of the boat. Witness further states that the men who stood by, and the men who assaulted him, are all strangers to him, although he thinks he could identify two of the men who struck him, if he could see them. This assault was altogether a political one, unprovoked, unjustifiable and outrageous in every particular, and it is his firm belief, that it was their intention to murder him. No steps were taken by the captain, officers or others of the steamboat Robert E. Lee to arrest these would be assassins. Upon witness' arrival in New Orleans he was attended by Dr. Hire, who for some time considered his condition a critical one; but under the Doctor's constant attention, he has so far recovered as to be able to walk about, but is still very weak and suffers from continual pain in the head. Witness fears that he may never recover from these injuries. He finally states that persons cannot live in the parish of East Baton Rouge who advocate the principles of the Republican party, though they may be in all othor respects upright, quiet and peaceable citizens.

Louis Francois states, on oath, that he was appointed Supervisor of Registration for the parish of East Baton Rouge; that on the 3d day of November 1868, about 9 o'clock A. M., he went to the poll to vote, when a policeman by the name of Charles O'Connell, stopped him and told him not to crowd the table. Witness then stepped back until the table was cleared, and then approached again to vote the Republican ticket, when he was caught by the shoulder by J. Bogan, who jerked him around and said, "stand back, G—d d—n you—if you want to have trouble you can have it d—n quick," and continued cursing him until he walked away from him, and waited until he was engaged in talking. Witness then went up and voted and left the poll. He then went to the court house to see how the election was going, and found the door on the north side crowded with colored people; there were at least a dozen of white policemen keeping them back, and preventing them from voting. At the same time the door opposite was clear and free for every white and colored man to vote the Democratic ticket. Seeing the imposition, suffered by colored Republicans, he spoke to the sheriff about it, who replied, that the crowd was so large that he could not help it, but that he would see that every one had a chance to vote. Witness remained at the court house until about 12 o'clock. He saw a colored man approach the table to vote, he was met by Mr. John Gass, (a Democrat), who asked him to let him see his ticket, and gave him another one, the man wanted the ticket he had taken from him. Mr. Gass then gave him a ticket and swore it was the one he had taken from him, and told him to vote it. The man voted this ticket. Mr. Gass had five or six tickets in his hand for the purpose of exchanging for Republican tickets, in order that the parties should vote the Democratic ticket. In the evening, about four o'clock, while witness was at the corner of the court house, he heard very loud talking inside of the house, and saw a great many people running from that side; then, came a great number of policemen and deputy sheriffs. An order was given for the policemen to fall in. Seeing there was going to be trouble he started to go away, when a policeman by the name of Benton Hillen caught him by the collar of his coat and said, "G—d d—n you, if there is anything done, I will knock you down!" (at the same time keeping his club raised over witness' head.) "Here, G—d d—n you, you are the ring leader!" Another policeman standing near by told Benton Hillen to let witness go. He replied, "No, I am going to hold him right here, and if there is anything done I will knock him down, and I am responsible for what I do." Finally the sheriff came up, and by his order witness was released. The sheriff's name is L. J. Bird. There were from seventy-five to one hundred policemen and deputy sheriffs on hand when the order was given to fall in, all armed with revolvers and clubs. The consequence of this display of power was that from two to three hundred intimidated colored people left the polls, who would have voted the Radical Republican ticket, if allowed a free expression of their political feelings. Witness positively knows that many of the policemen and deputy sheriffs on duty that day would lose no opportunity to inflict violence on the Republican colored people, at the slightest imaginary provocation. The colored people, knowing these facts, hastened to get away as soon as possible, for fear some excuse would be made for commencing an assault upon them, especially when they saw such a large number of officers drawn up in line between them and the court house. Many of the colored people saw witness under arrest, and knew that his life was in danger in case any disturbance should take place. Many of them told him, on and before election day, that prominent Democrats told them that if they voted the Republican ticket they would be discharged off the plantations. There were a great many colored men prevented from voting, because the commissioners would say that a letter was left out of the name, which would be on the poll book, although the number on the registration paper would correspond with that on the poll book. Deponent further believes that these objections were made to shut out Republican ballots, and that no hindrance would have been given to white men holding papers in the same condition to vote the Democratic ticket.

Seventy-seven (77) electors state, on oath, that they are duly registered voters of the parish of East Baton Rouge, Louisiana, having been registered at the court house, first (1st) precinct of said parish, and that they were prevented from voting on the 3d day of November, 1868, by an armed body of men, who threatened colored voters and caused them to leave said precinct; they further state that had they been allowed to vote, they would have voted for General U. S. Grant, for President, and for C. B. Darrall for Congress.

Four hundred and forty-five (445) electors of East Baton Rouge, Louisiana, state on oath, that they are twenty-one years of age, born in the United States, and had resided one year in the State and ten days in the parish, next preceding the election of November 3, 1868; that they were not and are not disfranchised, that they have not been able to register under the existing laws of the State for the reason that the office of the Surpervisors of Registration was closed, and they were therefore deprived of the right of suffrage; they also state that had they been allowed to register and vote, they should have voted for General U. S. Grant, for President, and for C. B. Darrall, for Congress.

Samuel George, states on oath, that he is a resident and registered voter in the First Precinct, parish of East Baton Rouge; that on November 3, 1868, he was present at the poll at the court house in Baton Rouge for the purpose of voting for President and Vice President and member of Congress; when he reached the door, (the poll being a few steps inside), he saw a number of policemen collected around the colored voters, and heard said policemen ask them to show their tickets, and upon their showing them, these policemen would change them for Democratic tickets. If they refused to show them, the policemen would take them away by force, and either compel them to vote the Democratic ticket or would not permit them to vote at all. Finding that many Republicans would not be sufficiently intimidated to vote the Democratic ticket, the Democrats became greatly exasperated, and one Wm. Garig, a commission merchant, placed himself on the north steps of the court house, and with revolver drawn, ordered the Democrats to fall in line, saying, "fall in, fall in men;" at the same time waving his pistol; the Democrats at once formed a line, facing the court house; all in said line then drew their revolvers, and drove the colored men from the polls; this was about 4 or 5 o'clock P. M.; there were between one and two hundred colored Republicans who would have voted for Grant and Colfax for President and Vice President, and for C. B. Darrall for member of Congress, who were thus driven away without being permitted to vote.

John Shields states, on oath, that he is a registered voter of the parish of East Baton Rouge; that on November 3, 1868, he went to the polls to vote for Grant and Colfax, for President and Vice-President, and for C. B. Darrall, for member of Congress, for the third district; when he arrived near the poll, assistant City Marshal Weiss said he must show his ticket. Weiss being an officer he showed him his ticket; Weiss then took his ticket from him, tore it up and threw it on the floor; a policeman, who stood by, handed him a Democratic ticket, and told him to vote it, but he refused; he tried again to vote, when one of the policeman offered him fifty cents not to do so, and when he insisted on voting, his ticket was taken away and torn as before; he then procured two Republican tickets, and advanced again; while waiting his turn to vote a large man (whose name he does not know) came out upon the steps, with a pistol in his hand, and called out, "fall in, fall in here, men, fall in line;" a line of white men was at once formed in front of and facing the door, with revolvers drawn; deponent believes that more than fifty men were in said line, these men then drove the colored voters from the polls, in confusion, almost creating a panic; witness saw no arms in possession of the colored men, nor any indication of disturbance on their part; most of the Republican voters then retired from the polls, not again attempting to vote; deponent is satisfied that his life was in danger if he persisted in voting the Republiean ticket, and he did not therefore again attempt to vote.

The followiug appeared in the New Orleans Bee, of December 12, 1868:

WARNING TO CARPET BAGGERS.

The Mayor of Baton Rouge publishes the following notice to the Supervisors of Registration for that parish, which they would do well to heed. It applies to some others as well:

MAYOR'S OFFICE, CITY OF BATON ROUGE,
December 7, 1868.

WHEREAS, In the report of William Baker, Chairman of the Board of Supervisors to Gov. Warmoth, on the late election, as published in the New Orleans Republican of the 1st inst., there is a statement touching the conduct of the officials and citizens of Baton Rouge, utterly false and malicious and mischievous in its design. And whereas the author of this statement claims to derive his information or opinion from a subjoined and printed communication from the Supervisors of this parish, I hereby make known to as many of those Supervisors as have signed said document or lent themselves to the work of maligning this community, and also to their aiders and abetors, who have furnished the data upon which this falsehood is based, that they owe their present immunity here in some measure at least, to the efforts which the officials of this place have made in the interests of peace, and to such protection to their persons as we have from time to time afforded them.

As the protection of the law and the forbearance of the community are appreciated in no other way by these persons than as a license for the perfidy and misrepresentation, I am compelled to say that while my oath of office, and I believe an ever present sense of duty, induces me to extend to all inhabitants and sojourners in the city the protection of the law. I shall for the future regard these miscreants as dangerous to the public peace and unworthy of public confidence.

That while we are bound and willing to throw around them the ægis of the law, their oft repeated and gross insults upon the citizens of Baton Rouge, render more and more difficult the duty of saving them from the just indignation of the subjects of their vituperation and abuse. They, as well as Mr. Baker and the Governor, know that in this instance we have been misrepresented.

Given under my hand and seal of office, the date above written.

(Signed) J. E. ELAM, Mayor.

BATON ROUGE—SUMMARY.

Number men maltreated...4
Number illegally deprived of their rights to vote, Nov. 3, 1868...277
Number prevented from registering, although entitled to do so...445

PARISH OF ST. LANDRY.

H. N. Frisbie, under oath, states as follows:

"In the spring of 1868, I was speaking in the parishes of St. Mary, St. Landry and Lafayette, in behalf of the ticket headed by Judge Taliaferro and Dumas, but for the Constitution also. In my intercourse with the citizens of these parishes, I was informed by parties of their plans and purposes, in the conduct of this and future elections. Among other things, I was told of their contemplated frauds upon the ballot box in the then coming election, and the particular manner in which said frauds were to be perpetrated, but what surprised me most was the general intention, as openly expressed to me by various parties in all of those parishes, to secure political control and predominancy by any means and at any cost, even to the sacrificing of all the leaders of the Republican party in those parishes; the only reason for not doing it then was the effect it might have upon the public mind of the North, endangering the success they so ardently desired in the coming Presidential election, but after that they would have control of the negroes at *any cost*, placing great emphasis upon these words, and looking very wise and knowing while speaking." Some two months since or more, witness had occasion to prosecute a colored man for the crime of perjury, who committed the crime, as witness believes, incited thereto by persons professing to be Democrats, and known to be malicious towards Northern men when not known to be Democrats. The case was made so clear after investigation and arguments by able lawyers that a Democratic judge was obliged to send him down for trial. A very few days afterwards Judge Abell and C. H. Luzenburg, (Democratic Judge and District Attorney,) caused a *nolle prosequi* to be entered and the man discharged, and this too without submitting the case to the grand jury, or calling for the testimony of the witnesses who were responsible parties and easily found. Nor could it be ascertained after careful inquiry, and from both of the parties above named, that any investigation was had, farther than to ascertain the politics of the parties.

This colored man, on the street and at colored Democratic clubs, boasted, or declared he was discharged because he was a Democrat, and witness was a Republican, and that no Radical could do anything to him, no matter what he might do, nor to any other colored man if they would be good Democrats. 'He knew it, for they told him so;' meaning thereby the Democrats. Witness charged and expects to to prove the Legislature, as soon as this election is passed, that the above named individuals, for partizan and political ends, did commit malfeasance in office by unlawfully discharging a person accused of crime.

Samuel C. Johnson, states on oath, that he resides in Washington, parish of St. Landry; that on the 28th of September, 1868, at about 10 o'clock A. M., he was startled by seeing quite an excitement in one of the white schools, the children evidently very much frightened, were running home; he also saw at this time armed white men riding through the town; he then left the town for his home about one mile from said town; he had been there but a short time when he learned that they were arresting all the colored men in Washington; he then went back to the town, as he heard that the white men had promised to protect the colored men in case of a riot; they did protect the colored people until the riot was over. Col. Thompson sent word to Washington, from Opelousas, to release all the colored men that were under guard, and allow them to go home. Witness shortly after left Washington to go to his home; on his way he saw the body of a colored man lying in the road; he was shot in the head and neck with buckshot; witness was informed by Joseph Gradney that more than thirty colored men were taken from under guard, in the town of Opelousas, and killed; Gradney also stated that he was compelled to join the Democratic party to save his life, and he was then on a Democratic horse, and had a red ribbon tied around his left arm; he was formerly a color-bearer in the Republican party; he also told him that the white people of Opelousas had killed W. Williams and James Pickett, both colored men, simply because they refused to join the Democratic party; parties continued visiting witness' house inquiring for him, and he heard of colored people being called out of their houses at night and shot; also shot down as they were passing quietly along the road; he concluded it best to leave, and on the 4th of October started for New Orleans;

he was informed that a man named Dupré killed two colored men on his plantation, because they had induced the other laborers to go to a barbecue on the 26th of September.

Henry Gardner states, on oath, that he resides in Washington, parish of St. Landry, Louisiana; that he was in said town on the 28th day of September, 1868. At the time the report of a riot in Opelousas was received, all the white residents commenced leaving town on horseback and armed with shot guns for Opelousas; about one hundred of them left Washington; he heard nothing further until these men returned the same evening; they reported the riot over in Opelousas, and proceeded to arrest all the colored men in Washington; hearing of this witness left his house and went to a neighbor's house to secrete himself; about a half hour after, ten or fifteen men came to this house, all armed with double barreled shot guns; he hid himself under the house; they seemed to know where he was. Mr. Hawkins (the sheriff) and Mr. Aaron Prescott, found him and ordered him to come out; they started with him to the prison, where they had the other colored men under guard; they had gone about two blocks, when Mr. Hawkins ordered the company to disperse and assemble again at Moundville, about two miles and a half from Washington. A young man in the company named Mr. Wm. Offut, saidthat he "would *not* go away, and leave a man there to be shot down like a dog." Mr. Stagg, one of the company, remarked that Mr. Hawkins had charge of the prisoner. Mr. Offut replied that he did not hinder him from taking charge of witness, but he was not going to leave him to be shot down like a dog; they then took witness on to where the other prisoners were and kept him there until the next morning. Mr. Aaron Prescott came the next morning and ordered all said prisoners to come out on the banquette; he formed them in line, and told them that Colonel Thomas had sent him word, from Opelousas, that everything was quiet, and that he would let them go, but if ever anything of the kind occurred again, they could consider themselves dead men. Deponent not putting much confidence in this, did not sleep at home that night; at about 12 o'clock the same night, a party came to his house, looking for him; they inquired of his wife for him, and not finding him, went away; witness went down town again the next morning, and was informed that

Mr. Hawkins, (the sheriff), had said that he had intended to kill him the night that he arrested him; witness then went to see Mr. Hawkins, and asked him about the matter; Mr. Hawkins told him, "Yes, it was my full intention to kill you before I took you down there; I never intended to take you there, a live man," and added, that all the company agreed to it but one; witness did not sleep at home for several nights; these white men came to his house three successsive nights, looking for him; the third night they entered his house, and not finding him, went into the next house, where deponent's sister lived, and afterward went to her brother-in-law's house, whom they called out, and shot about a block from his house, the first shot only wounding him, they fired five or six shots into his body, finally killing him; witness then left town, and remained hidden in a cane field for twelve days, waiting for an opportunity to escape; he finally procured a "dug-out" and succeeded in getting to New Orleans.

Napoleon Lastraps states on oath, that he is a resident of Opelousas, parish of St. Landry; that on Monday, September 28, 1868, between six and seven, P. M., while on his way to the office of the "St. Landry Progress" newspaper, he was stopped by fifteen or twenty men, one of whom, Mr. Solomon Davie, insulted him and said, "See what you have done. I have always told you all that it would bring something of that kind," and then asked "where are the rest of the Republican leaders?" Witness answered that he did not know. Davie told him that he believed he was lying, as many had done already. . Witness said that he did not want to have any trouble with him whatever, and turned to walk away. After he had proceeded about fifteen or twenty yards he was halted by one of the party above mentioned, who asked him if he had any arms. He answered that he had a pistol. The man told him to give it up, that he would be responsible for it. A lady was standing in the door of her house near by, and witness asked her if she would allow him to remain there during the night, as he feared to proceed farther. He remained, and at about 11 o'clock a party of thirty or forty armed white men came to the house, and knocked at the back door very loudly and rapidly. Witness told them to wait a moment and he would open the door. After he had opened it, one of the party walked through the hall and opened the front door, and admitted the President of the "Seymour Knights," Solomon Loeb by name, who asked witness if there was any ammunition or arms in the house. He answered that he knew nothing about it, being a stranger, and only stopping there for the night. The party then commenced to search the house, two or three of them trying to raise a fuss with witness all the time. In going to search the back yard and store room one of them said "make the son of a b—h (meaning witness) go into the rooms first with the light, and if any one is there concealed, they will fire on him first."

After completing the search there the party went over to the "Progress" office, compelling witness to accompany them. When they arrived in front of said office they asked witness where the key was. He answered that he did not know where it was. The President of the club, Solomon Loeb, heretofore mentioned, then said "We are authorized to go into this house." While they were standing waiting to get in, said President told witness that if he wanted to live in that parish he must join the Democrats, adding, if he did not he must leave the parish, or if he remained he would be killed, and further advised him, if he wanted to live, to join that party, because in this parish "we have a white man's government, and it has got to be a white man's government." The party then entered said office compelling witness to go into each room first with the light.. Said Loeb was the first man who destroyed any property in the office. Loeb then asked witness where Emerson Bently was. He answered that he did not know. Loeb said "we are the men that not only talk, but when it comes to taking the gun we are ready to take them." He continued talking insultingly. Soon afterwards witness was allowed to go, but was advised to keep himself very close, as this party would do him harm; he followed this advice, and the following week went to the parish of St. Martin. While there Charles Bell, the Secretary of his club, was killed between Breaux Bridge and St. Martin, while trying to make his escape, by a party of white men who were stationed there as "pickets," watching for the leading Republicans who were endeavoring to escape from Opelousas. After killing Bell they said "we will now go for the other one" (meaning witness), who being advised by his friends of his danger immediately returned to Opelousas. In the parish of St. Martin the colored people were compelled to take an oath to have nothing to do with the Republican party in order to save their lives. About the 28th day of October witness left Opelousas and came to New Orleans.

Beverly Wilson states, on oath, that he lives at Opelousas, parish of St. Landry, Louisiana. On the 26th of September, 1868, the Republican party held a public meeting at Opelousas. That on the 28th day of September (3) three white men, armed, named Jim Dickson, John Williams, and one Mayo, brother of the druggist, went to the Methodist Church, where Mr. Bentley, the editor of the St. Landry Progress, was teaching school. One of the three guarded the doors and the others went inside, and, approaching Mr. Bentley, told him to sign a paper, which he held in his hand, the substance of which was a perfect denial of some remarks that Mr. Bentley had made in his paper a few weeks before. Mr. Bentley then asked him if all the fuss would be done away with, if he would sign the paper. The answer was, "We will tell you about that after you have signed it." Mr. Bentley then signed the paper. The three men then fell upon him, beating him in a terrible manner with sticks and any thing they could lay hands on. One of the party made the remark, "Let's put our mark on his face;" but they did not do it. The children then rushed out from the building, terrified, telling every one they met that Mr. Bentley was being killed. Many of the children living on the edge of town, the news soon spread to the adjoining plantations; the colored people hearing the news armed themselves with what they could lay their hands on, and proceeded to Opelousas to protect Mr. Bentley, as he was looked upon as the leader of the Radical Republican party; but when they had reached the edge of town they were met by John Simms and Charles Thompson, who told them to go back, as the fuss was all over. They went back. Another crowd of colored men from other parts of the parish were met by a band of white Democrats. The band asked the colored men where they were going. They said, they wanted to go into town to protect Mr. Bentley. The white men told them to lay down their arms; when one of the colored men said, "I am the chief of this band; boys, fire!" which they did, killing three horses, but hurt no person. The white men returned the fire, killing one colored man dead and wounding two or three others; the rest of them were taken prisoners and lodged in the Opelousas jail. They were afterwards brought before Dr. Thompson, who ordered them to be shot. Sheriff Hays being present prevailed upon Dr. Thompson to rescind his order for the time being. The following night ten of these colored men were taken out of jail and shot dead, and left upon the ground for some two or three days before they were buried. They were finally buried in the following manner: a hole was dug about a foot deep, laying the bodies therein and covering them over with earth so as to leave some portions of their body out of the ground: some had their feet, some their arms, uncovered, upon which the *buzzards were feeding.* On the 29th of September, 1868, a band of armed white men broke into the office of the St. Landry Progress, and took the type and threw it into the middle of the streets; they then broke up the press and all the furniture that they could lay their hands on in the office. There they found the roll book containing all the names of members of the Republican clubs in the parish. They took the names of all the prominent Republicans and went about hunting them up. Those that they could find they killed on the spot; others who hid themselves in the swamp and bush saw armed white men approaching, burning up their houses and furniture. As for the number of colored men that were killed, deponent cannot exactly say; but he has been told by respectable white men in the parish, that the number cannot be less than (200) two hundred, and all those that wanted to have any protection for their lives, were told that they *must join the Democratic party.* During the late registration, every colored man belonging to the Democratic party was obliged to take his certificate of registration to Mr. Mayo, the druggist, and leave it with him, which they all did, to the best of witness' knowledge and belief. Deponent does not know a colored man that did not do it, as they thought that if they did not they would be looked upon with suspicion, that is, as Radicals, which is equivalent to being an escaped murderer in this parish. All the so-called colored Democrats were furnished with protection papers by the Central Hancock Club, and were told that no white man would hurt them when they showed this paper. This paper was given to almost all the colored men, and witness' reads as follows:

"PROTECTION."

"Opelousas, October 5, 1868.

"This is to certify that Beverly Wilson is a member of the First Colored Hancock Democratic Club of the First Ward, and is entitled to the friendship, confidence and protection of all good Democrats.

"(Signed) LEON MANSO, President.

"Approved, T. L. MACON,
"President Democratic Central Committee.

"Approved by Central Hancock Club,
"(Signed) WM. H. ELLIS, Secretary.

"Approved, J. H. OVERTON,
"President Central Democratic Committee,
"Parish St. Landry.

"Approved, J. H. Halsey, Chairman."

It is a perfect reign of terror in St. Landry for colored men; they are now taunted every day with the expression, "Now, where is your protection—the Yankees do not care anything about you." Deponent is now living in the city of New Orleans, and is trying his best to get something to do, as he is afraid to go back, and wishes to make enough money to send for his family; he does not know what will become of the colored people in that parish if something is not done very soon for their protection. The white men disarmed all the colored men in the parish before they commenced firing on them.

Emerson Bently states, on oath, that he is a native of the state of Ohio; that he is in his nineteenth year; that he has resided in Opelousas, St. Landry parish, La., for the past ten months; that for seven months he was engaged as English editor of the "St. Landry Progress."

That on Monday morning, Sept. 28th, 1868, three white men, armed with pistols, appeared at the back door of the Methodist Episcopal church, used by witness as a school house. At least two of them were members of the Seymour Knights.

One of them named J. K. Dickson asked witness to step to the door, which he declined to do. Dickson said "just as you please, sir," and stepping up into the doorway took from his pocket a copy of the "St. Landry Progress" of the 20th Sept., 1868, containing an account of a Republican meeting held at Washington, parish of St.

Landry, on Sept. 13, 1868, and asked him if he was aware that a party of gentlemen on Sunday last, Sept. 13, went to Washington armed for self protection, in consequence of speeches that had been made in Opelousas Radical Republican clubs, and reports that had been circulated throughout the community that the Radicals intended to burn the town of Washington. "We warned you," said he "that in case you lied about that affair, you conld not escape our revenge. Notwithstanding our warnings you have published statements that are both malicious and false."

Witness said, "do you mean to say that I lied in that report?" "Yes sir !" said he, "g—d d—n you, I do," and struck witness several blows with a heavy cane on his shoulders and back. One S. Mayo, lately constable of Opelousas, had at this time gone to the front door. When Dickson commenced striking witness, the pupils commenced jumping out of the windows, some of them passed through the door where Mayo stood, who pointed his pistol at them; witness was soon entirely alone with these three men. Dickson struck him about fifteen times with his cane, cursing him meanwhile in an outrageous manner, calling him a "d—d Radical dog;" Mayo and John Williams encouraged him, saying, "Give it to him, Dickson; g—d d—d him, use him up; there are three of us." Dickson then drew from his pocket a document which he read to witness; in effect it was an acknowledgment that deponent's editorial report of the Washington meeting was false and malicious, to be signed by him as editor of the Progress; Williams placed a chair at the table and said: "Now, g—d d—d you, sit down and sign, or we will have satisfaction;" witness hesitated to do so, when Williams said: "Let's do it right; let's do it thoroughly," and taking the cane from Dickson, struck him a number of blows; witness asked them what part of that editorial report they considered false; Dickson replied, "we do not want to talk with you; sign that, or we will use you up;" being at their mercy, and feeling that they were about to resort to extreme measures, he asked Dickson if they would go away and let him alone if he would sign the document; he replied, "yes; until you lie again;" witness then signed the paper and they left. As witness passed out he met a large crowd of men, principally friends, who had come to see about the disturbance; he did not observe that any of them were armed; the children had spread the report through the town that "they are killing Bentley;" one of the first men he met was the Deputy Sheriff, who inquired what had happened; he told witness that he could do nothing until he went before a Justice of the Peace, and procured a warrant for the arrest of the parties. B. R. Gantt, a member of the Democratic Executive Committee of the parish, advised him to go immediately before a Justice of the Peace and make affidavit. As the streets were thronged with citizens, witness advised his friends to return to their homes; he afterward met Judge George R. King and Dr. James Ray, both prominent Democrats—Dr. Ray being a member of the Democratic Committee; both expressed the desire that this should be considered merely a "personal affair," and that he should allow the law to take its course; that there was no necessity of its being the cause of a public disturbance; witness told them he should do so; and went immediately to the office of Justice D. P. Hill and made affidavit against the three parties that had assaulted him, and then went to the Progress office; on the way he saw numbers of his friends collected in groups; he advised them to go immediately to their homes, which they did; he saw also armed white men moving about town; he then went up stairs in the Progress office and lay down, feeling at the time quite ill; some of his friends advised witness to order the clubs to come immediately to Opelousas and revenge the outrage; he told them no, that he had received assurances from members of the Democratic Committee that they wished the law to be enforced, and that Dr. George Hill had met him and told him to go home, that a lawyer would be procured and that he need not trouble himself any further; Dr. Hill is a Democrat. Deponent does not know that any word was sent to any Republican clubs, ordering them to come to Opelousas. About 1 o'clock he heard very exciting talk down stairs, and recognized the voice of Dr. Little; he said, in effect, "Mr. Donato, you have sent for the clubs to come to Opelousas to revenge the whipping of that scoundrel Bentley; a party of gentlemen caned him for half an hour and did not give him half enough, and now you wish to bring men to murder our wives and children; we own this town; this has been going on long enough; now see if you can take it." At this time some one entered the office, and stated that they were fighting down town. A friend came to witness and told him that he must conceal himself; that Dr. Little and about twenty armed men were below; they concealed him in the loft of a barn in the yard of the Progress office, where he slept until about half-past 8 P. M., when he was aroused by voices and people walking in the yard; he recognized the voices of members of the "Seymour Knights," and heard Solomon Loeb (the President of the club,) say: "We are going to kill every man who has been engaged in deceiving the freedmen and trying to create enmity between the races." Men with lights were searching the barn, mentioning deponent's name frequently with curses; they came to the door leading to the loft where witness was secreted; it was locked, and not finding the key they proposed to break down the door with an axe, when one of them remarked: "He is not there—there is no loft to the barn;" another then said, "Come on boys; let's go and get François D'Avy;" they then left after posting sentinels around the office and yard of the Progress; he heard numerous parties pass and repass, halted by the sentinels; he also heard shots fired. At 7 o'clock the next morning a friend came and told him that he must leave that place, that they were returning to search for him; that they would kill him; that Mr. Durant, the French editor of the Progress, had been killed, and François D'Avy had been shot during the night; witness had just left the barn and concealed himself in the weeds of a garden in the rear when a large body of armed men came and searched the loft thoroughly; during the day he saw bodies of armed white men riding through the town and heard several shots in different parts of the town. Tuesday night, September 29, 1868, about 10 o'clock, witness heard parties of men passing to and from the Progress office, loading a wagon two or three times with material, and dumping it into the street and elsewhere; he could not distinguish any of the parties as they proceeded in silence not calling each other by name. On Wednesday they visited the office several times; about evening a large number of them came; they appeared to be fixing a seat on a wagon; he heard parties say they were going to burn old Bentley; a colored child said "please don't kill him, he is my teacher." For thirty-three hours deponent had nothing to eat or drink; at night he ran across the prairie to a field, when he was pursued by an armed body of white men. On Thursday night, assisted by friends, he escaped to the country; on Saturday night following, he was surrounded in a gully, but escaped; on Sunday night he remained on a plantation about five miles from Opelousas; he sent men each day to Opelousas to ascertain the particulars of the disturbance; he heard that prisoners were placed in the jail during the day and at night they were taken out and shot; armed men went from house to house seizing arms in the possession of colored people, and that every prominent Republican had been killed or forced to leave. Colored men had to pledge themselves to vote the Democratic ticket or abstain from politics. Drs. Thompson, Little and Estarge were the leaders of the white men, and ordered prominent Republicans to be killed. Colored men were obliged to wear a red ribbon for protection. The number estimated as having been killed ranged from fifty to a hundred, and some were quite positive that no less than two hundred were killed and wounded. F. Perrodin, a Deputy Sheriff, was a leader among the rioters, and gave protection papers to colored men on condition that they would discountenance the Republicans and abstain from politics. For weeks it was common talk that if they could kill off the leaders of the Republican party they could control the colored vote.

Linden E. Bentley states, on oath, that he has been engaged as foreman of the St. Landry progress. On Monday morning, September 28, 1868, a colored boy came to the office and told him that armed men were at the school house of his brother, (Emerson Bently, editor of the Progress) trying to kill him. He started immediately and met his brother coming toward the court house with a crowd of colored persons. He told witness that three men came to the school house and said to him that he had been publishing a lying account of a meeting held by the Republicans, at Washington, La., in which some remarks were made of "rebel spirit exhibited." These three men then commenced beating him with a cane.

Witness states that his brother then went to the office of Dr. Hill, Justice of the Peace, to make affidavits against said three men, whose names are Mayo, Dickson, and Williams; witness then returned to the Progress office, and was soon followed by his brother; shortly afterward white men, mounted and armed, came into town from every direction, and congregated near the court house. Armed patrols were sent around town to disarm the negroes. The freedmen were also coming into town armed, but witness' brother, and others, advised them to return to their homes and keep quiet, which most of them did. At about 12 o'clock an armed and mounted crowd of white men, 30 or 40 in number, accompanied by Mr. O. H. Violett, former agent of the Freedmen's Bureau, came to the Progress office and demanded to see Messrs. Gustave and Cornelius Donato, (proprietors of said paper) who came in, and Dr. Little, acting as spokesman for the crowd, told them that they, (the Messrs. Donato) had called in the freedmen, armed for the purpose of massacreing the women and children of the white people, because Bently had had a caning which he deserved, and that they had sent out couriers to tell the freedmen to arm and come to town; that a courier had been captured who was on his way to Washington to bring the Republican club at that place, to Opelousas, armed. The Messrs. Donato denied that they had in any manner tried to excite a riot, or had sent a courier to Washington. At this juncture a white man came in and said: "they are fighting at Hilaire Paillet's," a plantation a short distance out of town, whereupon the crowd mounted and left. Deponent's brother concealed himself and deponent closed up the office and went to John Brown's house where he was boarding. He knew nothing of the fight except from report. He heard that one white man and two or three colored men were killed, and several wounded on each side. Armed pickets were placed over the town, and persons entering or leaving the town were challenged. Monday night, at about 11 o'clock, a band of fifteen or twenty armed men came to the house where witness was staying, and demanded the key of the Progress office. Their leader, Pat. Ward, had a revolver, cocked, in his hand; he approached the table where deponent was sitting, and asked, "are you Bently's brother?" He answered that he was. Ward then said: "you are a pretty radical son of a b—h, ain't you?" Deponent does not doubt but that he intended to shoot him but for a young lady, who placed herself between them, and held his arm. Said Ward was drunk at the time. Witness informed this gang that he had left the back door of the office open, and that a man named Jesse Hutchins was working in the office. After a while the crowd left and he saw no more of them; soon after, at about twelve o'clock, he heard two shots fired in quick succession, in the direction of the residence of Mr. F. J. D'Avy, a leading Republican of the parish; about fifteen minutes after this Mr. D'Avy came running into the house, in bare feet and shirt sleeves, with his hand on the side of his head: a ball had grazed his head, near the ear. Witness saw Mr. D'Avy pass the house on his way home, the next morning; he had not been further molested.

On the same night above mentioned Mr. Durant, French editor of the Progress, disappeared, and was not seen nor heard from until Wednesday, when it was reported that a crowd of white men took him from his house into the woods, and it is supposed murdered him. He was a citizen of France.

Witness remained at home until Wednesday morning; he then went down to the court house, with Clement Camp, a fellow workman, and obtained permission from an old gentleman, who seemed to be acting as provost marshal, to go to the Progress office to get some clothing; he found the material destroyed, the press broken, and the type strewed about the floor and in the streets. Having been advised to leave deponent started at ten o'clock that morning on the steamer J. S. Blackford. On the way down Bayou Courtaubleau he saw white men riding about armed with shot guns, revolvers, etc.

Pierre Young, thirty-seven years of age, a registered voter of the parish of St. Landry, Louisiana, states, on oath, that he was born in Opelousas, Louisiana, and was the slave of one Dr. Thompson's wife's father, (Caddie Dupré). He has been working a crop of cotton on government land, near Washington, in said parish. On the 29th day of September, 1868, a large force of white men, about two or three hundred in number, armed with pistols, guns and swords, came to his place, headed by one Camillie Petrie (sheriff of Washington), Dr. McMillan, Capt. Prescott and Yorick Vallard; Camillie Petrie asked witness where his fire-arms were; witness replied that he did not have any; when Petrie said, "You d—n son of a b—h, you lie, you have got some;" witness still persisted that he had none, when he again said, "You d—d son of a b—h, if you don't go and get them for me I will cut your head off," he had a sword in his hand at the time. Said Petrie then went away and returned in a few moments with three colored men, one of whom was Henry Clay, president of a colored Democratic club, the other men's names were Natchey and King; Henry Clay asked witness for his arms, witness replied that he had none. Clay then said that it was a d—n lie, that he did have arms. Natchey then said to witness, "Who gave you the right to come on government land." Dr. McMillan then spoke, and said, "You black son of a b—h, you have no right to be working on government land, go work for your master; if you don't do it, in a few days we will kill you." Witness made no reply and walked away from him. The next night, at 8½ o'clock, sheriff Petrie came to witness' house with ten white men armed, and asked witness' wife where he was. She replied that he had gone to the country. Petrie then called her a "black, lying b—h," and said he would put her in jail, and that he would kill witness. They then went away. During this time witness was hiding in the bushes, not ten paces from his house. Witness also states, that on the 29th day of September, 1868 Paul Lambert and a son of Mr. Achille Dupré, and Pierre Gradny, and Sustan Lambert, went to Achille Dupré's plantation and took Francois, a colored man, from the field, and asked him for his weapons; he replied that he did not have any. Paul Lambert then stepped up and calling him a lying son of a b—h, shot him dead. They then went to the house of another colored man on the same plantation named Willis Johnson, when Paul Lambert asked him if he would vote the Democratic ticket; he replied that he belonged to the Republican party. A son of Achille Dupré, (a boy of fifteen), then drew a pistol and shot him (W. Johnson), dead, the ball entering just over the right ear. They then left and went to Paul Lambert's plantation and took a colored man named Wilson Deacon and his son, a short distance from their house and shot them dead. The said Wilson Deacon had voted the Democratic ticket, and witness believes that he was killed so that these white men could get their crop of cotton, which was a fine crop. When Mrs. Wilson Deacon asked these men why they had killed her husband, they replied, "by order of Dr. Thompson." She then asked them how she was going to make a living, since they had killed her husband, and they replied, "the best way you can, but you can't take your crop off my land." Yorick Vallard told witness that if the colored men did not vote the Democratic ticket, the white people would kill them off. The colored men were obliged to vote the Democratic ticket or run the risk of losing their lives. Witness states that there were about three thousand colored Republicans in St. Landry parish, but that he does not know of one who voted the Republican ticket. Witness states that he has knowledge of over one hundred and fifty (150) colored men who were murdered during the recent riot last September in this parish. Witness further states that he saw guards placed over the dead bodies so that they might be made food for buzzards, they were left lying on the top of the ground, and in the ditches and swamps. About 9 o'clock in the evening of the 29th day of September, witness was standing about one hundred and fifty feet from the Opelousas end of the Washington long bridge, when he saw two or three hundred armed men coming over the bridge with a colored man by the name of Victor Dufau as their prisoner; when they came to about thirty feet of the bridge, they halted and placed the said Victor Dufau against some brush by the road. A white man, one Capt. Prescott, of Washington, parish of St. Landry, gave the order to a colored man Natchey, in their party, to load, prime, aim, fire. Said Natchey did fire, and killed the said Victor Dufau. A few days after the riot witness was met by Sheriff Petrie, who asked him to be a Democrat; witness told him that he could not, as he belonged to the Radical party. Said Petrie then said that witness would be a dead nigger if he did not vote the Democratic ticket. Witness was fearful that the threat would be carried out, and took the first favorable opportunity to leave the parish, taking to the woods during the day.

S. A. Miller states, on oath, that since the 1st day of July, 1865, he has been a resident of St. Landry parish, State of Louisiana, and known as an ex-soldier of the federal army, and in politics a Republican. Deponent aided the loyal men of the parish to favor reconstruction of the State of Louisiana, according to the acts of Congress. And on the 17th and 18th days of April, 1867, he lent an unflinching aid to carry our constitution. Was at the polls on the 17th and 18th days of April, 1868, and saw an outrageous attempt on the part of the opposers of reconstruction to intimidate the colored men from voting the Republican ticket.

Deponent came to New Orleans in the latter part of July, 1868, and on the 29th day of October, 1868, was employed by Hon. C. B. Darrall, candidate for Congress, to take some tickets to the parish of St. Landry for distribution, and work for the election of the Republican candidates.

He arrived in Opelousas about 4 o'clock in the afternoon of October 31, 1868. Mr. Malone, driver of the mail coach, told him that on arriving in town he had better go to Col. Thompson and get a Democratic certificate of protection, or else his life would be in danger, as he was known to be a Republican. Mr. Malone also advised him to go to "Hayes' Hotel," and then he might not be molested during the night. Deponent went to this hotel. Mr. White, one of the proprietors, gave him a room. A few minutes afterwards Mr. James G. Hayes. the proprietor, came in and told him that his political career had been too obnoxious to the people of the parish for him to stop at his hotel, unless he could show a certificate of protection from the Democratic head quarters, or something to that effect. Deponent left the hotel, and went over to the office of the Freedmen's Bureau. While there Mr. Violett, ex-agent of the Freedmen's Bureau for the parish of St. Laudry, approached him and said: "god d—n you Radical son of a b—h, you reported me and had me removed, so that you might have that office for your radical purposes. About that time deponent was handed a letter reading as follows: "Mr. Miller: You must leave town immediately." Signed, "Young Democrats." Just then a great many people came over to said office, and made all kinds of threats against him. These men wanted to know if he did not know better than to come there when the people were so excited, and bring tickets for radical purposes. Many of these men were armed with large revolvers. Charles Moss approached deponent with revolver in hand, and told him that he could not see the "election through." Deputy Sheriff Perodin, and a man that claimed to be one of the town council, came to deponent, the latter saying: "Mr. Miller, you must get out of this corporation immediately." Witness asked him to let him wait until the next morning, so that he could take a stage or boat. No, says he, "you must go now, as you have come here as a Republican, we cannot keep the people down unless you do." Witness then appealed to them as a citizen and resident of the parish, to have protection from the civil authorities until he reached the limits of said parish; he replied "that Deputy Sheriff Perrodin would see him safe as far as the corporation limits." Witness then started to leave the parish with Capt. Dutton, A. S. A. C., and the Deputy Sheriff as his guard. As they were on the stage road going toward Grand Couteau, and near the town line, deponent saw a great many horsemen coming from town, whom he recognized as residents of Opelousas; they all had large revolvers hanging on them, and moved on both sides of deponent, forming a complete circle around him. Deponent was now some little distance from town, when Capt. Dutton and the Sheriff halted to return home; he then bade them good bye, and asked them if they did not think it was a hard looking chance for him to escape from a crowd of horsemen like that? The Deputy replied, "you should have known better than to have come here, when people are so excited." A horseman then came up, and said, "I will take charge of this man now." Deponent asked him if he was an officer? He replied "yes." Deponent then went with this man. On his way three horsemen, Charles Moss, Gill Cochran and G—, junior, kept close behind deponent. Witness called the Deputy Sheriff's attention to these men. The Deputy admitted that Charles Moss had said to him a short time before, that he would kill deponent, but said that the said Moss was a low puppy. The Deputy Sheriff halted these men and told them to go back to Opelousas, that they were not following them for any good. Cochran replied that he was "going squirrel hunting, and he be d—d if he would go home." Just then some colored men were passing on horseback. Witness tried to hire a horse from them at any price, but these men were afraid to recognize him, although he knew them well, so he had to content himself on foot. Witness was now completely surrounded by horsemen. The Deputy Sheriff, Mr. C. C. Dusion ordered them to halt, and come to him. After much persuasion on the part of said Deputy, three of these vile wretches came forward, and were ordered by the Deputy to go home. They replied, in fact, swore, that they would not; that they had a right to go squirrel hunting; and told the Deputy that he had no business out there. Deponent was continually passed and repassed by these men; they would halt at times and allow him to pass; then they would pass him. Deponent while passing Charles Moss' plantation, which is about three miles from town, was met by said Moss' brother. The Deputy Sheriff represented this young man to be good and quiet, and said that he would order him to take back those two men that lived in town. The Deputy gave said order, directing him to take Cochran and Gaurrique jun'r to town. Cochran drew his revolver and said, "he be d—d if he would be taken back." The Sheriff made him and G—, jun'r stop there and he went on. After deponent and the Deputy Sheriff had gone about a quarter of a mile further. the Deputy told him that he (the Deputy) must go back home, (deponent was now about eight or ten miles distant from Grand Couteau), and that he (deponent) must now go into the woods and make his escape the best way he could. The Deputy promised deponent that he would watch on the road so as not to let Charles Moss or any of those town rats go after him, for Charles Moss had said previous to deponent's leaving Capt. Dutton's company, that he would "kill that Radical Miller that night." Deponent asked the Deputy if he would not accompany him as far as Grand Couteau. The Deputy replied that he could not. Deponent then proceeded on his way alone, the Deputy returning to Opelousas. Deponent had gone about forty steps, when he saw Charles Moss coming towards him on a grey horse, with his revolver pointed at him. Said Moss had just passed the Deputy Sheriff, and said Deputy called upon Moss to halt; Moss not doing so, the Sheriff fired at him, and run his horse full speed after him and shot again; the horse stumbled down and threw the Deputy Sheriff into the mud and water. The Deputy then called out to deponent telling him to get out of the way the best he could, for if Moss come back on them he could give himself nor deponent no protection. Deponent then crept through the fence to an adjoining pasture on his hands and knees until he reached the middle of it; he then took the clothes out of his satchel and put them inside the bosom of his shirt, and buttoned up his coat so as to hide the white as much as possible. Deponent heard men whistling to each other in the woods, and saw Charles Moss running his horse as fast as he could toward Opelousas. Deponent crawled from the pasture into the woods, and had just got into some briars when he heard the hoofs of a great many horses on the other side of the pasture, coming from the direction of Opelousas, the moon shining brightly he saw at least forty horsemen together; they patrolled the road; five of them on horseback passed within forty feet of the briar bush where he was hiding; they went on the other side of the stream. Deponent heard the hoofs of horses coming from Opelousas, and heard one of the horsemen say, "here is where the d—d Radical went through the pasture." At this time there was a continual arrival of horsemen, sometimes two at a time. Deponent remained in the briar bush about two hours, and made up his mind to move through the picket line, and moving down toward a little opening, saw Charles Moss sitting about forty yards ahead of him on his grey horse. Deponent crawled away from him about three rods into the briars; he then saw a white man with a black mask on his face, his hands were white. Deponent made a noise in the bush; the man in mask raised his gun and took aim, but deponent laid perfectly quiet, hugging the ground until the man in mask took down his gun; he then gave a low whistle, and deponent saw something moving around from one side of the tree to the other about thirty paces from him; presently this figure gave a low whistle, and about two minutes afterward some one came to him dressed in a white gown, or something similar, and threw something over a limb of the tree about four feet above him; it was then about day light, and deponent started in a half run, seeing the person dressed up in the white robe climb up the rope until he reached the limb of the tree which he sat on. Deponent stopped, hearing something running down on his left in the brush; he then started again, seeing that they were trying to flank him, deponent, went to the same pasture from which he had made his escape first, and seeing some small houses in the distance, went toward them; a colored man cried out, "who is there?" Deponent beckoned his hand at him to hush, and then turned back toward the fence, and crawled along the ditch for a couple of hundred yards, and then laid flat down on his back in said ditch, which was about one foot deep; presently deponent heard a man say, "have you seen that man pass through there?" Some one at the house replied, "no, could you not shoot him?" The sun was shining on deponent, he did not move an inch one way or the other, except when he could hear them going through the grass and briars a short distance out side of the fence. He lay in the ditch most of the day; finally the men rode off, followed by a pack of dogs, barking. Deponent could hear the new volunteers ask the question, if they "had not killed that d—d white Radical yet?" and say, "here is a fresh track;" and then they would run and call their comrades, and dogs. Sunday night, as soon as deponent thought it was as dark as it would get, he crawled to the road, crossed it, and entered the plain prairie; he had proceeded about two hundred yards, when he heard a squad of horsemen coming towards him; they passed on; deponent kept back of all the fields until he got a little beyond Capt. Pratt's plantation, where the large prairie opens; after going some distance into it, deponent looking back, saw eight or ten horsemen place themselves along where he had already passed; he moved on, almost out of strength. From Saturday morning at 9 o'clock, until Monday at 7 o'clock, deponent only had a bowl of coffee. He is satisfied from the determination of the people of St. Landry parish, that a Republican could not live there, and declare his political sentiments, for if he did his life would be in peril and his property stolen. Deponent also states, that he was informed by many, that colored men were killed nightly And in conclusion, states that terrorism exists throughout the parishes of St. Landry and Lafayette, Louisiana.

Charles E. Montamat states on oath, that he was appointed supervisor of registration on the 3d of October, 1868, for the parish of St. Landry; that between the 12th and 20th of October some planters came with colored men to the office in numbers of twenty and twenty-five in clubs, to receive their certificates of registration, these men worked for these planters, the colored people had badges of Seymour and Blair on their coats, also badges of red ribbon on their coats. They delivered their certificates of registration to them personally. The planters who brought these colored men for their certificates, demanded from them their certificates. Through *fear* they were obliged to give them up. On the day of election, November 3, 1868, the colored voters came to the polls to vote; their employers came with them and gave them a democratic ticket and told them to vote that ticket. On the 1st day of November, 1868, one S. A. Miller, a Republican, came from New Orleans, for the purpose of distributing Republican tickets and voting, as he was a citizen of that parish. Mr. Miller came to the house where deponent was boarding. Deponent met him on the gallery and shook hands with him. Some six men followed behind him. Mr. Miller told deponent he came from the sheriff's house (Mr. Harris), where he had applied for board and lodging (it being a boarding house). He was refused. Mr. Miller stated that he wanted to see the Captain of the Freedmen's Bureau. While deponent was talking with Mr. Miller in the Captain's office a man named G. Violet called said Miller on the back gallery, where some very abusive language was used to Mr. Miller by the said G. Violet; this said G. Violet was discharged from the position as agent of the Freedmen's Bureau for interfering in politics. A notice was given to Mr. Miller to leave the parish in ten minutes, when he started to go away. Some thirty (30) men had gathered together on the gallery. Mr. Miller, seeing so many men around him, asked the Captain to give him protection. The Captain replied he had no protection, but would accompany him (Mr. Miller) two miles out of the town. The Captain with the deputy sheriff proceeded with Mr. Miller two miles out of town where they left him. The planters forced their laborers to vote the Democratic ticket whether they were willing or not, by misrepresentation and intimidation. Deponent heard that the reason why the Democrats wished Mr. Miller to leave the parish was that he was a leader of the Republican party.

John Baptiste Antoine (colored) states, on oath, that he is a resident of New Orleans, and a registered voter in said city; that on or about the 27th day of October, 1868, he went to Opelousas on business connected with the Republican party. When he arrived at Opelousas, a colored man named Charles Prescott advised him to leave immediately; that he was in danger. A white man asked witness what he came there for. He answered that he had come to see his friends. The white man then asked him if he was a Republican or a Democrat. He answered that he was a Democrat. The white man said that was right, adding that "every nigger that they found to be a Radical they would kill; that they would not allow any Radicals about that place; every nigger that would join the Democratic party to drive the carpet-baggers out of the place would be safe; but if they joined with the carpet-baggers they would be killed." Deponent saw a party of white men take a colored man named "Toney" from his house, and after taking him a short distance, they shot him in the head and body with buckshot, killing him instantly—this occurred at about 11 o'clock, P. M., on October 28, 1868. The only provocation was that he was a Republican, and had been heard to cheer for Grant and Colfax. A day or two previous to the election these same white men discovered that deponent was a Republican and a discharged Federal soldier. He was informed by his colored friends that they, said white men, were hunting for him, and they would surely kill him, as they never spared a colored Republican who came there from the city. Witness managed to escape by hiding in the woods until dark, he then rode rapidly to Berwick Bay, and arrived in New Orleans without further molestation.

On September 29, 1868, the office of the "St. Landry Progress," a Republican newspaper, was destroyed by a crowd of armed men.

ST. LANDRY—SUMMARY.

Number killed, positively sworn to	55
Estimated by different parties and the Democratic papers	150 to 200
Number shot, positively sworn to	4
Number otherwise maltreated, positively sworn to	8

REMARKS.—Under the state of lawlessness and intimidation existing it has been impossible to procure full evidence from this parish. The probabilities are that the larger estimates are nearest the truth.

PARISH OF ST. MARY.

Josiah Fisk states, on oath, that on the election of Col. Pope, as sheriff of the parish of St. Mary, witness was requested by said Pope to go to Franklin, in said parish, to act as his legal adviser. Witness was at that time a resident of New Orleans, and practicing law in said city. When he arrived at Brashear City, he received a message from Col. Pope, saying that the people had become hostile, and had resolved that no Republican should hold office or have a house in the parish; also advising witness not to bring his family, but to go alone, and not let any one know that he knew him, (Col. Pope) or was seeking him until he (witness) had secured a house, as he would not be able to get one if he did. On witness' arrival at Franklin he sent his son to the hotel to secure rooms; he was told that they could be accommodated that night, and if suited, the landlady told him she would let them have any three rooms in the hotel that he desired. Witness remained at the hotel that night (September 1, 1868), and in the morning the landlady informed him that she had received orders not to rent any rooms, unless she could rent half the house, which would have been about twenty or thirty rooms. After a private interview with Col. Pope and Mr. Roberts (editor of the Attakapas Register, who had also been refused a house), witness went to the landlady of said hotel, and told her that he would rent the half or the whole of the house, if she would rent it. She replied that she had received instructions not to let him have any rooms in her house at all. Witness having heard of a house to rent back of town, sent his son to the agent (one Demortie) with money to pay the rent in advance. Said Demortie inquired who wanted the house, and was informed that Mr. Fisk wanted it. He replied that he would not rent the house without proper references. Witness then went personally to Mr. Demortie, who told him that he wanted some one to vouch for him. Witness replied that he knew of no one, but would pay the rent in advance, to which Demortie replied, "I will tell you plainly, I will not rent my house to any but a Democrat, and I ask you plainly are you a Democrat or Republican?" to which witness replied, "I am taking no active part in politics at present, but I am a Republican." Mr. Demortie then told him he could not have the house at any price. Witness, however, found a house occupied by a widow lady, and had agreed upon the terms, and offered the money, when she told him that she would like time to consider and find out about him, for if he was a Republican she would be afraid the Democrats would either kill her or burn her house. So witness could not get this house, but afterwards procured rooms at the house of Mr. Baldwin.

Witness was informed that the Democrats were pledged to kill or drive away every Republican officer in the parish, and at the request of Col. Pope he never appeared on the streets with him (Col. P.) except once, and then they were obliged to separate on account of the crowd gathering, hooting, and yelling "here comes Pope, the carpetbagger, and his scallawag lawyer." A few hours before the murder of Col. Pope and Judge Chase they were both at the court house. Witness met Judge Chase at the door and spoke to him about the threats that had been made. Judge Chase told him that one of the crowd had told him that they had concluded not to murder him (Chase) as he had resided so long in the parish, and being a planter, but that they would certainly kill Col. Pope and all the balance of them. While talking witness saw three or four men directly opposite the court house talking in a violent manner and looking threateningly at them. Witness called the judge's attention to these men, and told him that they would kill him. He replied, "Yes, I believe they will kill me."

Sometime afterward witness was in a room in town when he received notice from men belonging to the Seymour Knights that they would kill him that evening (October 17, 1868). A man in the room advised him to leave immediately, which he did as soon as he saw which direction the "Knights" took, he taking the opposite direction, riding rapidly for home. Witness thinks he could identify several of these men. There are two roads leading from Franklin to Mr. Baldwin's place, which form a junction before reaching the house, and it was at this junction that they intended to kill witness, but riding rapidly he had just passed this point when the club came up; but finding they had missed him, they returned to Franklin, seperating, and some going to the house of Col. Pope and some to the house of Jack Moore, a colored man and President of a Republican club, whom they searched for, but he having gone to a place about fifteen miles distant to spend the night, they did not find him. All the leading colored men had to take to the swamps, not daring to return home until they were assured of protection by the military. Pickets were stationed on the road so that witness could not get to Franklin from Mr. Baldwin's place. He, however, escaped by crossing the Teche and wading through the swamps to Grand Lake and taking a skiff to Brashear. He stayed all night about three miles from that place, and was here met by a man named Slack, who told him that he could not get to Brashear, as the Democrats had pickets out. The military arrived at Brashear the next morning, and witness then finding it safe proceeded. Witness knows nothing concerning the murder of Col. Pope and Judge Chase except what he has learned from his wife and others, and from such information, he states that Col. Pope and Judge Chase were together on the gallery in front of Pope's room which was in the rear of the hotel and on the second floor. The murderers came along under the gallery softly until they reached the stairs, up which they rushed and fired several balls into Col. Pope before he had a chance to rise, when he jumped for his room into which he fell dead. Judge Chase struggled with them on the gallery and stairs, they firing at and stabbing him during the time. He fell on the bank of the bayou a few paces away. Previous to this one evening a man had been stationed at a bridge (which witness passed on his way home) for the purpose of killing witness, but being detained in Franklin later than usual that night, tho man thought he had missed him and started for town, but as witness was riding rapidly toward home he met the man who said, "You old scallawag, you are late to-night, but I will get you yet," and drawing his pistol exclaimed, "I'll give you h—ll now," and fired at witness, but missed him. He then yelled after him, that he would "jayhawk him yet." There never had been a word between this man and witness, and no violent language had been used to engender any ill feeling. He further states that on the 18th, the day after the murder of Pope and Chase, he was informed of the names of some of the murderers, and wrote out an affidavit and writ for their arrest, but as the sheriff was dead, and he could have no communication with the coroner or any constable, he found that in order to have the parties arrested it would be necessary to deputise a colored man to execute the writ. He also had satisfactory proof before him that the murderers, assisted by a large number of their Democratic friends, were drawn up in line of battle, and that they had all the streets leading into Franklin picketed, and were sending the women and children out of town, as though preparing for battle. He also had proof that secret societies were formed all over the State, binding themselves by a pledge or oath to kill all the leading Republicans in the State and to protect each other at all hazards, and that the pledge was acquiesced in and sanctioned by the Democratic party of this parish. He also had proof that the Democrats had been receiving arms and ammunition for several weeks before the murder of Col. Pope and Judge Chase, and that the merchants in Franklin had refused to sell powder to Republicans. He was satisfied from the proofs before him that if he issued the writ, and an attempt was made to execute it and arrest the murderers, it would bring on a regular battle between the Democratic and Republican parties, and although the Republicans numbered about one thousand the most, yet most of them were unarmed, while the Democrats were armed, he deemed that the contest would be unequal, and not being willing to have unarmed Republicans slaughtered he refused to give out the writ, and has it now in his possession.

Josiah Fisk further states on oath, that he is a duly qualified Justice of the Peace, of Ward No. 3 of said parish of St. Mary. Upon being informed of the murder of Col. H. H. Pope, and Valentine Chase, he wrote an affidavit and a warrant for the arrest of the murderers, but he could not get any officer or any other person to attempt to serve said warrant except a colored man. He ascertained that the murderers were well armed and drilled, and was satisfied that any attempt to arrest them, especially by a colored man, would result in the death of those making the attempt, and he did not issue the writ. In connection with Mr. James Baldwin, the founder of the Baldwin University, at Berea, Ohio, and the Hon. John Page, of Jefferson, who was at Mr. Baldwin's house; he addressed a communication to the commander of the Post at New Iberia, in said parish, stating the facts of the murder, and the situation of affairs in Franklin, and soliciting aid from him. In a few hours the messenger returned bringing a reply, of which the following is a copy, to wit:

HEADQUARTERS POST OF NEW IBERIA,
New Iberia, La., Oct. 18, 1868.

Messrs. Fisk, Baldwin and Page:

SIRS—Your note of this date has just been received. In reply I would respectfully beg leave to state, that the position in which I am placed as a Post Commander, is one which will not allow my taking any steps in any matter unless it be to assist the civil officers in keeping the peace. Strict orders have been issued, which prohibit military commanders from taking any action, unless it be upon requisition from the Sheriff to assist in quelling a riot. The case presented by you does not come within the scope of my orders. However, knowing that this case is a serious one, more so than any that has come to my notice, I shall telegraph to New Orleans for orders. I would be much obliged if you would furnish me with all the particulars of this case, with names of witnesses, in order that I can make a full report by letter.

I am gentlemen, most respectfully,

Your obedient servant,

(Signed) STAUNTON WEAVER,

1st Lt. 20th U. S. I., Commanding the Post.

Mr. Fisk then addressed a communication to General Rousseau, of which the following is a copy, to wit:

PARISH OF ST. MARY, Oct. 18, 1868.

Major General Rousseau, Commanding the Department of the Gulf:

DEAR SIR—The undersigned respectfully represents that a mob went to the room occupied by Col. H. H. Hope, in the town of Franklin, and parish of St. Mary, and killed him and Valentine Chase. Col. H. H. Pope was the Sheriff, and Valentine Chase was the Parish Judge. The Coroner elect has failed to qualify, which leaves a Justice of the Peace the highest officer in the parish. The mob is armed and bids defiance to the civil authorities. I am a Justice of the Peace of said parish, and respectfully solicit your aid in furnishing troops to assist the civil authorities in dispersing said mob, and in arresting the murderers, and preventing the town of Franklin from being burned. Yours respectfully,

(Signed) JOSIAH FISK,

Justice of the Peace 3d ward, parish of St. Mary.

Being satisfied that it was not safe to remain longer in that parish, witness came to New Orleans; upon his arrival General Rousseau sent for him and made inquiries as to the situation of affairs in Franklin, and wound up the interview by stating that he was satisfied that we ought to have two companies sent to Franklin, but that deponent must call on him through the Governor. Deponent then addressed a communicaton to the Governor, of which the following is a copy, to wit:

St. Mary Parish, October 20, 1868.

To His Excellency H. C. Warmoth, Governor of Louisiana:

A mob in Franklin, parish of St. Mary, on the night of the 17th of October, 1868, went to the room occupied by Colonel H. H. Pope, Sheriff of said parish, and in cold blood, without any words or quarrel, shot and killed him, and also killed Valentine Chase, Parish Judge of said parish. The Coroner elect of said parish has not qualified, which leaves a Justice of the Peace the highest civil officer in the parish. As I am a Justice of the Peace of said parish, and as said mob is now armed and bidding defiance to the civil authorities, and as the civil authorities here are unable to disperse said mob, or arrest the murderers, I deem it my duty to call on you for assistance in arresting the murderers and in dispersing said mob, and to restore peace and quiet. Yours, etc.,

JOSIAH FISK.

Witness wrote a communication of which the following is a copy, to wit:

Parish of St. Mary. November 5, 1868.

To His Excellency H. C. Warmoth, Governor of Louisiana:

The undersigned most respectfully represents, that on the 17th day of October, 1868, a mob went to the residence of Col. H. H. Pope, in Franklin, parish of St. Mary, and killed him and Valentine Chase. On the night of the twenty-eighth of the same month, a mob, composed in part of the same persons, went to the plantation of Mr. James Baldwin, near Franklin, and tore down the doors of the cabins and drove all the colored people from the plantation. Women with little children in their arms had to leave their homes, and hide in the woods and swamp, to save their lives. They then broke down the gate that led into the yard inclosing Mr. Baldwin's residence, and tried to get into his house, but failed. They left with curses, threatening to return again. From the violence and threats used, Mr. Baldwin did not deem it safe for him or his family to remain there. They left the plantation, and a large crop of sugar cane. The only excuse they gave for murdering Col. Pope and Judge Chase, was, because they had the presumption to hold office, one as Sheriff, and the other as Parish Judge, under the Constitution adopted under the reconstruction acts. The only reason they had for wanting to murder Mr. Baldwin and his family, was because Mr. Baldwin had donated twenty thousand dollars toward the building of an Institution for the education of "niggers." The murderers are at large, and bid defiance to the civil authorities. They have killed or run every officer from the parish that held office under the present Constitution, except myself, and they threaten to kill me if I issue a writ for their arrest. Nearly all the white men who would not join in the conspiracy against the new State Government, and all the leading colored men have been killed, or, to save their lives, have had to flee from the parish. When the white mob appears at the negro quarters, if they do not run, they are accused of inciting a riot, and are shot down without mercy; if they run and hide to save their lives, they are branded as cowards. A great number, both white and colored, are now refugees, and dare not return to their homes. In consideration of the above facts, I most respectfully solicit your aid as the Executive officer of the State, in procuring troops from the United States Government, to aid the civil authorities of this parish in arresting the murderers and in bringing them to trial.

Yours respectfully,

(Signed) JOSIAH FISK,

Justice of the Peace, 3d ward, parish of St. Mary.

Witness had proof from Mr. Baldwin, his wife and daughter, and others, of the truth of every fact stated in said communication. The Mr. J. Baldwin who was driven from his plantation, as stated in said communication, is an aged man between sixty and seventy, and the man who founded the Baldwin University at Berea, Ohio. He donated one hundred and fifty thousand dollars for the University at Berea; and had donated twenty thousand dollars towards building an Institution of learning on the plantation near Franklin, from which he and his family were driven. He had also made a standing proposition, pledging himself (in addition to the twenty thousand dollars) to give as many dollars as the Methodist church or any person would give, for the benefit of said Institution. Ten thousand dollars had also been given by Mr. B——, from France, and twenty thousand had been given by individuals mostly residing in the Northern States to purchase the plantation adjoining Mr. Baldwin's for an orphan's home. The plantation had been purchased and a large brick building commenced. The walls of the front building were up, the roof on, and they were about commencing to plaster it when Col. Pope was killed. In consequence of the excitement, and threats made, the hands all quit work, and the building was deserted.

The mob acknowledged that they made a charge on the asylum the night that they made the attack on Mr. Baldwin, but found no one there.

Mrs. Vashti H. Fisk states, on oath, that she was at the house of Mr. John Baldwin, near Franklin, St. Mary parish, Louisiana, on the night of the 28th of October, 1868, when she heard the firing of guns and pistols about the negro quarters; shortly after a mob or company of men came upon the gallery of the house and kicked at the door and called Mr. Baldwin several times. Mr. Baldwin, who was then in bed, asked them what they wanted. They replied that they wanted him to come out; they wanted to talk with him. He told them to come in the morning if they wanted to see him. They then said they wanted some coffee. Mr. B. replied that his daughter and her child were sick, and could not make coffee. They replied that they would be back in an hour and would have coffee, or they would take possession of the place. They swore and talked in an angry and rough manner. After they left the doors were barricaded with trunks, lounges, boxes, etc. On returning they tried to open the door, but failing, they left. In the morning, finding the gate broken down, the doors of the negro shanties knocked down and the negroes driven away, and deeming it unsafe to remain, witness, in company with Mr. Baldwin's family, consisting of Mr. Baldwin, his daughter and her child, packed up what they could carry of their clothes and went to the bank of the Teche, where they stayed till the morning of the 30th of October, when a boat coming down, they got on board and came to New Orleans, leaving the furniture at the house. Mr. Baldwin's daughter had been very sick.

Prince Davis states on oath, that he is a resident of Franklin, parish of St. Mary; that on the evening of October 17, 1868, he was in the club room when several persons came to the house, and one of them, named Thomas Gorda, looked in the room and then returned to the crowd and said something to them, they then hallooed "hurrra for Pope, the d—d son of a b—h." The crowd then left and went to the tavern where Col. Pope was; a short time after they left, witness heard the report of pistols at the tavern, and soon after left the club-room and started to go home; at the corner near his house he overtook two colored men, one named Morris. While speaking with them, Fred. Gates, Dan. Caffrey, George Gravenburg and some other white men came along and said "who is that?" Morris replied, "it is the old man Morris," when Caffrey said "we have killed Pope and Chase, is that anything to you?" Morris said "no." They then inquired for Wash. Williams' house. Morris warned Williams that they were after him, and he left.

John Fields states on oath, that he has been a resident of St. Mary parish since November 1865. At the Constitutional election held in April, 1868, he was elected Justice of the Peace for the fourth ward. On the 11th day of March, 1868, he purchased a horse from James Cook, and paid for the same; he rode said horse through Pattersonville, Franklin and Jenerette, electioneering and attending Republican club meetings; after it was ascertained that he was elected, he was accused of stealing said horse, arrested and put in jail without any trial. He offered A. J. Rosencrans, C. B. Darrall and Col. H. H. Pope as security for his appearance to answer said charge, which was refused. He was still confined in the parish jail in the town of Franklin on the 17th day of October, 1868, when Col. H. H. Pope, sheriff, and Valentine Chase, parish Judge, were murdered. The jail is situated directly opposite to the tavern where the above murders were committed. Deponent heard the report of pistols, and immediately afterwards the crowd came running from the tavern to the jail. They came near to the window of the cell where deponent was confined, and one of the crowd remarked to the others, "We have killed Pope and Chase, and we had better now kill the negro Justice of the Peace." Some one replied, "We had better, go in." One remarked "If we go in he will cripple some of us, so that they will find us out." The reply was, "We were in there the other day and searched the cell, he has nothing to cripple us with." Another said, "If that negro hits you with his fist there will not be much more left of you." One said to another, "Come, let me hold you up, and you shoot him through the window." He replied, "No, he might jerk the pistol out of my hand and shoot me before you could let me down." The reply was, "We have got him where we want him. If Grant and Colfax are elected we will go in and kill him while Kramer (the jailor) is sweeping out the jail. If Seymour and

Blair are elected we will take him out and tie him to a stake and shoot him and let his friends see him. Come, let's go and kill Jack Moore and Wash Williams. We must let none escape." The question was then asked, "Where does Fisk stay?" The reply was "He stays at the Baldwin Place." The remark then was, "If we can not get him to-night we will get him some other time." Deponent knows three of the persons engaged in the above conversation personally. Some of the others he knows by reputation, having heard their names called. Deponent was arrested and put in jail in Franklin on Saturday, the week after the election in April, 1868, and remained there until the latter part of June, when he, together with three others confined in the same cell, not liking the fare very much, found means of making their escape. Deponent remained out of jail until the latter part of August, when he was advised by Col. Pope (in consequence of the political excitement and threats which had been made against deponent and other Republicans) to give himself up and be put back in jail. He gave himself up under a promise from Col. Pope that he would help him to get out in a short time on bail. During the time that deponent was out he was in disguise at night and frequently dressed in women's clothes, and passed amongst the Democrats and saw their signs, heard their pass-words and threats against the Republican party and against particular members of that party whom they named. Deponent is able to give some of the signs and pass-words. They pledged themselves to let none escape except such as would take an oath to support Seymour and Blair. Deponent heard them mention the names of several Republicans that they intended to kill, among which were those of Pope and Chase. The club known there as the "Seymour Knights" were pledged to sustain each other at all hazards, and if one happened to be arrested they were pledged to assist him, and if necessary, in order to clear him of a charge, they were to swear that he was not in the place where the offense was alleged to have been committed, or anything else that was necessary to get him clear.

The following extract from the Cincinnati Gazette, containing a brief memoir of Judge Chase, and a letter from him to the Hon S. D. Campbell, are here inserted:

[Special Correspondence of the Cincinnati Gazette.]

HAMILTON, OHIO, October 23d., 1868.

The people of this community are deeply affected by the announcement first made that one of their former fellow-citizens, Judge Valentine Chase, was murdered by rebels in St. Mary parish, Louisiana, on the night of the 17th ultimo. Mr. Chase was a native of this county, and at one time represented this and Preble counties in the State Senate. He was a graduate of Miami University, and for some years practiced law in this city. In 1851 he was a prominent candidate of the Democracy of this county for the office of Lieutenant Governor. About six years after that he married a lady in Brashear parish, Louisiana, where he shortly afterward took up his residence. He resided there until the war broke out in 1861, when his Union sentiments made him an object of rebel wrath, and he was driven out of the State. Coming back to this city effectually cured of his Democratic proclivities, he at once took active part in the Union cause as editor of the Hamilton Telegraph. As sufficient evidence of his peaceable and conservative character, I may state that the proprietors of the Telegraph at one time threatened to discharge him because he would not resent personal assaults. At the close of the war he returned to Brashear parish, and was elected Parish Judge by the Union party—a crime for which he forfeited his life. The following letter written by him to the Hon. L. D. Campbell, just a fortnight before his assassination, will be read with painful interest, as the testimony of one who was standing on the brink of death, and as it were prophesying his own sad fate. His death is the best evidence that the prediction he makes with regard to the purpose of the southern rebels in the case Seymour and Blair are elected, is well founded:

INGLEWOOD PLANTATION, Sept. 3, 1868.

Hon. L. D. Campbell:

It is with deep feelings of anxiety that I address you this note of inquiry. Are we rushing headlong into another revolution? The inquiry may surprise you if you are a stranger to the wild fury which is hurling this community into a state of anarchy, and is inaugurating a reign of terror similar to that of 1861. The leaders are becoming bold, and openly avow their intention to murder all the newly elected State and parish officers, or drive them from the

State. Mexico is often alluded to as a sample of what we are coming to. They look to the Democracy of the north to support them. You are there; tell me, are these hopes baseless, or well founded? What stand do the conservative Union men of the North take? Whom do they support, and what are the prospects for Seymour and Grant? For, on this issue depends, in my judgement, the extent to which this insurrection shall be carried. That it will be inaugurated I have no doubt. *There is an extensive secret organization pledged to it.* It is claimed this organization extends from Maine to the Rio Grande, If Seymour should be elected they expect, from the principles announced in General Blair's letter, that he will aid them in the overthrow of all the State governments South. And even should he fail, they will try it, and thus throw the country into a state of anarchy. If the Democracy of the North assist them as a party, it will be extensive; and God help the country. If it shall be confined to this section, blood will flow for a while, but a timely interposition of the army will suppress it. Give me your views. I know that you are always looking ahead, and I know that you are in confidence with the present administration, and can give me some assurance of the prospect that lies before it of preventing this great calamity. These insurrectionists think that because President Johnson was opposed to the reconstruction acts, he will be slow to check their overthrow by violence. I hope this is not the case. I believe he has been persecuted, but still I believe he will not be untrue to his country for the purpose of avenging himself on a party.

Please let me hear from you soon, and direct your letter to Mrs. Thos. J. Cocke, for if directed to me I should probably never get it. The bitterest rebels have free access to the post office here, and it is believed are playing their old game.

My regards to your family and all our friends.

With great esteem, I remain, Yours &c.

V. CHASE.

The following are extracts from the "Planters' Banner" of October 10, 1868, and are inserted as illustrative of the public sentiment which preceded these murders:

"Where are the carpet-baggers of St. Landry? They are where the carpet-baggers of St. Mary will be one of these days. * * * * The recent disaster of the radicals in St. Landry, and the dwindling of Loyal League clubs in the parish, have had a terrible effect on the little rat Pope. He looks on the streets as though he had been chawed up by a terrier. He has a complication of diseases—his liver don't act, he has the cholic, the toothache and the yellow jaundice, and don't feel very well himself. If he dies, the shell of an English walnut would make a good sarcophagus in which to convey his precious remains to his Northern friends, or if he is to be buried on Southern soil, as he has no "forty acres" of his own in which to be buried, he should be put in a pair of oyster shells and buried at low water mark where the tide ebbs and flows twice in twenty-four hours." * * * * * * * * * * * * * * * * * Speaking of a Republican meeting held near Franklin, a few days previously, it says: "That was Pope's funeral procession, and the funeral processsion of the radical party in St. Mary. * * * * * "Blank certificates will be prepared, and every colored person who votes the Democratic ticket in November, in St. Mary, will have one of these certificates filled and duly signed, as a proof that he is in harmony with the white people of the country, and it will entitle him always after to be considered the friend of the white man and entitled to the white man's friendship and protection. Those colored people who stick to the carpet-baggers till after the election will have the door shut in their faces. They will be too late." * * *

The "Planters' Banner" also published the following in reference to these murders:

"Since the shocking events of the night of the 17th, all parts of our parish have been diligently patrolled by armed police every night. Most of the negroes now show a disposition to vote the Democratic ticket, and live on friendly terms with the white people of the parish. Many say they do not intend to go to the polls or to vote next Tuesday, but will work in the field all day." * *

"The bloody event of last Saturday night we fear is but the prelude to bloody events all over the South. It is the foretaste of an irrepressible conflict between Radical office holders and the people of the South, which we fear it will be impossible for conservative men to restrain.

The Times has the following atrocious sentiment referring to the murder of Colonel Pope:

"The homicide of certain persons, who have been installed exclusively by the votes of the negroes and a few white strangers and outcasts, in highly responsible judicial offices in the country, are due to the exasperation produced by a system of oppression, wrong, insult and spoliation, which were never exercised toward a brave and spirited people without producing like results."

In connection with this horrible outrage, the Crescent made the following comment:

"An indication of the terrible and irretrievable failure of the Radical scheme of reconstruction."

The remains of Colonel Pope were brought by his friends to New Orleans, where a large concourse of ex-army and navy soldiers and citizens, and the following officers of the United States army: Generals Rousseau, Ayres, Hatch, Buchanan, Neill, Tompkins and Beckwith; Colonels Keeler, Russell, and McClure, and Captains Baldy, Burbank and Major Hutchings, escorted them to the boat which was to bear them to his former home.

The following resolutions were adopted by a meeting of ex-army and navy soldiers: * * * * * * * *

We, the ex-soldiers and sailors, late of the United States army, and many residing in the State of Louisiana, have learned of the assassination of Col. Henry H. Pope, at Franklin, in the parish of St. Mary, with astonishment and horror. Were this an isolated case of brutal and cowardly murder, it might be passed over as one of those atrocities, which might, and occasionally does occur in any country or community, but when it constitutes only one instance of a long series of similar outrages actually perpetrated, and in conformity to the threatened designs of extended organizations, whose cardinal principles seem to be violence and bloodshed committed upon individuals, solely for political opinions, the occurrence becomes one which should excite alarm in the bosoms of all good citizens, and should arouse every lover of civilization and peace, to the most determined efforts, in arresting and bringing to condign punishment those who participated in, or give countenance to these crimes against the peace and dignity of the State, and against the sacred rights of humanity. That our united opinion may stand publicly recorded, we do therefore concur in the passage of the following resolutions:

Resolved, That we shall ever remember the good qualities of Col.

Henry H. Pope as a soldier and a citizen, and now proclaim to the world that in both capacities he bore himself as became an American patriot.

Resolved, That we condole with his widow and all his family friends, and assure them that our hearts are filled with the most poignant grief for their irreparable loss.

Resolved, That we feel that in the fall of our late comrade in arms we recognize that the cowardly hand of the assassin is raised against us all, and that we are called upon to meet the emergency with the same patriotism and courage which animated us in going forth seven years ago to meet the armed enemies of our country.

Resolved, That we assert and shall maintain our right to live in this country and to have our opinions, to express and vote them on all occasions freely, on the general ground that we are citizens of the United States, and on the special ground that we have assisted in bearing the flag of our country in victory from the Potomac to the Rio Grande.

Resolved, That we appeal to the Government of the United States, whose honor we have maintained upon many a sanguinary field, for protection in our persons and property, and in the free exercise of our political rights as men and Americans.

Resolved, That we appeal to the General commanding the United States forces in this State to use the troops of his command, to his utmost ability, to give security to his late comrades in arms, and to afford them safety in loving and advocating the principles of justice and the sacred cause of our common country. * * * *

The Republican has the following remarks upon the occasion:

* * * "It was an occasion of the deepest solemnity and grief. In the presence of such a profound affliction, party spirit was melted into patriotism, and minor differences sunk in the recollection of the gallant career of the departed soldier whose hearse stood before us draped with the flag of his country which he had so nobly defended."

The Planters' Banner thus refers to the destruction of a Republican paper:

"Last Sunday night the Radical press and type of this place were destroyed by the hands of persons at present unknown to the public, and the editor and printer left the next morning on the Peerless."

ST. MARY—SUMMARY.

Number of killed, positively sworn to........................ 2
Number of maltreated, positively sworn to..................... 3

PARISH OF ST. BERNARD.

Brevet-Major Kinzie Bates, 1st United States Infantry, states, on oath:

Question—(By Mr. Campbell,) State, if you please, all the facts in your knowledge with regard to the troubles in St. Bernard parish, in the month of October last.

Answer—On Monday morning, the 26th day of October last, at about 2 o'clock in the morning, witness was directed by the commanding officer of the post at Jackson Barracks to proceed to the court house of the parish of St. Bernard, with his company, to quell a riot that was said to be going on there, and to be guided in his actions by Circular No. 2, from Headquarters, Department of Louisiana. (Deponent does not remember the date,) He marched to the court house, a distance of sixteen miles, and arrived there about 8:30 A. M. While there, he received a message from Mr. Thomas Ong, living about two miles distant, requesting him to come to his (Ong's) place, as his life was in danger. He placed eight men in a wagon, and directed the balance of his company to follow him on foot. As he approached Ong's place, he noticed about a dozen white men armed, sitting in front of the gate; as he reached the gate about sixty mounted men, armed with double-barreled shot guns, came up; they had some freedmen prisoners; Mr. Ong came out and placed himself under witness' protection. Witness asked this party what their object was, and was informed they were a sheriff's posse who were arresting the supposed murderers of Pablo Fillieu. Leblanc, the deputy sheriff, came up and spoke to witness. Witness asked him, at once, to disperse his posse, adding that he would take care of the parish. They then marched over to the court house with their prisoners, and witness saw no more of them. There was a very bitter feeling existing amongst these people against Mr. Ong. The sheriff of the parish, whom witness had not seen before, came to him and desired to make some arrests. To prevent any further trouble, witness furnished him a squad of men under a discreet non-commissioned officer; he made some twenty arrests on the different plantations. These men witness took charge of, and fed with rations belonging to his men. After he had established a guard at the court house, which he was unable to do, before he placed them in charge of the civil authorities of the parish. During that morning a fight occurred upon the plantation of General A. L. Lee, some miles below, and Dr. Lee, father of General Lee, was taken prisoner by a party of Sicilians. Witness knew nothing of this affair until late in the afternoon, and having his hands full, he could not divide his small force of twenty-four (24) men to send a detachment down there. That night, however, Dr. Lee was brought up and placed under his protection. A large number of negroes gathered on Mr. Ong's plantation, under the protection of the military authority, many of them stating that they were afraid to remain at their homes. Witness remained there three days. The parish remaining quiet, he was relieved by another company of his regiment, and then returned to the city.

A few days afterwards, Brevet Major General Rousseau sent witness back to the said parish to make a full investigation, which he did as far as the excited state of affairs would permit. He made a report to the General, on his return, and as far as he can recollect, the following is a synopsis of it: On Sunday, the 25th October, 1868, there was a Democratic meeting at the court house of St. Bernard parish, composed of the Constitution and other clubs of the parish and the "Seymour Infants," of New Orleans. These clubs were marching up the road in the afternoon, when a Metropolitan policeman, and ex-soldier of the United States army, by the name of Michael Curtis, came riding down the road; as he passed these clubs, he shouted out "fight, fight down the road." Some one in the procession called upon him to halt. He paid no attention to it, and rode faster, when he was fired upon, but not hit; he sprung from his horse, and while climbing over a fence, was shot through the head and instantly killed. His pistol was by his side, one barrel discharged. Deponent has been told that a coroner's inquest rendered a verdict that he came to his death by a pistol shot inflicted by his own hand. A short time after this the same procession came in contact with a freedman, who was shouting for "Grant and Colfax." He was pushed or assaulted in some way, when he drew a revolver and shot a man through the shoulder. He was instantly shot down and killed by some member of the procession. Another freedman was killed the same afternoon, but deponent does not remember the particulars. That night a number of freedmen from the plantations down the road attacked the house of a baker by the name of Pablo Fillieu, and after a desperate fight, killed him, burnt the house, completely destroying its contents and his body. Numbers of the citizens came out armed and fired upon the negroes, and they ran back to the plantations where they worked.

Dr. Lee's statement of the trouble at his plantation will be found in deponent's report at Headquarters, Department of Louisiana. There were two white men killed (Curtis and Fillieu), and witness obtained the names of eight freedmen, which, however, he does not now recollect. It was impossible to find out the exact number of killed, as many of the freedmen were hidden in the cane. Lieutenant Spaulding, the officer who relieved deponent during his absence from the parish, in order to assist him in making out his report, visited the different plantations and conversed with the freedmen. They were adverse to making any affidavits or statements. The above statement was obtained by conversing with a number of the people of the parish. Deponent farther States, that in his opinion the presence of the United States troops protected Mr. Thomas Ong from personal injury.

Question—(By Mr. Campbell.) State, if you please, the reason why the freedmen, in your opinion, were adverse to making any affidavits or statements.

Answer—From what Lieutenant Spaulding told me, and what I saw myself, they were evidently under the impression that they would be marked and suffer bodily harm.

On Tuesday, November 3, 1868, a freedman on Mr. Cofield's plantation, while at work digging potatoes, was taken by a party of Sicilians, numbering five or six, to a canal in the rear of the place and stabbed to death. When deponent left he heard a coroner's jury was investigating the affair.

A. G. Thornton states, on oath, that he is a citizen of the State of Louisiana, residing in the parish of St. Bernard; that he was elected Parish Judge on the Republican ticket for the above parish, at the election held on the 17th and 18th days of April, 1868; that for three years previous to his election he was a practitioner of medicine in said parish; and that for a large portion of this time he was the only physician there. Witness is acquainted with all the leading men in the parish, having lived in the State for over twenty years, and was always treated kindly by them up to the time he was elected to the office of parish Judge. Some six weeks previous to the election held on November 3, 1868, there was a Democratic meeting held at the court house of the parish, where the white men lost no opportunity of insulting the colored men during the day, often brandishing knives and pistols in their faces. This conduct caused the colored people, and the few white Republicans living in the neighborhood, to greatly fear them. After the meeting broke up they formed themselves into a procession and marched down the road. Witness saw many of them flourishing pistols in the air as they were passing along, and has no doubt they were *all* armed. They insulted every Republican they passed, and upon seeing witness they cried out, "There goes a scallawag." The same day of the procession a large body of men, headed by Recorder Gastinel, of the parish of Orleans, were in the vicinity of the court house. About 1 o'clock he (Recorder Gastinel) came over to witness' residence (which is about two hundred yards distance from the court house), accompanied by some of his company, and took seats on the gallery. While sitting there the "long roll" was beaten at the court house, whereupon the whole crowd started down the road, yelling and making the most outrageous noises. Many of them were on horseback. Upon their arriving at Mr. Turner's place they surrounded his house, broke down his fence, and then started, as they said, "in pursuit of the d—d black son of a b—h of a Republican who stopped the negroes from coming to their meeting," referring to witness, as he afterwards learned from good authority; being under the impression that he resided at Mr. Turner's place, as seeing Recorder Gastinel on witness' gallery, they took it to be the house of some Democrat. [Gastinel and his friends had their horses and carriages in witness' front yard.]

At the meeting held by the Democratic party there were but five or six colored persons present, and he knows positively that there are only four colored men who are Democrats in the whole parish only one of whom is old enough to vote.

From the day of this meeting it was plain to see that it was excessively dangerous for either a white or a colored Republican to walk the streets by day or night. It was so much so that witness refused to visit the sick after dark, although often called upon. After this the Democrats held their meetings at a sugar house, a mile below the court house. On Sunday, the 25th day of October, 1868, there were about thirty men whom witness took to be "Innocents" of New Orleans, who came down to the meeting, and it was in this neighborhood the riot commenced, by the killing of two negroes. About three o'clock in the evening a crowd passed witness' house, on their way to the court house. Witness' front doors and windows were closed, but the crowd stopped at his gate and cursed him with the most obscene oaths for at least fifteen minutes, and then went away. After they had been gone about twenty minutes, Michael Curtis, a Metropolitan policeman, and an ex-soldier of the U. S. A., was shot dead by a party of these white men from the court house while he was making his way to witness' house for protection. Said Curtis was on his way from Mr. Ong's with a note to Antoine Chalaire, the sheriff, who was supposed to be at the court house, requesting this official to summon a posse of men for the purpose of preserving the peace; witness had already given the same order to the sheriff, who gave him no answer at the time. A day or two aftewards, said sheriff told witness that he was powerless to act, but witness believes he did not want to, as he is a Democrat. Witness did not see any negro with a gun or other fire-arm, or making any hostile demonstration during the day; nor does he believe there was a negro out with a gun in any portion of the parish on that day. Of the thirty-five (35) negroes who were murdered during the riot, witness could not learn of one who had a pistol or gun on his person; he does not mean to say that there were only thirty-five negroes murdered during the riot, as he has no doubt there were many more, but that was the number officially reported to him.

On Monday, October 26, 1868, a band of about thirty (30) white men, armed, came to witness' house in the morning, just after the United States troops had passed, on their way to Mr. Thomas Ong's residence, to give him protection, and took his hat, two guns, table knives, carving knives, and many sundry household articles; they also upset the mattrasses on the beds; in one case, making three little children, who were sick, get up, that they might, as witness presumes, search between the mattrasses for money or silverware. During the day of the riot armed white men patrolled the parish, demanding of the colored people their registration papers and money, which they gave up under penalty of death. This information witness received from a number of the negroes themselves, and has every reason to believe the truth of their statements. Witness has no hesitation in saying that it would have been the height of folly for Republicans to have attempted to vote on the 2d of November, 1868, in St. Bernard parish. Within a mile of the court house a negro was cut to pieces in a horrible manner, with a bowie knife, until he was dead, because he would not "Hurrah for Seymour and Blair" when he met a party of white men; this witness has from negroes and could, if necessary, give the name of two Democrats, whom he heard say, "After the soldiers leave, we will kill every d——d Republican, white and black, in the parish." Witness further states, that it is impossible for him to act as parish judge for this parish, either in civil or criminal cases, as neither of the parish officers or witnesses will pay any attention to his official orders, and furthermore, that he is the only officer in the parish who has taken the oath of eligibility, and that Philogene Jourda, the clerk of the court, Antoine Chalaire, the sheriff, and all the constables, are inimical to him in feeling on account of his politics. Some weeks ago Governor Warmoth appointed for the parish a full police jury, six magistrates, six constables and an assessor. Most of the police jurors have been murdered, and every one of the other appointees have been frightened away by being charged in some way or other with producing the riots, which charges are known to be false. Of all the appointments made by the Governor, not one of them has yet come forward to qualify, although witness has often notified them to do so. There has been no police jury in this parish for many months.

Thomas Ong states, on oath, that he is a citizen of the State of Louisiana, and is a resident of the parish of St. Bernard; that prior to the last registration in this parish, certain white men visited colored men, and told them "they must come over to the Democratic party; that if they voted the Republican ticket they would be killed;" and in some instances planters and other employers threatened to discharge the colored men if they did not vote the Democratic ticket. Prior to a Democratic meeting held at the court house in said parish, on or about September 20, 1868, at which a large number of the "Innocents" and other "roughs" from New Orleans, attended, there was an attempt to create a riot. A call was made for a Republican meeting to take place at the court house, on the 27th of September 1868. The negroes in St. Bernard and in the upper part of Plaquemine parish, were told if they attended this meeting "it would be at their cost," as the white people of the parish were determined they (the negroes) should not attend Republican meetings unless they attended Democratic meetings also. The white people numbering from one hundred to one hundred and fifty (100 to 150) on that occasion assembled on the "Millaudon Plantation," a point the Republican procession would have to pass in going to the court house. They were armed with double barrelled shot guns, and had on the premises a large quantity of prepared cartridges, with from nine to sixteen buck shot in each one. As the procession was returning to their homes, two or three negroes, whom the Democracy had succeeded in entrapping, were sent out to insult them as they passed the sugar house. Some three or four carts containing arms, covered with hay, belonging to, and driven by white men, passed witness' house early in the morning of the day the Republican meeting was held. The colored men were unarmed at the meeting; and on the road witness had told them not to carry arms, that if found with any they would be arrested immediately and confined until the meeting was over. A system of intimidation was carried on all the time, until the whites assembled on the public road in an armed body, Sunday October 25, 1868, and commenced the slaughter by killing colored men. The colored people had been generally informed that on this day they would have a chance to join the Democratic party; if they did, they would be protected; if they did not, and attempted to vote on the day of election they would be killed. They were also threatened with wholesale massacre on that Sunday night. In regard to the burning of Fillieu's house, witness has been informed by good authority, that the colored men, who had been threatened with death, at the hands of the whites, were on their way to Marreros' plantation for defense, and that while passing Fillieu's house they were fired on—some say as many as three times, others five. For the succeeding three days, bodies of armed white men prowled around the parish, killing and maltreating every colored man that appeared on the road, and not content with this, went to their residences, robbed them of their money, provisions, clothing, registration papers, and in some instances, the discharge papers of discharged soldiers, were taken. This they did notwithstanding the presence of United States troops, who were there to aid the civil authorities in preserving the peace. On Tuesday, October 27th, 1868, a body of white men arrested four colored men, and after taking them about two miles from their homes, released them and told them to "run for their lives;" and when they started all four were fired upon; three of them were killed, and the other was severely wounded, but succeeded in making his escape. About 4 o'clock P. M., Sunday the 25th of October 1868, witness fearing a disturbance, dispatched a letter by a member of the Metropolitan Police force, addressed to the Sheriff of the parish, apprising him of his apprehension of a disturbance, and demanding his presence with a posse in that part of the parish, to preserve the peace. The policeman above mentioned, was shot from his horse and killed by men in the Democratic procession; his name was Michael Curtis; he was a discharged United States soldier, having been five years in the service, and during that time he had participated in all the heavy fought battles of Virginia. He was a member of a New York regiment. The citizens of the parish knew from said policeman's reports that he had been a volunteer soldier in the service of his country; in fact, he never disguised the fact, but rather made a boast of having aided in conquering the rebellion, and therefore felt that he had a right to live in any portion of the country where the stars and stripes wave. The killing of Curtis greatly exasperated the blacks, as they knew that he was one of the men who had fought for their freedom. The men who chased Curtis on the road and shot at him, were all on horseback; they and the man that shot him, are known to the authorities, but none of them have been arrested. The men who committed the horrible outrages on the 27th and 28th October, 1868, are also known to the authorities, and are allowed to go unmolested; but nearly one hundred colored men and women, who were suspected on very flimsy grounds of having been present at the burning of Fillieu's house, have been arrested, and after a mock examination before a magistrate, were committed to prison to await their trial before the District Court, and were conveyed to an adjoining parish for safe keeping; there, after a lapse of some days, they were taken before a Democratic Judge on a writ of *habeas corpus*, and released from custody, on the grounds that the commitment was not sufficient to hold them. Witness firmly believes that there were at least twenty (20) negroes killed during the three (3) days rioting. During the last Registration, one Edmund Villery, a large sugar planter in St. Bernard parish, had been refused registration, and deponent happening to meet him in the road just after being refused, he became very much excited, and in a conversation with deponent said, "that the d—d niggers had refused to register him as a voter, but they were registering every d—d black son of a b—h who presented himself;" at this he (Villery) became very violent, and brandishing his cane, said "that if every white man in the parish was like him, no d—d nigger should vote, he would kill them all first; he would murder them before they should vote." This he repeated several times.

It is in evidence, that on the 25th of October, 1868, between the hours of 10 o'clock, A. M., and 6 o'clock, P. M., in the vicinity of the court house of St. Bernard parish, when the Democratic "Bumble Bee" club, with some of the "Innocents" of New Orleans, were marching down the public road, two colored men were sitting on the track which run along this road, the above named clubs "hurrahed for Seymour and Blair." The colored men took no notice of it. One of the men in the procession struck one of these colored men on both sides of his face with his right hand, while he held a six shooter in his left hand, cocked; he knocked the colored man down, and taking his revolver in his right hand, pointed it at him. The colored man drew *his* revolver and shot said man in the shoulder. The colored man was immediately shot dead by the other members of the club. As the other colored man, who was sitting with deceased, started to run, he was shot dead also. At this time the general shooting of all colored people commenced; also of all white men that they could get a chance at, who were known to be Radicals.

ST. BERNARD—SUMMARY.

Number killed, positively sworn to..................from 38 to 68
Number shot, positively sworn to........................ .. 1
Number otherwise maltreated, sworn to...................... 4

PARISH OF CADDO.

Solomon Thomas, states on oath, that he resides in Shreveport, Caddo parish, Louisiana, that on the 14th of October, 1868, he was standing in Mr. Eugene's grocery, on Texas street, with Mr. Robert Gray, a Justice of the Peace, elected on the Radical ticket, but who was never allowed to take his seat by the Democrats. Two white men by the name of Hugh Curry, a planter, and Charles Worsel, a Constable, First Ward, entered the store. Curry asked Mr. Eugene the price of apples; at the same time gave Worsel a wink; said Worsel went to the door leading into the yard, and taking aim with his revolver fired at Robert Gray. The ball entered his left breast, from the effects of which shot the said Robert Gray died soon after. The Chief of Police, Joe Brison, and Deputy Sheriff Edmund Sturgis were on hand before he died, and had him conveyed to the infirmary, where deceased made a full statement before he died in the presence of these two officers; but they made no attempt whatever to arrest the murderer, Worsel; they were in favor of having Gray killed. To witness' positive knowledge, Republicans, white or colored, cannot live in Caddo parish without the risk of being killed at any minute, day or night. About five minutes after Worsel had shot Justice Gray, he aimed his revolver at witness; fortunately the cap snapped. Witness ran from him and secreted himself under the house; it was Worsel's intention to kill him. Not finding him, he (Worsel) went with a squad of white men, all armed, to a grocery situated at the edge of town, and spreed it for two or three hours. He then returned to town alone, and said to a crowd of white men: "If there is any man that has got anything to say because I killed a nigger, now is the time to say so." Dr. Moore, of Shreveport, immediately joined him, and they went to the grocery; Dr. Moore treated the crowd, amounting to fifteen or twenty, and told them whenever they met a Radical nigger that would not "give in" to shoot him down. Gus. and Wm. Worsum and Dors. Bickem pursued witness twenty days to kill him, and searched for him day and night. To his knowledge every colored man in Caddo had to vote the Democratic ticket; the polls were surrounded with armed white men; bands of them went to every colored man's house, and took his arms away—none of which have since been returned. The only colored man that voted the Radical ticket was named James Watson, and he was killed the same night, report says, by young Watson, a son of Col. Watson, and Henry Allen, Col. Watson's brother-in-law. Witness saw the dead body of James Watson and assisted in burying him; he was shot in three places. The said James Watson was respected by both white and colored citizens of the parish; he was not an officer of any political club: witness never heard him talk politics, and knew him to be a quiet and peaceable man; *he was murdered simply because he voted for Grant and Colfax.* He was about twenty-three years of age, and was born and raised in Caddo parish. About the 12th October, Wm. Wright, Sam Wright, Edmund Sturgis, Mr. Ziegler and Mr. Shidet, with a young man named Johnny, went up to Tom Johnson's brick yard and took five colored men away from their work; after tieing their hands, marched them down to the plantation of Mr. Reuben White, then they crossed Bayou Pierre, and reaching Red river these five colored men were placed on the river bank standing up and riddled with bullets by the above named parties; witness saw the bodies floating in the river. In the course of a month at least twenty-five or thirty dead bodies of colored people have floated past Shreveport.

M. P. Hunnicut, states on oath, that he was a member of the Board of Supervisors for Caddo parish during the late registration; he heard white men question colored men in regard to how they would vote at the approaching election; if the colored man did not answer he was put down immediately as a Radical, and was told, if he voted "the G—d d—d Radical ticket" they would kill him. A man by the name of Calhoun gave a great deal of trouble by coming daily to the Supervisor's office and taking blank oaths to "fill them out," as he said, "for Democratic niggers," but that he would not let Radical niggers have any; witness remonstrated with several gentlemen in regard to the way this man was interfering with the Board; and the said Calhoun hearing of it told parties "that he would blow that G—d d—d son of a b—h's head off before he left town." This man kept interfering with the Supervisors until about two days before they closed their office. On the last day of registration a man by the name of Wright, brother of the Clerk of the Tenth Judicial Court, came into the office, took a blank form No. 1, and erased the words "twenty-one years old;" witness taking the blank, said: "I will make it out for you;" he then admitted that he was only twenty years old. Witness then tore the blank up. A colored man then came in; Wright asked him if he was going to vote the Radical ticket; the man made no reply; Wright then said: "You are a G—d d—d Radical—vote that ticket and we will kill you." Witness spoke up and told the colored man to vote as he pleased. Wright then said: "Maybe he will not be allowed to vote as he pleases," and was much excited. He then abused witness in a very disgusting manner. A package of Republican tickets, on board the steamboat Lizzie Hopkins, arrived at Shreveport at 2 o'clock Saturday evening; witness applied at 4 o'clock to the clerk of the boat; he referred him to the discharging clerk, who showed him on his book where he had delivered said package to dray No. 87 to be delivered to him; the clerk informed witness that the driver knew him, and would deliver them to him. Upon inquiry witness found out at the Controller's office, that there was no dray numbered "87;" that "59" was the highest number licensed. On Monday morning, November 2, witness made complaint to several members of the Democratic Committee about this matter; some of the members went to the boat, and blaming the clerks, finally had them delivered to him from this boat. He afterward found out that they had been secreted on the boat. Receiving these tickets so late he was not able to distribute them to Republicans so as to give them a chance to vote. Another lot of tickets, sent to him by the Hon. J. P. Newsham was not received until the day after the election. The letter that was sent at the same time, however, was received on the morning of election. The wrapper on the tickets was completely torn off. On the Presidential election day, November 3, 1868, witness gave some Republican tickets to a colored man, by request, in the presence of two white men. The colored man was followed by the two men, the tickets taken away and torn up, and they gave him a Democratic ticket, telling him "if he did not go and vote the same they would kill him." The colored man's name is Monroe Jacobs—the white men were strangers to witness.

Sinclair Potter states, on oath, that on or about the middle of October, 1868, while he was sitting at home with his wife in Shreveport, at about 8 o'clock in the evening, four white men, armed with guns and pistols came to him, and told him not to run away from the house, if he did, they would shoot him. One of these men, with a sword in his hand, approached him and took hold of his ear. Deponent tried at this time to get out of the house by the back door. One of the party seeing him, raised his gun and said, "Old man there is no use of your trying to get out, your house is surrounded." A colored man by the name of George Saunders occupied the house with him. These men went into his room and took his wife and made her go with them all over town, looking for a colored man by the name of "Charley," whom they said "they wanted to kill," as he had been in the riot over in Bossier parish. About the 3d day of October a soldier came to deponent's blacksmith shop, and told him that he had buried five (5) colored men that he found dead a little back of his camp; he said he saw them shot down by a squad of white men, numbering about fifteen (15), and that they were not arrested, and that they refused to bury the colored men that they had killed when ordered to do so by the commanding officer; that on or about the 25th of October, a white man by the name of Lipp, who keeps a dry goods store on Texas street, called him to his house and told him his life was in danger in consequence of being connected with the Radical party, and deponent hearing of so many colored people being killed, left Shreveport and came to this city. No Republican meetings were held in or about Shreveport for at least a month before the Presidential election. A white man, whom deponent has known for over a year, (but could not recall his name,) told him to leave the Republican ranks as his life was in danger; and if he would come over and join the Democrats, he should not only have all the money he wanted but also a house to live in. The man that told deponent this is a carpenter by trade and owns real estate in Shreveport. To witness's own knowledge at least twelve colored men have left Shreveport in consequence of political oppression.

CADDO—SUMMARY.

Number killed, positively sworn to 42
Number otherwise maltreated 4

PARISH OF EAST FELICIANA.

John S. White states, on oath, that he was appointed Supervisor of Registration for the parish of East Feliciana by Mr. Baker, chairman of the said board. On the election day the polls were opened at half past seven o'clock A. M., and everything seemed to go on peaceably until about nine, when he heard a body of white men make the remark that "every d——d Radical s—n of a b—h that voted the Radical ticket would have his head blown off," at the same time presenting pistols to two negroes. Shortly afterwards witness went over to the court house. A man by the name of Evans White, town constable of Clinton, came up to him and said, "I don't want any Radical tickets distributed here, and if you have any, you can throw them away as soon as possible, or I will drive you away from the court house," at the same time pointing his fist at witness's face. There were about ten white men standing around the polls; they commenced shouting, "Kill the d——d Radical s—n of a b—h! Kick him out!" etc. Witness immediately left the court house, and on going down the street was accosted by a crowd of colored men who were driven away from the polls because they wanted to vote the Republican ticket. A colored man by the name of Henry, who had been appointed as Commissioner of election, told him that he had been taken from his house, and shown his grave in which he would lay, should he accept the position of Commissioner. From most every precinct in the city, witness has heard similar reports of the most discouraging character, and states that the intimidations and frauds committed in this parish are too numerous to mention. Out of at least 1800 colored men who would have voted the Republican ticket, he believes there were only 650 who had the least chance. He further states that every one was requested to show open tickets before they put them in the box, thus keeping away a great many Republican voters from the polls.

Zeno Johnson states, on oath, that on the 26th of September, 1868, he went with 140 colored men to Jackson, Louisiana, to register according to the laws; and there the supervisors, named

Berthune, Meyer, and J. L. White, told them they had no blanks to register them. At the same time they registered all the white men that presented themselves. Some white men hearing witness and others finding fault with the supervisors for refusing to register them, told them to "clear off." About forty of them then went away, the balance remaining. About the 29th of September the Board removed to Clinton and refused to register the colored men there also.

Herman Morrison states, on oath, that eighty-one colored persons were refused registration by the Board of Registration; that they are all twenty-one years of age and over; that they were all born in the United States, and have resided in the State of Louisiana one year next preceeding the 3d day of November, 1868, and residents of the parish of East Feliciana, ten days next preceeding the 3d day of November, 1868, and that they are not disfranchised by any acts of Congress. That they were not able to register under the existing laws of this State for reasons that were beyond their control, whereby they were deprived the privilege of voting on the 3d of November, 1868; and had they been registered as the laws direct they would have voted for U. S. Grant and S. Colfax, the Republican ticket. He farther states, that he was one of the party of eighty-one that were refused registration; that at the poll held in the First Ward in the school house, presided over by John East, Tom Jefferson and ——, as commissioners of election, there was fraud practised in this; that the commissioners said there were only nineteen votes for Grant and Colfax, when in fact, to his knowledge, forty-nine colored persons voted the Republican ticket; furthermore, that Mr. Tom Jefferson, who is a justice of the peace and who was one of the commissioners, and who claimed to be a Republican, did so far forget his oath of office and position as to deceive a great many colored voters by giving them Democratic tickets, which he told them were Republican ones. They voted the said tickets, believing at the time they were voting the Republican ticket. As witness was going to the polls he was halted by a man with a revolver in his hand, who said to him, "You are the fellow I am looking for; I want your arms." He said "I have none." He immediately searched witness from head to foot. Witness asked him for his order to search him. He held off his revolver and said "there is my authority." Witness said, "I thought you ought to have a written order." He replied in a fierce manner, "I have my verbal orders from the commissioners of election." One of the men who was standing by the man that searched him, was Mr. Robert Newport. Eighty-one signatures corroborate the above testimony, as it appears by the petition sworn to before L. A. Fuller, 5th Justice Peace, parish of East Baton Rouge, La.

The following action of the Democratic planters of this parish, was printed in the Republican. It confirms the accounts given by the colored men:

At a meeting of the planters of East Feliciana, held at Clinton on the eight instant, the following resolutions were adopted:

Resolved, That we will not employ for the future any freedmen who shall hereafter vote the Radical ticket, nor shall we rent lands, advance supplies, or assist in any manner such persons. A certificate from the employers will be necessary to show that any freedman has voted the Democratic ticket, or has voted at all. We will always give our preference to those who voted the Democratic ticket, and are members of the Democratic club.

Resolved, That we will not patronize any professional man, or trade with any merchant who does not bind themselves to be governed by the above requisitions.

EAST FELICIANA—SUMMARY.

Number maltreated	5
Republican voters excluded from registration	121
Republican votes fraudulently thrown out	30
Republican voters illegally excluded from voting	1150

PARISH OF WASHINGTON.

Charles Benedict and David Hennessy state, on oath, that they are citizens of the State of Louisiana, and residents of the city of New Orleans, and that they were supervisors of registration for Washington parish during the recent registration; that on the evening of October 6, 1868, they arrived in Franklinton, the county seat of said parish; they rode into town on a wagon driven by a colored man by the name of Joe Magee. He asked witnesses if they were the "registrars." They answered "yes." Mr. Benedict then asked this colored man how things were in the parish. He answered, "all the colored people are Republicans and will vote that ticket if the white people will allow them to." Witnesses opened their registration books at the court house on the 7th of October, 1868, registering but few whites or blacks during the day. They at once saw that the colored people were completely under the control of the whites. The following day they commenced registration at 8 o'clock, A. M., and registered quite a number of colored voters. During the day witnesses were repeatedly called out of the office by colored people, who asked them "what they should do," as they had been told if they did not vote the Democratic ticket they must leave the parish. The citizens had refused to grind their corn, and refused to sell them goods, even when they had placed their money on the counter. Witnesses saw an instance of the latter in the store of John R. Wood. From this date colored women would come into witnesses' office and tell them that their husbands and brothers wished to see them at night at some designated place, that they might receive advice as to what to do; that they were on the verge of starvation, as they were obliged to send their corn to Covington, parish of St. Tammany, some forty miles distant, in order to have it ground. Witnesses advised these people to put up as much as possible with all these inconveniences until after the election. They replied, "We are all Republicans—every one of us. The white Democrats will not let us vote that ticket; they will kill us, they say, if we attempt it." On the 14th of October, 1868, witnesses opened their registration office at Beulah church, third precinct, and registered about (100) one hundred colored men there. During this registration there were from fifteen to twenty (15 or 20) white men in the church all the time, who were continually making threats against the colored people if they did not vote the Democratic ticket, saying "We will kill every d—d nigger in the parish if they do not vote as we want them to," and "They've got no blue-coated, d—d Yankee sons of b——s now to protect them. We rule our own parish now." On Sunday, the 18th of October, 1868, witnesses met some seventy or eighty (70 or 80) colored people in the woods, just below the church, near a creek, who accosted them saying, "Our white friends cannot blame us; we will have to vote the Democratic ticket to save our lives." On Monday the 19th of October, witnesses registered more colored people at the above named precinct who reported that their houses had been visited at night by bands of armed men, who told them "they must go to the polls and vote the Democratic ticket." These colored men told witnesses "they did not want to vote at all, if they could not vote the Republican ticket."

On the 22d of October, the Board of Registrars, of which witnesses were members, returned to Franklinton court house. On Friday evening, 23d instant, there was considerable excitement in town caused by the people running to and fro. About 10 o'clock, P. M., a colored man came to witnesses' room and told them they had better leave town as soon as possible, because he had heard several of the citizens say they were "going to kill them" as "they were nigger lovers and had visited the niggers at night." Witnesses remained, but saw that their pistols were in good working order. About 12 o'clock that same night, some sixty or seventy (60 or 70) armed men, with masks on their faces and white sheets on their horses, passed the house in which witnesses were and proceeded to the residence of a colored man by the name of Isham Buckhaulter, who is one of the leading colored men in the parish. They broke down the doors of his house and entered it with lighted torches, and demanded of him his Republican tickets and his registration papers (he had not yet registered). They took about one hundred tickets, which he had for distribution, and destroyed them. This party, who were of the Ku Klux, next went to the house of Robert Magee, who is another leading Republican, and took from him about the same number of tickets and destroyed them. On the following evening this same party went to the house of George Washington Burrows, a colored man, and took some fifty (50) Republican tickets from him, after shamefully beating him and breaking down the doors of his house. The following morning witnesses went to the postoffice, about 10 o'clock, and as they were going away, they saw a colored man beckoning to them from the edge of the woods. Mr. Benedict remarked to Mr. Hennesy that he (Hennesy) had better go on, and that he (Benedict) would go and see what the colored man wanted. On his way there, he saw four white men on horseback, armed with double-barrelled shot-guns. He found the colored man hidden behind a tree, crying, who stated that a squad of "Ku Klux" had been to his house the night before and "beat his old father almost to death." Witness told him, he could do nothing for him, that he was watched just as much as the colored people were. This colored man stated that his father was beaten because he denied that witnesses had been to his house on several occasions. His father denied it, because he knew witnesses would be assassinated if it was known they had visited him. This same gang of Ku Klux patrolled the parish for five nights, committing outrages on the colored people. On the morning of the 3d of November, 1868, the colored voters were brought into town by armed white men. A man by the name of Hapgood came in with a pair of "six shooters" at his side. Pulling out a revolver before the crowd, he said, "Show me the black Republican son of a b—h that dares to vote the Republican ticket, and I will shoot him on the spot." Then he commenced distributing Democratic tickets to all the colored men, and made them vote that ticket, with his revolver pointed at their heads.

Witnesses registered in the parish two hundred and fifty-six (256) colored men. These men would have voted the Republican ticket unanimously if they had been permitted to do as they wished, but *not one* Republican ticket, was cast in the whole parish. There were some thirty(30) colored hands on the plantation of Mr. Brumfield (a white Republican) who did not register, as they stated they knew they would not be allowed to vote as they wished; Mr. Brumfield did not register for the same reason. Mr. R. Babington, who is the postmaster at Franklinton, Washington parish, was the secretary of this gang of "Ku Klux." He gave all the colored men a certificate signed R. Babington, secretary, "certifying that the bearer had voted the Democratic ticket and upon presentation at any store they could buy goods." Any colored men not having such certificate could not get the necessaries of life at any price. On the 5th of November a colored man named Elijah Andrews met Mr. Benedict (one of the witnesses) and his wife, on the road leading to squire Richardson's; he was crying; Mrs. Benedict asked him why he was crying? He answered that "he had been driven away from his home by one Wm. McGee, who had come to his house with a double barreled shot gun and wanted to know why he had not been to the election?" He told McGee that he was sick and not able to go; whereupon, McGee took his registration paper away from him and told him to "get out of the parish inside of five days or he would kill him." This colored man's statement was verified by Mrs. Squire Richardson, who lives near his house. There is a family of white people living about ten (10) miles from Franklinton, by the name of Mushgrove, consisting of a father and four sons; they are a desperate set. They came to Franklinton on the 4th of November, and remained three or four days, committing all kinds of depredations on the colored people. In their tours around the town they would insult and knock down every colored man they had a chance at; they split one colored man's head open with a club and left him lying on the ground; these same men halted before Mr. Hennesy's (one of the witnesses) room and fired two shots through it, which fortunately injured no one; they then galloped off. Witnesses further state that their lives were continually threatened while they were attending to their official duties as supervisors of registration and election, and that they fully believe that it is impossible for Republicans, especially white ones, to live in Washington parish, as the most prominent white citizens swear that no white or colored Republicans shall obtain a foothold in their parish. Postmaster Babington, before mentioned, has taken and subscribed to the "recantation oath" which is now on file in the office of the Hon. Geo. E. Bovee, Secretary of State.

WASHINGTON—SUMMARY.

Number maltreated.................................... 7

Number of Republican voters prevented from voting by intimidation.................................... 256

PARISH OF BOSSIER.

Henry Taylor states, on oath, that he is a citizen and duly registered voter in New Orleans, Louisiana, and that on the 29th of September, 1868, while he was at Shady Grove, Bossier parish, he saw a colored man on a gallery; a strange white man approached, and remarked to the colored man that he was a d—d Radical. The colored man replied that he was a Radical, when the white man drew a pistol and fired at him. He fell, but was not hurt. The white man then got in his wagon and covered himself up, but the colored men hearing the shot fired, ran from their quarters to the wagon and taking the white man out chained him and kept him as a prisoner, intending to take him to Bellevue and turn him over to the civil authorities. Captain Curtis, and other citizens of Bossier parish, clubbed together that night and unchained him. He then went off, and brought back with him from ninety to a hundred men, armed with revolvers, shot guns and rifles. When they arrived at the Shady Grove Plantation, they commenced firing at the colored people, killing eight (8) men and two (2) women. The women were killed while pleading for their husbands. After this they took seven men to the springs, six of them were killed, and one of them was shot and left for dead, but was able to return to the plantation. These white men learning that they had not killed all the men they took from the plantation, returned and killed the wounded man and his wife. They also saw some carpenters at work making coffins for the dead, whom they killed with their tools in their hands while at their work. The killed at the Shady Grove plantation amounted to eighteen men and three women. This armed band of white men took all the arms on the place. The colored men did not use any weapons or bad language. At Gum Springs, these men met a colored man, whom they ordered to take his hat off, which he refused to do, when they put a chain around his neck, cut his throat and hung him up to a tree. He remained hanging to this tree for three days, when he was taken down and buried by the colored men, at the request of the planters; said colored men being afraid to go near him until requested to do so by the white men. This band of white men went to the preachers' houses and brought them out by force, and beat them with their guns, and made them swear never to preach the gospel again. These preachers were so badly beaten that the people were obliged to carry them home and put them to bed; it was supposed that they would die. These white men said that they would kill all the "nigger men" and then they could rule the women. Mrs. Catharine Taylor's child died and she was obliged to get protection from the white men to bury it. These white men who committed the murders were composed of citizens of Bossier parish, and many of them leading planters. On the 7th of October some fifty planters, well armed and mounted, went to Benton, Louisiana, and held a meeting. They started out in squads to different plantations, killing men and women—twenty (20) colored men were killed that night. While the colored men were picking cotton in the fields they were shot down, without knowing who killed them or for what they were killed. The colored women ran away from the Shady Grove plantation with their children, leaving everything. When witness returned to said plantation he saw about twenty-five white men there, some in the cabins and others standing about with their guns in their hands, and heard them say that they intended to kill every man, woman and child on the Dixon plantation (eighteen miles from Shreveport, Louisiana), near Carolina Bluff. The remaining colored men who were on the plantation left, for fear of losing their lives. Witness then left with his wife.

Isaac Young, a resident and duly registered voter of Bossier parish, states on oath, that he was a laborer on Dr. Vance's plantation; that on or about the 30th of September, 1868, about day light in the morning, a party of white men, among whom were John Vance, Thomas Vance, Calvin Vance, Whitfield Vance, Captain Carter, James Brownlee, —— Ogden, William Haynes, Griffin Cheatham, Marsh Griffin, John Arnold, Bob Stinson, William Agent, Joe Graham, Tom Marks, Bill Marks, Andrew Marks, George McCauley, and James McCauley, all residents of Bossier, came to Dr. Vance's plantation and took from there the following named colored men: Simon Crawford, Alex. Arnold, Jeff. Williams, Steve Vance, and two others named Steve and Bob. These latter they took to Benton and killed, and the rest they killed at Gum Springs, a few miles above. Witness saw said John Vance kill one Henry Chambers, at the gate on Dr. Vance's plantation. Vance shot him first in the breast, when Jim Saunders shot said Chambers three times. The shooting was because of the said John Vance asking Chambers to go with him to Benton, and on Chambers refusing, Vance fired, but missed, when he again fired, hitting him in the breast. Chambers then jumped at and caught Vance by the shoulder, and fell with him struggling. Saunders then shot Chambers three times Chambers was not armed. After the shooting, as a colored man named Alfred Green came out of the gate to see what the trouble was, Vance threw his pistol at him. Vance and Saunders then left. Witness heard all of this transaction himself, lying concealed under the house of Dr. Vance; he had fled from the place in the morning to avoid being taken away with the others, and had returned and concealed himself under the house. Friday, October 2, 1868, in the night, about twelve o'clock, Fred Kinney came to witness and told him that the white men (Vance and others) had released him (Kinney) for the purpose of finding him (witness), so as to betray him into their hands. Kinney also told witness that Dr. Whitfield Vance ordered the colored man Bob to be killed, saying that he was too much of a Radical for him, when a large bowie knife was put on his shoulder and driven down into his heart. The blood spurted about his head and he fell dead on his back. The white men then made the colored men kneel down about the deceased and look into his eyes, and then ordered them to carry him to the side of the road, saying that they would make buzzards meat of him. Kinney also stated to witness, that as these white men were going to Benton they met two colored women on horseback, whom they took from their horses, and, taking their lariat ropes, hung them to a tree near by, and then ordered the colored men to take their bodies to the side of the road and cover them with brush. The origin of this difficulty was, that on Sunday, the 27th of September, 1868, a white man—a stranger to the people—stopped at the negro quarters, on the Shady Grove plantation, and wished to purchase corn. This stranger inquired of an old colored man who was lying down in front of his quarters what his politics were. The old man not answering him, he raised his gun and snapped one barrel at said colored man. He then fired the other barrel, but the colored man turning over, the shot entered the door. The colored men then arrested this white man for the purpose of taking him before the civil authorities; but on Monday morning a body of armed white men came and released this man, and took him to a justice of the peace, but refused to allow any colored men to go to give testimony. No evidence being against him he was released. This white man reported around that he had been whipped and robbed by the colored men on the plantation, and on the strength of his report he and others took witness' horse and four other horses as a compensation for the alleged robbery, when in fact nothing had been taken from him. This was the same party who took away and murdered the colored men, as above stated. For two weeks after these events witness was pursued and searched for by these white men, but succeeded in eluding them, and, believing that his life was not safe in the parish, he came to New Orleans. These white people had a spite against witness, as he was a Republican and had assisted the Republican party. The name of witness was mentioned among others as an object of revenge. William Haynes, told witness's wife that he (Haynes), Jim Chatham, and Whitfield Vance, would give two hundred dollars ($200) reward for him (witness), dead or alive. The object of these persecutions was to make the colored men vote the Democratic ticket, which witness has since learned they were compelled to do.

C. W. Keeting, a resident of Shreveport, Caddo parish, Louisiana, twenty-seven years of age, states, on oath, that he is Deputy United States Marshal, for the District of Louisiana, and that on the 30th day of September, 1868, he was called upon, by a number of citizens of Shreveport, to make an application to the commanding officer of the post of Shreveport, Captain Chas. E. Farrance, for a detachment of United States troops, to aid in suppressing a riot, then said to be going on in Bossier parish between white and colored citizens. About 6 o'clock in the evening witness proceeded to the bayou, near the Shady Grove Plantation, Bossier parish, with a company of United States troops, under the command of Captain Coes; upon arriving there witness found about seventy-five citizens of Shreveport armed, and nearly all mounted. Witness saw no colored man in the vicinity; the white men had pickets thrown out; witness went to the commanding officer of these men—one Captain Nutt—for information in regard to the riot, and was told by him that the trouble originated a few days before, by a white man from Arkansas shooting among some colored men residing on the Shady Grove Plantation; that the white man was arrested and held a prisoner by the colored men, and afterwards released at the request of citizens of the parish; that this white man proceeded to his home, and procured the assistance of about forty or fifty other white men, and returned to said plantation early in the morning of the 30th of September, 1868, and commenced firing on the colored people, killing one and wounding four or five others. They then started toward Benton, with quite a number of colored men as prisoners. About 11 o'clock A. M., of the same day, the colored men of the Shady Grove plantation, and from other plantations in the vicinity, to the number of about fifty, armed themselves and proceeded to the bayou, near Mr. Bari's plantation, and arrested two white men named Brownlee and Ogden. The colored men stated that they were going to take them to Shreveport, as they were with the Arkansas men that did the shooting on the Shady Grove Plantation that morning. They had proceeded down the road but a short distance when the order "fire" was given by some one in the party, and both Brownlee and Ogden died from the effects of the wounds received; then the colored men returned to their homes. Witness left the troops at the ferry, near the Shady Grove Plantation, and rode towards Benton in company with Captain Nutt and two other citizens of Shreveport, where they arrived about 12 o'clock at midnight; witness found about one hundred white men assembled at that place armed, but no colored men were to be seen here nor were there any on the plantations from the ferry to Benton, a distance of about five miles. Early the next morning about two hundred white citizens from the different sections of Bossier parish, reported to Captain Nutt, armed and mounted. As many of these men were under the the influence of liquor, and talked of killing the colored people that had left the plantations and were supposed to be armed and hid in the swamps, witness told Captain Nutt that if these men would go home, that he (witness) would take a detachment of United States troops mounted and go to the swamps and counsel the colored men to return to their plantations, and then all those that were guilty of any crime could be arrested by the proper authorities. Captain Nutt favored this plan, but the white citizens of Bossier seemed determined *to hunt the colored people in the swamps themselves*, and as witness well knew that they would shoot every colored man they found with arms, he would have nothing to do with them. The Sheriff of Bossier—Mr. Hill—arrived a short time after, and witness returned to Shreveport, leaving him in charge; Mr. Nutt and many others left for their homes when witness did. On the 1st day of October some of the white men from Arkansas returned to Bossier and killed five colored men who had taken no part in the riot whatever. For about a week after this, armed citizens rode through the parish shooting colored men; they said they had the names of all the men that were in the party that killed Brownlee and Ogden, and that they were determined to kill every one of these men they could find. Five (5) colored men were taken from the brickyard of Mr. Johnson, near Shreveport; three of them were shot and their bodies thrown into Red river. One colored man that had been wounded was taken from Mr. Smedley's plantation and killed. The colored people of Shreveport and vicinity were greatly frightened, and thinking that their whole race was about to be murdered, left for other portions of the State. It would be impossible to state the correct number of killed, but from the best information that could be obtained by the Agent of the Freedmen's Bureau and witness, the number of killed in Bossier parish and about Shreveport, Louisiana, from the 30th day of September, 1868, to the 7th day of October, 1868, will exceed one hundred (100).

George Harris, a registered voter and a resident of Bossier parish, La., and for the last ten (10) years a preacher of the gospel, states on oath that he is President of a Republican club in Bellevue, Bossier parish. That about the 20th of October, 1868, witness first heard that Democrats were going to kill him because he was a Radical. Elias Cong, Tom Gillmore, Elias Connell, Jim Hearn, and Thomas Hutchinson, who live on their plantation, between Bellevue and Red Shute, said that the Democrats would kill all the niggers before they should vote the Radical ticket. Just before the election witness saw, about seven miles from Bellevue, towards Shreveport, one colored man, his wife, and two other women, (one of whom was pregnant) lying dead in a house. They were all shot. A colored boy, about fourteen or fifteen years of age, was also dead in the house; he was cut with a knife in the side. Witness saw, about the same time, three colored men lying dead on the top of the ground. They had been shot, and evidently left there for the buzzards to feed upon. Witness saw the dead bodies of two colored men and one woman floating down Bayou Red Shute. Witness having heard that the Democrats were going about the parish killing the colored people, and having heard so many threats against his life, left for New Orleans, traveling eighty (80) miles through the woods, and avoiding all roads that were much traveled. The colored people were all terrified, not knowing when their time would come to be murdered.

BOSSIER—SUMMARY.

Number killed, positively sworn to..........................162
Number shot, positively sworn to............................ 1
Number maltreated, positively sworn to...................... 6

REMARKS.—It is estimated that many more persons were killed in the Bossier "negro hunt" than the above estimate.

PARISH OF OUACHITA.

REMARKS.—The following affidavit refers to matters embodied in a former report, and is inserted for the purpose of correcting some errors in that report:

Hon. O. H. Brewster states, on oath, that he is thirty-six years of age, a citizen of the United States, and a resident of the parish of Ouachita, State of Louisiana. That before the election of April 17 and 18, 1868, he kept a store at Trenton, in said parish. That he represents the said parish in the lower House of the Legislature of Louisiana, having been elected on the Republican ticket by the Republicans of his representative district. That a short time after the elections of April, 1868, five houses, situated about three miles from Trenton, were set on fire by a party of white men in disguise; it was said there was fifteen or twenty of them. They were dressed in black robes, and their faces painted black. The houses burned were occupied by colored people, except one, where lived a white woman, who had several children; it was quite currently reported that this woman was living with a colored man. Every respectable person with whom witness talked about this outrage strongly condemned it, except one merchant of Trenton; he approved it, saying "that he was glad of it; that the persons living in those houses were a parcel of thieves; that he had often missed property that he supposed had been stolen by the inmates of said houses." A colored man named Jordan Hunter was one of the principal tenants of one of those houses, and was, during the night they were fired, shot at (it is said a great number of times) and wounded in four (4) several places, dangerously, but not mortally. Witness knew him well, and had often traded with him; he was a very honest man, and Southern men, who had known him from his boyhood, gave the highest praise to his character. The day after this outrage had been committed, Hunter left for Monroe, and his wife, after having vainly sought shelter about the town, and after having been turned out everywhere, came to witness, and he gave her the hospitality of his house. The excitement ran very high for several days among the colored people who came to witness for advice; he persuaded them to bear these things patiently, and not to commit any excesses. A few days after a meeting largely attended by planters and merchants was held, and a series of resolutions condemning thieving among colored people, and murdering and burning among the white people and other outrages perpetrated by secret Klans, having been introduced by Capt. Jos. P. Crosby, a very influential and prominent citizen of the parish, and unanimously adopted, it quieted the whole matter. That action had a very good effect, as witness has never heard of any other disturbance in that section since, and he thinks if intelligent and well inclined Democrats would take similar steps everywhere in Louisiana, it would contribute a good deal to re-establish law and order in the State. In regard to Franklin Sinclair, the colored teacher, who was murdered on the 16th of April, he was a candidate on the Republican ticket for Representative, and witness was chosen in his stead, after the news of the sad event reached the Republican headquarters at Monroe. When witness came to Monroe on Friday morning he was quite astonished to find the Republicans voting for him, as he had had no intimation of any nomination. Franklin Sinclair was very highly esteemed by the Southern people who knew him, and almost every white man with whom witness conversed on the subject, expressed his regrets at this foul murder, and allowed that since they knew him they had not seen him out of his place once. The only offense Southerners could find him guilty of, that witness ever heard, was that he had been teaching a negro school. In regard to the conduct of the election, on Friday night, April 17, 1868, witness received a note from Mr. Butler, commissioner of elections at Forksville, setting forth that there had been such threats and so much intimidation used against the Republicans at that poll, that he dared not continue the election the next day without some protection, and requesting witness to make application at headquarters for troops, in order that every citizen might be protected in the free exercise of his rights. Troops were not sent, however, and witness does not know whether that poll was opened the next day or not. In witness' precinct at Trenton, everything went on very fairly, the Deputy Sheriff stationed at the poll, a Mr. Coats, a Democrat, who stood there during the whole time that the election was going on, freely acknowledged to witness, after the polls had closed, and the election was concluded, that everything had been fairly conducted, and that he did not see any illegal voting by either party.

The Hon. Frank Morey states, on oath, that in the month of October, 1868, a few days before the Presidential election, a colored man named Mitchell Allen, a prominent member of the Republican club at Monroe, Ouachita parish, who was employed as a fireman by the North Louisiana Railroad Company, was assassinated at Girard Station, Morehouse parish. There was strong circumstantial evidence pointing to a well known character about Monroe, name unknown, who was known by the soubriquet of "Red Henry," as the assassin. Said "Red Henry" has since that time, been killed in Arkansas.

[From the Republican.]

The Monroe Intelligencer gives us a pleasant view of affairs in that section on the day of election. It is another proof of the perfect security with which Republicans could vote:

The following is as correct a statement of the trouble at the Filhiol box, on the day of election as we have been able to get. Everything went on quietly, and nearly two hundred votes had been polled when the commissioners started to dinner. On their return, they found that about thirty strange white men on horseback, accompanied by one colored man, and fully armed, had arrived in front of the polls. On re-opening the polls, a colored man voted a Republican ticket, and the crowd of strangers being informed of it immediately called on the colored man in their company, whom they called Bob Stiff, to pitch into him. Stiff immediately knocked this colored man down with a stick, but after he had been struck once or twice the man succeeded in making his escape. While this was going on a difficulty occurred between another colored man and the strangers, who were about to kill him, when Mr. P. Carrington interfered, and saved his life at the risk of his own. Shortly after this, the party of strangers mounted their horses and rode down the road; they had been absent but a short time, when some firing was heard in the direction they had taken. On their return they stated that a colored man named Culpepper, in Mr. Filhiol's field, had fired at them, and that they had killed him in consequence. In proof of this they exhibited a stick in which some shots were lodged. At night there was considerable apprehension of difficulty among both races, but nothing serious occurred, excepting the burning of a schoolhouse belonging to the colored people on the Bres plantation, and of the corncrib, with twelve hundred bushels of corn on the Faust plantation. A colored man, whose name we have been unable to learn, was shot in the mouth. That night about fifteen colored men came to town for protection, which was extended to them by the sheriff. On Wednesday warrants were issued against a number of the men, who were said by the colored men to have been implicated in the difficulties of the night. On Wednesday night Sheriff Wisner, and Mr. Dobson, acting as his deputy, with some cavalry, started down to arrest the accused, whom they brought to town on Thursday. The prisoners immediately gave bonds for their appearance for trial on Friday. On that day the case was continued until Monday.

On Friday three of the principal witnesses in the difficulties of Tuesday night, named Simon Peterson, Daniel Webster and Orphey Johnson, all colored men, started down the river to go to their homes, and stopped on the Copley plantation for one of them to see his wife, when they were taken out of the cabin by a party of eleven white men. Four of the white men took them to the deadening in the rear of the plantation and there told them to kneel down and say their prayers, as they would be killed. Instead of doing this they broke and ran, when fire was opened on them by the whites, and Peterson and Webster were killed, but Johnson succeeded in making his escape Johnson came to town on Friday evening about dark, and his story created a great deal of indignation among all classes of our community.

Mr. Duffel, who has charge of the Copley plantation, makes the following statement as to what occurred prior to taking the men out of the cabins: The white men came riding to his house furiously and stated that they had been fired on by some negroes from the corner of the fence, and that the negroes had hid themselves in one of the cabins, and unless they were brought out immediately, they would burn up the quarters. Mr. Duffel went in search of the negroes, and found them hid in the loft of one of the cabins. A shot was fired at him, said by the colored men to have been by accident, when he told them that they must come down or the cabin would be burned up, with them in it. The negroes then came out and were taken away by the four white men, as stated by Johnson. The names of these four men are Pinckney Faust, Marion Faust, Beaver and John Faulk.

Warrants were issued on Saturday for the arrest of the four accused, and on Sunday morning Sheriff Wisner started out with a posse for their arrest, but did not succeed in finding any of them. The bodies of the two killed colored men were found on Sunday afternoon by some colored men, together with the dead bodies of their horses.

The case of the parties arrested by Sheriff Wisner was continued on Monday until Thursday.

OUACHITA—SUMMARY.

Number killed 4
Number shot 2
Number maltreated 3

PARISH OF RAPIDES.

W. F. McLean states, on oath, that he is a citizen of the State of Louisiana, and resides in the town of Alexandria, Rapides parish. That he is the editor and publisher of the Rapides Tribune, the official journal of the parish; that the first issue was made on the 3d day of October, 1868, and on the evening of the same day he left for New Orleans, to obtain type and material for the purpose of completing his newspaper and job office. He afterwards returned to Alexandria with new type and material for the purpose above specified, and with two additional printers. On the night of the 15th of October, 1868, the office was broken open by a mob, and portions of the press—which rendered it useless—and all the new type and material, with a large quantity of the old type, was by them thrown into Red river; all of the old type and some of the new that was in the cases was scattered in the street, together with the cases. The civil authorities took no action in the matter whatever. The loss in material alone sustained, amounts to about three thousand dollars ($3000). The loss of business, and the expense incurred amounts to about two thousand ($2000) more. On the 31st day of October, 1868, witness again left for New Orleans, for the purpose of refurnishing his office with type, material, paper, etc., and again arrived at Alexandria on the morning of the 15th of November, with the material specified. On the night of the same day his office was again broken into, and all the type and material and portions of the press—so as to render it useless—together with his trunk, clothes, papers, books, and everything of a movable character, was taken out and destroyed. This loss amounts to about three thousand dollars ($3000). The business being entirely destroyed, the loss of business is about two thousand dollars ($2000); but cannot be properly estimated in consequence of the complete destruction of the office. It is impossible to print a Republican paper in the said parish, without the immediate protection of the military forces. Witness was appointed Mayor of Alexandria, by Governor Warmoth, (under and by authority of the act incorporating the town of Alexandria, approved September 29, 1868,) a short time before the general elections, but declined to act as such, believing it best not to attempt to exercise the authority of the office, during such exciting times, or until the election was over. When he returned, on the 15th of November, he stated to some friends that he would issue his proclamation on the 17th and enter upon the discharge of the duties appertaining to the office of Mayor. This fact becoming known to the acting Mayor, and other members of the Democratic party, they commenced a series of abusive assaults during the day, (15th inst.,) and at night assaulted witness, with missiles of every description. The night was very dark, so much so that witness could not recognize any of the parties. Some friends of witness told him on that day, that there were many parties who had told them "to advise him not to exercise the functions of the office; that he would not be allowed to do so, and if he attempted it he would not live a week." John McBride, a printer in the office, was with witness when he was stoned. McBride had been frequently told by parties, to suggest to witness, that he had better not attempt to exercise the duties of the office. Judge John Osborn, District Judge of the Ninth Judicial District, told witness that the "Ku Klux Klan," robed and masked, had visited and stoned his (Judge Osborn's) dwelling at night, in Alexandria, twice in one week, about the second week in November. The same acts were perpetrated on Judge Barlow, parish Judge; and such threats were made by them against him that he was obliged to seek the houses of friends at night, to save himself from assassination. Both of the above named Judges were elected to office on the *Republican ticket*, at the election held on the 17th and 18th days of April, 1868. On the 17th day of November, in Alexandria, Mr. C. W. Boyce, late president *pro tem.* of the State Senate, and now Justice of the Peace, was asked who he voted for, on November 3, 1868. He replied, "for Grant and Colfax." Thereupon he was knocked down and beaten. The party that assaulted Mr. Boyce is well known to the civil authorities of the place, but so far they have failed to act in the matter. After assaulting Mr. Boyce, the same party drove him across the river, to Pineville, where he resides. Acts of violence of this kind are of frequent occurrence, and no notice whatever is taken of them by the authorities, and it is believed they have been committed with the knowledge and consent of the acting Mayor E. R. Boisatt, and other prominent citizens of the parish. Mr. T.

J. Colamy, chairman of the Board of Supervisors for said parish, informed witness that while counting the votes, the day after the election, a mob outside of the sheriff's office threatened to hang the members of the Board of Supervisors, and many other acts of hostile demonstration, were committed for the purpose of intimidating the parties who had charge of the election returns. A large number of both white and colored voters, were obliged to vote the Democratic ticket for fear of bodily harm, who otherwise, would have voted for Grant and Colfax at the late Presidential election.

RAPIDES—SUMMARY.

Number maltreated..7

PARISH OF ST. TAMMANY.

Charles B. Evans, states, on oath, that he was a member of the Board of Supervisors for the parish of St. Tammany during the late registration in this State. That two colored men came to him on the 4th day of November, 1868, and requested him to have some white men arrested, that lived in Washington parish. These colored men stated that on the night of Sunday, November 1, 1868, a party of men, disguised and armed, came to their house in Washington parish and took them to the swamp. They were asked how they were "going to vote;" they replied, "Radical." They were then tied to a tree and whipped with sticks, and left in this situation until Tuesday morning about 9 o'clock. They only had one meal during their confinement. They were told, upon being released, to go and vote, and leave the parish, and mind that they "did not lose their lives while doing so." They then went to the polls with the intention of voting, and were asked by a colored man how they were going to vote; they remarked, "Radical." One of them was immediately knocked down by this colored man. The Republican tickets that were sent out to the different precincts for distribution among the colored people, never reached them, because the other two members of the Board, Mr. E. Linderman and Captain J. H. Ingraham, employed Democrats to distribute them. When deponent held them to account for this negligence, they replied, "that they could not find anybody else to go;" but witness knew very well that they could have found plenty of honest, colored Republicans, who would have been glad to have undertaken the trust. One of the returning officers, appointed by the other two members of said Board of Supervisors, while on his way to "Bayou Chitto," got drunk, and had his ballot box taken away. This officer's name was E. Shean, and tickets that had been intrusted to him to deliver among the colored people, were not received by them.

The following is an official statement of Wm. Baker, Chairman of the Board of Registrars, as to the conduct of the election of November 3, 1868, in the Parish of St. Tammany:

The parish of St. Tammany is no exception to the other parishes where intimidation has been resorted to. The report of the supervisors shows conclusively that citizens in that parish no longer enjoy the privilege of the ballot. "A week or ten days before the election the Ku-Klux Klan rode around parts of the parish and threatened and intimidated the voters." "The editor of the St. Tammany Vindicator had to fly from the parish to save his life." Houses of known Republicans were visited as a part of the system of intimidation and surveillance. The Democrats announced that no white man should vote any but an open ticket. Out of 1465 registered voters 261 failed to vote. Yet the white and colored population of the parish are about equally divided. The registrars conclude as follows: "We are satisfied that had there been no intimidation used, the Republican majority in the parish would have been at least two hundred."

ST. TAMMANY—SUMMARY.

Number maltreated.. 2

PARISH OF UNION.

J. E. Trimble states, on oath, that he resides in Union parish, State of Louisiana; that on or about September 1, 1868, in the town of Farmersville in said parish, a Democratic club, organized under the name of "The Central Democratic Club of Union Parish," notified the colored people, that, in case they became members of the Democratic club, and voted their ticket, they would be protected from the Ku-Klux, and they would issue to them protection papers; and in case they should not vote, they must surrender to the club said protection papers. Many colored people were induced through fear to become members of this, and other Democratic clubs throughout the parish. Several colored members of this organization came to deponent, stating that they were members of this club, but desired to vote the Republican ticket, if they could safely do so. At precinct number two (deponent was informed), the colored people were marched in file to the polls, under the leadership of the officers of their club, to vote the Democratic ticket, previously prepared for them. As Chairman of the Board of Registration for the parish of Union, the returns, made to witness in his official capacity, from Marion, precinct number six, were informal, in this, that there was no certificate of the Commissioners of election of that precinct accompanying them, as required by law; at said precinct about one hundred and seventy-six ballots were polled, all Democratic. On or about the 18th of April last, while attending the election at the Downsville precinct, a colored man named "Jack," to whom witness had furnished Republican tickets, was threatened with violence, and through fear he left the place to return to his home. As soon as it was discovered that he was gone, a party of three white men followed him, and overtaking him on the road, struck him on the back of the head with a heavy stick or club; he ran off through the woods, when he was fired at with pistols. Upon reporting the above to the proper officers, no action (so far as deponent knows) was ever taken in the matter.

UNION—SUMMARY.

Number maltreated..1

PARISH OF BIENVILLE.

W. H. Honnens states, on oath, that he is a resident of the parish of Bienville; that on the 28th day of May, 1868, a party of seven white men came to his house on their way to Pine Bluff Landing, asking if they could do anything for him at the landing, on the arrival of the boat. He gave them a letter to deliver on the boat. On their return they stopped at his house, and called him out. When he went out, one of them, named Hardy Took, fired at him. The ball hit him in the head, and knocked him senseless. When he recovered he found that he had fourteen wounds, twelve of which were in his hip and thigh. His wife came out upon the balcony, and begged them to spare his life, but they continued to fire at him, until she called the colored people for assistance, when they left. The following morning the same party passed his house, and one of them, named H. Shehee, came and inquired how he was, if he was badly hurt. Having been informed that these men would come back and complete their work, he left the parish as soon as he was able to move, leaving his furniture, house and property, to the mercy of these people. Since he came to New Orleans he has received information that they have driven his colored workmen away from his place, and prevented them from gathering the crops. On the same day, May 28, 1868, a party of white men took a colored man named Moses Lawhorn, from his house to the woods, and there murdered him. After killing him they cut off his head to make sure that he was dead; the only provocation was that he was a Republican. About a week after witness left, he received information that a party of unknown white men, had shot a colored man named Robert Vickers, because he did not attend a Democratic meeting, which he had been notified to attend. All the colored men in the parish are notified to attend these Democratic meetings, and failing to do so, are visited at night, taken out, and either whipped and beaten, or murdered.

BIENVILLE—SUMMARY.

Number killed, positively sworn to 1
Number shot, positively sworn to 2

PARISH OF WINN.

D. M. White, being duly sworn, deposes and says, that he was an Assistant Sub-Assistant Commissioner of the Freedmen's Bureau in the parish of Winn. About the latter part of August (1868) a party of armed white men went to the house of Hal Frazier and his son Brantly Allen, colored, the latter teacher of the freedmen's school, near Frazier's mill, and called them to come out; as they did not answer, these men went to the window and fired several times into the house, but fortunately without hitting them. They were compelled to leave the house and conceal themselves in the swamp in order to preserve their lives. The colored men are threatened with violence if they do not vote the Democratic ticket.

SMITHFIELD, December 12, 1868.

W. B. Phillips, Esq.:

DEAR SIR—A most horrid murder was committed by two white men at Frazier's mills, in Winn, fifteen miles from here. Two colored men by the name of Hal Frazier and Robinson, were sent to their final resting place without a moment's warning. Hal Frazier was an honest colored man, and owned a saw mill, but was a strong Radical. Capt. White has been driven away from Winn parish, and they tried to decoy me to Alexandria, for the purpose of assassinating me. The fact is, Phillips, if you was here I would not give two bits for your hide.

* * * * * * * * *

Yours truly,

(Signed) W. S. CALHOUN.

S. B. Shackleford states, on oath, that he is a resident and duly registered voter of Rapides parish, State of Louisiana; that previous to 1860, one Hal Frazier (colored) was a slave of one John Frazier, of Winn parish, and that said Hal Frazier bought and paid for himself, and has since purchased a saw mill with machinery attached and about 2000 acres of land, of said John Frazier, his former owner. That about the 8th of December, 1868, a double murder was committed at said saw mill on the persons of said Hal Frazier and one Jesse Robinson. That ———, of Winn parish, told witness that in a conversation with John Frazier, about fifteen days previous to the murder, said John Frazier asked him (———) to leave Frazier and come and work for him. He (———) replied that he was working for Hal Frazier and could not leave. John Frazier then replied, "D—n you; you and Hal Frazier will both smell bullet packing in less than ten (10) days; we will break up that nest of Radicalism!" Witness is of the opinion that said John Frazier and one Doctor Cockrell, son-in-law of said John Frazier, were accessories to the murder of said Hal Frazier and Jesse Robinson.

Calhoune's Plantation, Rapides Parish,
December 10, 1868.

General A. L. Lee, Editor of New Orleans Republican.

Dear Sir—I write to inform you of the latest rebel outrage in Winn parish, perpetrated on two colored men named Hal Frazier and Jesse Robinson. On the morning of the 8th inst., two strangers went to Hal Frazier's saw mill—as they said—to buy a bill of lumber. Not finding Hal at the mill they left. Yesterday, at about twelve o'clock, they returned, and finding Hal there, engaged him in conversation about the price of lumber, etc. One of them took Hal from the mill to measure some lumber, while the other remained near Robinson. While Hal was kneeling down, drawing a plan for the house the stranger wanted built, the man pulled his pistol and when Hal raised his head he was shot, the ball entering under his right eye and coming out at the back of his head. As soon as the pistol was shot the man in the mill drew his pistol and shot Robinson through the back and once through the head. As soon as they found Hal was dead, one of them took his pocket book, which contained some three or four hundred dollars in money and valuable notes. They then mounted their horses and rode off. Hal Frazier was a hard working man and owned the saw mill and considerable property, in land, stock, etc. No one had anything against him, except that he was a thorough Radical; it was on that account he was murdered. I left the parish, as I know that I will be murdered in the same manner as Frazier was, as some parties have threatened to "fix" me the same way.

I am respectfully, etc.

D. W. WHITE,

Late Supervisor of Winn parish.

WINN—SUMMARY.

Number killed positively sworn to............................2

Number maltreated positively sworn to.........................3

PARISH OF PLAQUEMINE.

Joseph Whittier, states on oath, that he was in the parish of Plaquemine on the 21st day of October 1868, and was working on the Fasinon plantation; he was going out hunting, when a white man seeing him, hallooed, "hurrah for Seymour and Blair;" witness answered, by hurrahing for "Grant and Colfax," when a white man came up and struck him in the face with a club; there were four other white men with him; he made no resistance, for there were too many for him. Witness ran, and they fired three shots at him, but he was not wounded.

PLAQUEMINE—SUMMARY

Number maltreated...1

PARISH OF TENSAS.

Nestor Smith states, on oath (at an inquest held over the body of Richard Hollis, who was killed at Ashwood, Tensas parish, Louisiana, on the 23d day of October, 1868), that he was standing behind the deceased in the store; a colored man who was standing beside him asked deceased who he was for? Deceased replied "I am for Grant, and will be for him until I die." At that, a white man by the name of Blanchard, who was also there, said "If that is your calamity, get out of here." When the shot was fired Mr. Blanchard was behind the counter. Witness saw the pistol in Blanchard's hand and saw him fire it.

The verdict of the jury in the above case was, "that the death of said Richard Hollis was caused by a pistol shot fired by a man named Blanchard, whose christian name is unknown, and who is a stranger in this parish;" and was signed by the following persons, viz;

W. M. McGALLIARD.
JOE CLARK.
H. E. MOORE.
his
ROBERT ⋈ CROOK.
mark.
his
CHARLES ⋈ KELLEY.
mark.

TENSAS—SUMMARY.

Number killed, positively sworn to........................... 1

PARISH OF LAFAYETTE.

The following is an official statement of Wm. Baker, Chairman of the Board of Registrars, as to the conduct of the election of the 3d of November, 1868:

"From the parish of Lafayette there does not appear to have been any interference with registration, but armed bands of men patrolled the parish and intimidated and prevented Republicans from voting."

PARISH OF CLAIBORNE.

From the Republican, November 17, 1868.

Sometime since a mob partially destroyed the printing establishment of the Homer Illiad, owned by Hon. W. Jasper Blackburn, M. C. This was done during the absence of Mr. Blackburn to this city, and Mr. Pratt, of Claiborne, a Democratic Representative in the present Legislature, very promptly and magnanimously offered to place at Mr. Blackburn's disposition the printing material of the Minden Democratic paper.

The publication of the Illiad was resumed again, and we now learn from Mr. Pratt that the establishment has been sacked a second time in the night, and this time completely demolished.

The people of Claiborne parish seem to fear the truth, and very unwisely demonstrate their hostility to the discussion of Republican principles, by destroying type and breaking up presses.

They are as bad as the benighted citizens of Franklin, Opelousas, and Alexandria, who have done the same thing once. The expense of this luxury will be paid by the tax payers.

PARISH OF ASCENSION.

Mark Shonberg states, on oath, that he resides in the town of Donaldsonville, parish of Ascension; that on Saturday, October 17, 1868, between the hours of eight and nine o'clock P. M., he saw Mr. F. Reno, L. Guin, and about forty other men, all white, armed with shot guns and revolvers. Reno told witness that they were going to shoot him on sight; afterwards said Reno sent him word he was going to shoot him himself. These men purchased all the fire arms in the town and put them in a secret place. Dr. Franklin, who was with witness that night, was told by some of those men not to go in company with witness, for they "wanted to shoot the d—d son of a b—h." The doctor answered them, "I have always been his physician and I will not leave him; he is a gentleman, and if you want to shoot him, you will have to shoot me." The doctor went with him to his house, and told him not to go out at night, for he was in danger from these armed men. The civil authorities belong to this party of armed men, and will use no means to protect the Republican citizens, but give these armed men protection. Witness is the postmaster appointed by the United States Government; he also has the warehouse, and landing of the steamboats, where his duty compels him to go. These men are watching him every night; they also patrolled the town every night; they stopped at his house at midnight and, knocking at his room door, called him to come out, when he went to the door they had gone; it being dark he did not see them. Witness was notified that he would be arrested, in the morning on false charges, in order that they could get the chance to kill him and raise a muss. Witness was told on Sunday night that, in order to accomplish their designs, he was to be arrested the next morning; he took a horse and buggy and came to New Orleans, leaving his family, property, and all that he had at the mercy of these men.

Morris Marks, Parish Judge, parish of Ascension, states on oath, that the white citizens of the town of Donaldsonville, in the parish of Ascension, are in every way and manner striving to create, by threats and open demonstration, and by their disloyal course to bring about dissatisfaction, and if possible riot and bloodshed between the two races. Every imaginable dishonorable, low and degraded means are put in practice, to bring about the ends of those who are leaders in this, and other diabolical outrages, that have been, and are being, perpetrated upon the loyal and law-abiding citizens of both races. Those of the civil officers of the so-called Democratic party are none other than those who still hold dear the rebel cause, and are in great measure the upholders of the course pursued. The paper called "The Drapeau," edited by Felix Renaud, assisted by one R. H. Bradford, both of whom are as mean as the meanest could be, are by their obnoxious publications, inciting the people to riot and murder which can be proved by the issues of the paper itself. At the meeting of a club of so-called Democrats, in the first ward of the parish of Ascension, of which H. L. Duffee is President, resolutions were proposed, and unanimously passed, to the effect that at the coming election those who are disfranchised by law, and consequently not registered, are determined to vote peaceably if they can, and forcibly if they must. Deponent is advised by his friends not to return to the parish, as his life has been threatened by those who are the leaders of the so-called Democratic party. As regards the election held on the 17th and 18th days of April, 1868, frauds of the grossest character which were perpetrated are daily coming to light.

Gustave Arnheim states, on oath, that he is a resident and registered voter of Donaldsonville, parish of Ascension; that his life, as well as that of every loyal citizen, is in danger, having been repeatedly threatened by a gang of armed men, of which Felix Renaud is the leader. They meet daily at said Renaud's bar-room, where they keep their arms deposited. Deponent and others have used every endeavor to prevent the disturbance, which this gang appear to so anxiously seek. He and others have, however, found it impossible for them to remain there without protection. This condition of things has been reported to General Hatch by the Bureau Agent stationed at Donaldsonville. To avoid a disturbance which this gang of unprincipled men had arranged, deponent left the place in a carriage on Monday morning and came to New Orleans to report to the Governor and petition for assistance, and to warn Judge Marks not to return to Donaldsonville, as his life was in great danger.

ASCENSION—SUMMARY.

Number maltreated..2

PARISH OF CATAHOULA.

M. J. Lemmon states, on oath, that he is a citizen of the State of Louisiana, and has been a resident of the parish of Catahoula for the past two (2) years. He was appointed agent of the Freedmen's Bureau for the above parish in May, 1867, and was relieved July 31, 1868. That J. A. Fanning arrived in the above parish on the 18th day of October, 1868, as chairman of the Board of Supervisors, in company with William Goodwin and Schuyler Marvin, as commissioners. Mr. Marvin being sick and unable to work, Mr. Fanning appointed witness in his place. The Board proposed to open their office on or about the 20th day of October, 1868, at Mossy Grove, on Black river. On that day witness was warned by James Dunckley, Jr., not to open an office there, for if it was done his wife would find him hanging to a tree some morning, and that the citizens would not permit it. Dunckley also said that witness had been distributing "incendiary documents" among the freedmen, (meaning the Republican papers of the State,) and that he understood that a Republican meeting was to be held at Mossy Grove, and if they should attempt it they would be driven away and badly hurt. This same day, or the day following, a letter was dropped in Mr. Fanning's hat, while he was at supper, warning him to leave the parish immediately. On account of these threats the Registration office was not opened at Mossy Grove; and witness firmly believes, from his knowledge of those men, that if it had been, they would have carried their threats into execution, and no doubt would have killed the members of said Board of Registration. But notwithstanding this, he determined to, and did hold a Republican meeting at Mossy Grove, advising the freedmen to come armed, as their lives were threatened, which they did. Witness thinks there were about two hundred freedmen in attendance. Just before the meeting commenced, about twenty-five white men, armed with double barreled shot guns, came to deponent's place, and, finding the freedmen armed, thought it advisable not to make any attack, and went away. The meeting was held and passed off quietly. Witness received a letter—found in his yard—warning himself and Mr. Fanning to leave the parish on or before the 26th of October, or they would be hung. Another letter was also received by witness on the following morning, containing similar threats. These letters were signed "K. K. K.," with a picture of a gallows. On the nights of October, 26th and 28th, a body of armed men came to witness' house, disguised with masks; but finding some freedmen up, and not seeing witness, left on both occasions without saying anything or doing any harm. To deponent's knowledge, a great many freedmen were discharged from plantations because they refused to join the Democratic clubs and vote the Democratic ticket. A few days before the election a party of three white men went to the house of an old colored man, in the night, took him into the woods, stripped him, tied him to a stake, and gave him a large number of lashes with a harness trace, and then told him to go, and if they found him in that part of the parish the next day they would kill him. He started to run and was fired at three times, but was not hit. The old man was so badly bruised from the said beating, that it took him three days to get to witness' house, a distance of fifteen miles; and from what he told and from witness' own knowledge of these people, he has no hesitation in saying that the sole and only purpose of these men was to get possession of the old man's crop, consisting of about twelve acres of cotton and the same in corn. Witness firmly believes that there have been from twenty to twenty-five freedmen killed during the past eight or ten months in Catahoula parish. About the 1st of January, 1868, three colored men were arrested on suspicion of having killed an ox, and while on their way to jail were met by the "Ku Klux," and taken from the parties who had them in charge. A few weeks after their bodies were found floating in a bayou. Mr. Newman, of Catahoula, (a brother of Mr. Isidore Newman, broker in New Orleans,) told witness that a party of white men visited his place about the first of this year, and killed all the colored men, women and children on the place, and then set fire to the house, gin and barns, which were thereby burned to the ground. Mr. Tallia-ferro, the chairman of our Board, told witness that he thought there would be at least seven or eight hundred (700 or 800) freedmen that would not register, on account of the threats that had been made against them, such as, "They would be killed," "be hanged," "be driven off the places," etc. And many were deceived by being told that it was not necessary for them to register again, that they could vote on their old registration papers, while others were told that they had plenty of time to register for the next three or four weeks, when the parties telling these lies knew positively that the Registration office would close in a few days, viz: on the 24th of October, 1868. Witness found his life in so much danger while residing in this parish, that he left on the 29th day of October and arrived in this city on the 31st. Witness further states that Republicans cannot live with any security in Catahoula parish. That the leading citizens of the parish were very sanguine that Seymour and Blair would be elected President and Vice President, and it was nothing unusual to hear them say—in fact it was their boast—"that after Seymour and Blair were elected, no G—d d—d Radical should live in the parish." The following are some of the names of the "Ku Klux Klan" of Catahoula parish and of the parties that came to witness' house, as before stated: James Dunckley, Jr., R. R. Brown, F. T. Leatherman, Frank Folk, John Lacraux, Michael Lacraux, Michael Beard, Joseph White, H. Ramsey, William Jones, Eugene Barrow, Rollins, and Turnage. All these parties were at witness' house, and he believes the man Rollins and his brother were the murderers of the three colored men arrested on suspicion of having killed the ox hereinbefore spoken of. That the said Rollins was very bitter against the colored race, and witness believes from what he has heard that he (Rollins) has killed at least thirty or forty of the said race since the surrender of General Lee, in 1865.

Hon. O. H. Brewster, member of the House of Representatives, State of Louisiana, states, on oath, that he left the city of New Orleans on the 21st day of October, 1868, for the landing, six miles below Trinity, Catahoula parish. On his arrival there he met Mr. Lemmon, ex-agent of the Freedmen's Bureau, and saw him pick up a letter in his yard; the letter contained the following words, as near as witness can recollect: "You and your Radical friend, Fanning, (present Bureau agent for this parish,) must leave this parish by the 26th instant, under the penalty of being hung;" it was signed "K. K. K.," and contained a picture of a gallows. On the 23d of October, 1868, witness visited Trinity and called upon the Board of Supervisors, and was informed by Mr. Taliaferro, who is a member of the Board, that there were about eight hundred freedmen who had not registered. This was on the 24th, and next to the last day of closing registration. Mr. Taliaferro believed these freedmen had been deceived by the planters for whom they worked, and that these planters had told said freedmen that their old registration papers would do, and that the registration office would not close on the 24th of October, 1868, but would keep open for three or four weeks longer. Mr. Taliaferro said he thought they would have a peaceable election in the parish, but there was no doubt the parish would go Democratic, on account of so many freedmen being deprived the privilege of registering. Witness says it was published in the papers that he would make a Republican speech that night at Lemmon's place. A few of the colored men who came to the place of meeting, came armed with double-barreled shotguns. He asked these parties why they came armed? They replied that "parties of armed white men had visited them on the plantations, and told them if they went to hear Brewster, or any other Radical speak they would kill them," and that hundreds would have come to the meeting if they had not been afraid of getting killed. The following morning Mr. Lemmon and witness found a letter in the gully, tied to a corn cob, containing a warning, as follows: "Lemmon and his Radical friend must leave by the 26th," signed "K. K. K. ! ! !" A day or two afterwards witness went to Ouachita parish to a point twelve miles below Monroe, to fill another appointment that had been published. Directly after landing, he met an old overseer, and heard him say to a boy on a white mule, "run quick and tell all of them." It was about a half mile to the store; after going there, and while conversing with Mr. Filhio, a crowd of men collected around, some of them showing their fire-arms, and surrounded witness. The man who seemed to be the leader said "I believe this is Mr. Brewster?" Witness replied, "Yes ! how do you do, sir ?" He answered "None of your business." Witness then said "there is no need of having any trouble; what is the matter ?" To which he replied "We want to notify you that you must leave this place to-day, or you will not live 'till night," or words to that effect. They also told witness that if he intended to hold a Republican meeting he had better come with a strong force, or they would not succeed. Witness told him he "would like to know why they pursued this course?" He replied (the leader) "because you belong to a party that is trying to excite the colored people to kill off all the white men, women and children; the colored people are quiet now, and we are determined to keep them so." Witness answered, "I refer you to my course in the State Legislature, to show you that I have worked for the good of the whole people, both white and black." He answered, "It makes no difference what your course has been, you belong to a party that wants to bring on a war between the two races, and we are not going to allow it, and we don't want any more talk about the matter." Witness went into Mr. Filhio's house, who recommended him to go away for fear these men would commit some outrages. Witness then left Mr. Filhio's house and started for Monroe, where he arrived in the afternoon, and then immediately went to Trenton. He had only been there a few minutes when two of his Democratic friends, whose names he would not like to give, told him his presence might make a disturbance, and he had better be on the lookout. Witness saw several colored men who told him they could not vote for "Grant and Colfax" and live there; that they would have to vote for "Seymour and Blair" to save their lives. Many of them told witness that their employers had taken their registration papers and would make them vote for "Seymour and Blair." Just after dark witness found the excitement so high that he started to return to Monroe, and while passing through the grounds that surrounded his house he was fired upon by white men, who had previously threatened that they would kill him before morning. He thinks these men were strangers to him and were from some of the hill parishes. Witness is perfectly satisfied from his travels through the different parishes of the State, that the Democratic party is controlled by a set of white desperadoes, and that honest Democrats are as much intimidated as Republicans. A day or two after witness went to Madison parish, and after passing Delhi, he was told by a Democrat that the "Ku-Klux-Klan!" had waited on a shoemaker, and warned him to leave in a certain time; he was then packing up to go. Witness found everything quiet along the river in this parish; he made speeches at Milliken's Bend and in other portions of the parish, and was well treated by the Democrats in each place. In coming down the Téche country through St. Mary parish since the election, witness says it was openly said by Democrats on board of the boat, that "if there was no other way to get rid of the Radicals, the Legislature would have to go up."

Abraham Jackson, colored, states, on oath, that he was obliged to flee from the town of Harrisonburg, parish of Catahoula, on the

3rd of November, 1868, on account of the demonstrations made by the Democrats toward taking his life; that for some months past he had been engaged in teaching a colored school in Harrisonburg; that about two months since he found it necessary to close his school on account of threats made against him by parties professing to be Democrats, since which time he had been engaged in cutting wood and doing any other work he could get to do. On Monday night, November 2, about 10 o'clock, witness being on the road, about three hundred yards from his house, he heard the sound of a body of men approaching, and being afraid, he crouched behind some rocks on the road side, which they passed. He judges there were a hundred of them, all armed with guns and revolvers; they went directly to his house and inquired for him; witness hearing everything they said from where he was concealed. A friend, who was at the house, told them he did not know where witness was; whereupon they threatened to shoot him if he did not tell. They then went to John Moore's (a colored man) house, and inquired for witness; Moore told them he did not know where witness was; and then told them that witness had read the Republican papers and documents to him so much that he had become a Republican, otherwise he would be a Democrat. These men replied: "God d—n him, he had better make his escape from here, for if we lay our eyes on him we will slay him." One of their number, a Captain Gillespie, said: "If he (witness) comes to the polls to-morrow I will blow his brains out," adding, "I will be there myself, and if Jackson enters the court house door I will shoot him." Witness knows of nothing they have against him except that he taught a colored school, and read the Radical papers to the colored people, and tried to enlighten them as much as he could; he has never heard them say they did not wish the colored children taught, but has heard them say they "did not want a black teacher in town." Witness says a large number of colored men have been found killed in the parish on account of their politics the past year. There was a band of men called "Ku-Klux" that went about the country in the night, and it was supposed those found killed met their death at their hands. Witness farther states, that there are about forty colored Democrats in the parish, and that they are allowed to carry weapons, but that colored Republicans are not allowed to carry them or have them in their houses; that on the day of the election he did not dare to go to the polls on account of the threats made against him the night before, and because the Democrats had said that none but Democrats should put their tickets in the ballot box.

The following is an official statement of Wm. Baker, Chairman of the Board of Registrars, as to the conduct of the election of the 3rd of November, 1868, in the parish of Catahoula:

"From the parish of Catahoula, the report shows, with a previous registry of at least twenty-five hundred for twenty-three hundred and seventy (2370) voted. Under the present registration not one-half of that number registered, and less than one thousand voted. This the Registrar accounts for by saying: 'There was such a system of imprecation, abuse, entreaty, espionage and threats and annoyances generally, that very many voted against their convictions and many more were deterred from registering at all.' 'The vote as given is not a fair expression of the sentiment of the people of this parish at all.' 'There was no absolute fraud in receiving or counting votes.'"

CATAHOULA—SUMMARY.

Number killed, positively sworn to........................	3
Number killed, estimated by witness........................	20 to 25
Number maltreated, positively sworn to..................	6

PARISH OF ST. MARTIN.

Wm. Dunn states, on oath, that he made a contract with Mr. Delahousay, in the parish of St. Martin, on the first day of January, 1868, to cultivate about sixty or seventy acres of land. Witness was treated very well before the election, which took place on the 17th and 18th days of April, 1868, but after the election, knowing that he voted the Republican ticket, said Delahousay came to him when at work and said that he had allowed him (witness) favors before, but now he should hold him strictly to his contract, and if the Constitution was adopted war would commence. On frequent occasions said Delahousay had threatened to shoot witness and his son and the men that were at work for him; one of whom, by the name of Emanuel Brown, was driven away from the place because he went to register. Several white men made threats against a colored man named Jack Johnson, because he took the New Orleans Advocate, and against witness, because he took the Republican. They also said if they could get witness and one or two other colored men out of the parish they could control the rest of the colored men in that portion of the parish where witness lived. These threats becoming so numerous, and the feeling against witness so bitter, and the election of November 3 being so near at hand, he sold out his standing crop at less than half its value, and left the parish, as he felt that a longer stay would endanger his life. Witness also states that many men were discharged from the different plantations because they had registered; and all kinds of threats were used by the Democrats towards the colored men to induce them not to register, telling them that if they did, they must vote the Democratic ticket, or they would be driven off the plantations. That the colored people were very much frightened, as they did not know what moment their cabins would be visited by bands of white men for the purpose of killing them. That during the first part of October, a band of white men visited the house of a colored man in this parish and killed him and his mother.

The following letter, from the Hon. A. R. François, a State Senator from this parish, is here inserted on account of the graphic history which it relates of the progress toward reconstruction in that parish, and because in its general outlines it is a very correct delineation of the state of affairs in the rest of the State during the past two years.

Mr. François is a property holder, an old resident, and a gentleman who was universally respected in his parish:

Hon. P. Harper:

Dear Sir—I have the honor to inform you that your communication of September, 1868, is received, and be assured that, with all my good will, I comply with your request. My pen is not one of an English grammarian, nor can I find language to describe all the rebuffs and sneers which my race and their friends have been compelled to bear in the parish of St. Martin from the Democratic aristocracy, for its seems to all observers that this parish is a small hereditary monarchy instead of a simple parish in a State of this American Republic. Since law in some shape or another has made its appearance in this section of the State, a single family have been the promulgators and interpreters of it according to their own views and to their own profit.

This great family began with the Bryants, but are connected with the Fournets, Garys and DeBlancs by intermarriages. Sir, is it necessary for me to give you a sketch of this intermixed family? I believe not; for if you wish to be minutely informed of the reputation of these small potentates, you have only to travel on the Têche from one end to the other, and inquire among all classes of people, and you will get a clear idea of the compact existing among this intermixed family. Not a single dark deed was ever committed in St. Martin except by the hands or at the instigation of this artful and cunning family. The policy of these Democratic leaders are questions of family, not of principle.

Now, sir, can I give you a description of all the abuses of which my race has been the victim in St. Martin? I know that it is impossible; but sir, I feel that it is my duty to tell you, that wherever you may go in St. Martin, you will discover by the attitude of the *cavaliers* of that parish, that a bitter feeling still exists against the United States Government, and all those who are willing to sustain that government, and they are yet unable to conceive how the negroes can possess any rights at all, to be respected. Sir, in St. Martin a white man in dealing, will cheat a negro without a single feeling of remorse. They will kill a negro without deeming it to be murder; to debauch a negro woman, they do not think seduction; to take the property of a negro, they do not consider robbery. And I speak truly when I say the lives of the negroes and their friends are but as the twice pressed grape—a thing fit to be trodden under foot by every brutal clown or thug among the St. Martin white aristocracy. And, sir, when abused, if a colored man demands justice and the respect due to all human beings according to their personal merits, the slaveocrats rise scornfully and call him an insolent dog, who barks at the white race, and who does not know that he is by fate doomed to be forever crushed like a vile worm beneath the heels of servitude and obscurity! It is a common expression in every still rebellious slaveocrat's mouth, that when chance shall be theirs they will have us racked for our insolence; will rend the flesh from off our vicious bones and bathe them in blood, and tear out our accursed tongues for ever having had the foolish impudence to demand equality with the Southern aristocracy before the laws, or to interfere with the great political questions of the South. Now, sir, you cannot conceive how little the white people of St. Martin who call themselves christians feel or care for the lives of the poor black men, who are truly christians. Nor can you ever know half the wrongs or the bitter mockeries which my race has endured in St. Martin; neither can you imagine the anger of the Southern people in this section of the State against the blacks and the northern people. You, nor any other, can have an idea of the base persecutions to which we have been subjected in St. Martin, except you were there, and experienced in your own person the horrors of confusion and desolation that we have sustained for many years past. Permit me to refer to the year 1861, when the great confusion of the rebellion began in our section of the State. The political agitators (especially the "intermixed family,") wished to find a pretext to bring the white people of the parish entirely in favor of the rebellion, and promptly did they excite others less skilled in political machinations to bring about the object of their wishes; therefore the great mass of ignorant whites were instigated against what they called a d—d Yankee. A white mechanic from the North, long a resident of the parish, employed at Fausse Pointe as a cooper, was denounced without the least proof, as an abolitionist, and was sent before the court for trial with seventeen colored men, whom he was accustomed to employ on Sundays to advance his business.

The court conscious that there was no evidence against the white man, who was the first to be tried, dismissed his case but the people excited by their skillful politicians came out en masse as a "Vigilance Committee," and hanged the white man at St. Martinsville. This dark deed took place near the Bayou known as the "Têche," the highest tree served as the gallows. He was hoisted by way of a pully, and it was terrible to see the agitators grasp the rope in their right hands and start on a double quick until the neck of their poor victim met with the pully. The masters of the seventeen colored men accused with this unfortunate man, demanded that the severest punishment be inflicted upon their slaves for having had any connection with "that Yankee." Was their process pursued regularly according to law? We cannot tell, but we do know that out of the seventeen negroes, six were hanged, as if it was done by law; for a sentence was read to them and the sheriff, named "Greig," hanged them with his own hands. The other eleven were sent to hard labor at the Penitentiary. In 1863, when the Union army made its appearance on the "Têche" and took possession of New Iberia, the colored people throughout the parish heard of it, and a party of about fifty slaves from "Breaux Bridge" started in a body with the intention of passing into the Federal lines, but when they got within fifteen miles of St. Martinsville the political agitators sent to New Iberia for Federal protection, saying that the negroes were in open revolution against the white race. At that time these Federal officers did not act consistently with their positions. A company commanded by Captain Wood was sent to act in conjunction with the people of St. Martin who were all armed. Both parties, Union and Rebel, fixed themselves in line of battle at the foot of the St. Martinsville Têche Bridge, over which the poor slaves had to cross, and when they got within two hundred yards of the bridge a deputation (the same that went to New Iberia after them) demanded the Federal officer to open fire on the rebellious negroes, but he refused, saying he could not say that those negroes were in rebellion against the white race. At this moment these fugitives recognized the United States soldiers and shouted hurra for Uncle Sam! The agitators exasperated, ordered their party to open fire on those defenseless black people, and the Federal officer so disgraced himself as to stand an impartial witness to that butchery of his country's best friends! and sir, the horrors did not stop there. A few in that small band of men were only wounded, and they were hanged to every post of the bridge. At that barbarous sight the Federal troops retired, but the bodies did not remain there, for the slaveocrats were not satisfied that the example should remain unperfected; a ditch was dug in the outskirts of the town and those martyred people were tied with a "lasso," some around their necks, others around their legs, then part were fastened to the tails of horses, others were seized by the agitators themselves, and all were dragged in triumph to the ditch, and inhumanly corded one upon another. This butchery to this day has impressed upon the minds of some heretofore slaves that the Yankees were not their friends, and are not even now, or they would not permit so many outrages to be practiced upon them even to the present time under their very nose. What if some persons do know about law, when the intelligent people of our parish ignore it, or interpret its meaning according to their own wills? But the colored people know one thing, and that is, that the Northern people are the victors, and should extend protection to the people that stood by them and whose rights are trampled upon every day.

On the 25th day of April, same year (1863), two colored men, Hamilton and Frederick by name, were hanged on Declouet's plantation without any process of law or any cause whatever, under the pretence that they were in the so-called rebellion against their masters and the white race. Another was shot dead by a Mr. Gardnier, Jr., because while a little tipsy he expressed his sorrow at the execution of those innocent men. Shortly afterward, in the same year, on Lastrapp's plantation, four (4) colored persons, a man, his wife and two children were shot dead because they were going to leave their master's plantation to join the Federal toops at New Iberia. March 4, 1864, Joseph Oliver, a respectable colored man, of good family, was taken from his home, about seven miles from New Iberia, under the pretence that he had dealt with the Yankees during their occupation of that place, and brought into the village by two white men named Norwood and Tiller, who called upon the people to unite with them in having said Oliver hung, but a few experienced men opposed to that mode of proceeding, directed the party to St. Martinsville, where a Confederate "court martial" was convened, but about a mile out of town, the party concluding it was going to too much trouble to obtain a judgment to have a "nigger" hung, resolved to execute him at once; accordingly they shot him dead on the spot, took his clothes, boots and money, and left his body naked on the ground. In 1866 a colored man was found hanged at "Grande Pointe." It is still a mystery who committed the deed, and no effort was ever made to find the guilty party. March 10th, of the same year, a fishing party, composed of a young man named Caytan, aged sixteen, a woman and two young girls were seated in a small boat fishing in the "Bayou Têche," in front of Onesiphore Delahoussay's plantation. The young man was at one end of the boat eating, when the report of a gun was heard, and he received a load of shot in his head from a gun in the hands of Onesiphore Delahoussay, Jr., who then had the whole party arrested on the pretence that they were stealing wood from his place. They were taken to St. Martinsville, to be placed in jail, but the civil officers seeing the absurdity of Delahoussay's pretence did not comply with his desires. The young man lost one eye as the result of this wound. His parents took the necessary steps to bring the case before the court, but lawyers refused to take charge, and judges refused to receive their affidavit, with the exception of one justice of the peace, in New Iberia, who received it, but no suit was brought because the constables refused to execute the warrant of arrest.

The same year a colored man named "Jean Louis" was killed in the woods at "Fausse Pointe," no effort was made by the authorities to find the criminal party, and the death of that man is still a mystery. The same year a colored girl was employed as a servant by a family named Melancon; after several months service a difficulty arose between the girl and Mrs. Melancon, the latter refusing to pay the girl her wages. She brought a suit before the justice of the peace at St. Martinsville and gained the suit. When she went back to Melancon's plantation for her clothes, Melancon seized her in a rage and whipped her unmercifully, asking this poor orphan girl if she did not know that she had no right to bring his wife, "a white lady," before the law? Thereupon the girl came back to make her complaint again before the authorities, but the judge refused to entertain her case farther. In 1867, at "Fausse Pointe," a colored man named "Jean Baptiste" was with a fishing party on the lake shore. He had absented himself for a few moments from the party, when the report of a gun was heard, and when his friends reached the spot he was found dead. His murderer, a white man, was standing near him with a gun, claiming as a reason for the act that the negro was stealing horses, which was false, and witnesses can testify to it.

Abundant evidence can be brought, if required, to prove all of the foregoing statements. In addition to all this there is evidence at the "Freedmen's Bureau" in New Iberia that numerous cases of murders and ill treatment of the colored people have not been investigated, nor prosecuted by the agents of the Bureau, since 1865. Lieut. Cornelius, for several years one of said agents, was very intimate with the slaveocrats of St. Martin, and instead of deciding cases himself, or sending them before some military authority, that would protect the freedmen, he would send them before the civil officers of the parish, or leave them unattended in his office; therefore no suits or prosecutions were brought against those disturbers of the peace, and lawfessness was encouraged and is continued until this time.

And now, sir, we have reached the great event of the election of the 17th and 18th of April, 1868. When the Union men, both black and white, were called upon to vote for a Republican form of government, by adopting a Republican constitution, under which to bring the State back into the Union; and here, again, we had all the hardest trials imaginable. Notices of election were not given, as the law requires, in the newspapers published in the parish; the first notices that were given were handbills posted in a few places, and these not until the 13th of April, and then not giving what was most important for voters to know, viz: the places where the polls were to be established; they only stated that polls would be established, for instance, at "Coteau," which is a portion of the parish eight or nine miles in length by five or six in breadth. Some of the registrars announced verbally that the Coteau poll would be opened at Cleophas Romero's store, but on the day of election it was transferred to Jos. Gario's, without notice. No mention was made in said handbills about the number of ballot boxes that would be used at each poll, and it was understood by the Republicans that the ballots "For," or "Against the Constitution" and all officers to be voted for under its provisions would be cast in one box, according to Special Order No. 65, Head Quarters Fifth Military District, which reads as follows:

"The ballots to be cast for or against the constitution shall have on them, printed or in writing, the names of the several officers voted for under its provisions," etc.

This order was not executed by the Registrars and Commissioners, some of whom required the ballots to be cast in three different boxes, others in one. In St. Martinsville, at the poll superintended by C. D. Olivier, Chairman of the Board of Registration for the parish, ballots were cast in three different boxes; those voting the

Republican ticket having cast their ballots in one box only, their votes were contested, and were not counted for Justice of the Peace nor corporation officers, whom the Republicans had really elected by twenty-five majority in the Second Ward.

The Republicans attempted in vain to obtain from the Registrars, C. D. Olivier, P. Bienvenue and J. B. Vandergriff, even verbal information (in the absence of written) as to the places where the polls would be established, and the number of boxes in which to vote. The invariable answer was, "Nothing has yet been decided by the Board;" and it is a well known fact, that the Democratic party was organized in secret clubs with pass words and signs; that C. D. Olivier was a member, and that they all were well informed as to how the election was to be conducted. The polls at St. Martinsville, Fausse Pointe and Bayou Plomb were surrounded by armed gangs of men, assuming a very hostile attitude, and said to have been under the control of the Sheriff; said forces were composed of white men, most of whom belonged to the secret Democratic organization. They were armed with double-barreled guns, pistols and daggers; their duty was to disarm every person who approached the polls, and this was violently practiced upon Republicans and apparently on Democrats. In this gang of armed men were some notorious guerrillas, who openly boasted of having killed the first Union soldiers on the soil of this State. During the two days of election they prevented colored Republicans from voting according to their opinions, and frightened the timed from the polls. When a Republican approached the polls he was violently searched and insulted.

The Commissioners of Election also acted entirely in a party spirit; three Democrats were permitted to come up to the polls to one Republican, and *then* the Republican vote would be refused for one cause or another.

These Commissioners, most of whom had been fraudulently registered, were, or pretended to be, ignorant of their duties as defined by military orders, and acting on their own responsibility, assumed the right of preventing about two hundred and fifty Republicans from voting (though they had their registration papers) on the following grounds, viz: Some were presumed to be too young, although they were willing to swear they were twenty-one years of age; others were rejected for being *too old*, or for having been born (as the commissioners claimed) in the State when under the French government, and therefore would be obliged to take out naturalization papers before they were entitled to vote. This was done without the least proof, and simply upon their appearance; some were prevented for alleged non-residence, although their registration papers showed that they were residents; thus the Commissioners prevented many Republicans from voting, and permitted Democrats to vote, although both resided on the same plantations; others had their registration papers taken from them, as the Commissioner claimed they were fraudulently obtained, because by some mistake in the types, the numbers on the printed lists furnished the Commissioners from headquarters, did not exactly correspond with the numbers of their registration papers. But with similar mistakes Democrats were permitted to vote. These last charges are brought especially against the Commissioners at St. Martinsville, who allowed themselves to be guided by the opinion and decisions of one Valsin Fournet, (of the intermixed family), who, although disfranchised, was permitted, together with many other disfranchised and disloyal men, to surround the ballot box for the purpose of intimidating colored voters and driving them from the polls. While this right was denied by said Commissioners not only to Republicans and loyal men, but also to Republican candidates.

On the second day of the election, April 18th, most of the persons desiring to vote at St. Martinsville being Republicans, the commissioners of election proceeded so slowly that when the polls closed, at least one hundred and fifty or two hundred of them had not had an opportunity to vote. The way this was done was as follows: The commissioners permitted Democrats and disfranchised rebels who were standing by, to challenge every Republican voter, upon the most frivolous grounds, and permitted all sorts of questions to be asked them, such as, the very day on which they were born, the name of their master before the war, or if they were christened in the Catholic church, or not, and made them procure their christening papers, to prove their ages. All these questions were asked in the most insulting tone imaginable. On account of these outrages the Republicans, at a late hour opened a separate poll, but not in time to take the ballots of all who had been refused the right to vote. Mr. L. E. Laloire, one of the deputy supervisors for the parish, took the affidavits of about sixty-two Republicans who had been prevented from voting by the commissioners of election. At "Fousse Pointe" the same system of intimidation prevailed;

Republicans were searched, insulted, and their lives threatened if they did not vote the Democratic ticket. One J. D. Broussard, a disfranchised rebel, who was allowed to register and vote, was, with E. Broussard, P. Traham, Alcè Dugas and Gustave Loreau on a committee appointed by the *secret organization*, to notify a white Republican named Ovide E. Smith, on the 16th day of April to leave the place within twenty-four hours, and he was forced to do so. The new list of voters was not revised by the Registrars of St. Martin, according to orders from headquarters, and the consequence was that about one hundred rebels fraudulently registered, were permitted to vote.

The Board of Registrars is to be blamed for having registered persons who had been stricken from the list by the former Board for reasons set forth in the registry books, with satisfactory evidence which had been furnished said Board, and especially for registering Dr. Alf. Duperier, whose name had been stricken from the list for the following cause, to wit: "Having been a member of the Legislature of Louisiana before the 21st of January, 1861, and afterward aided the rebellion by a loan of one thousand dollars to arm and equip men to prevent the advance of Federal troops."

The registrars allowed rebels to register although they were clearly disfranchised; also many who were under age. Also persons of foreign birth without producing their naturalization papers, who had been rejected by the former Board because they could not produce said papers. They went so far as to register one J. Dorville Broussard (heretofore mentioned), who was elected (as the present) parish Recorder, and whose antecedents are well known to the whole community, and especially to C. D. Olivier, Chairman of said Board of Registrars.

J. D. Broussard was State Assessor before the 21st of January, 1861, and afterwards served as an officer in the rebellion, and also held civil office under the Confederate States government.

Auguste Maris was a postmaster before the 1st of January, 1861, and served as a commissioned officer in the Confederate States army, and afterward rebel postmaster for the parish of St. Martin, and yet this Board of Registrars permitted this "celebrity" to register and vote, although an order from headquarters ordered his name to be erased from the list, which order was not complied with until after he had voted.

In many instances the Registrars refused to grant new registration papers to colored voters, who had lost their certificates, because they could not remember the numbers, and many were refused the right to vote on that account.

The Board of Registrars did not open their office on the days nor at the places mentioned in the notices given by them, and thus a good many colored citizens were deprived of the chance to register, while Democrats were initiated into all the secrets of the Board If you could have a committee appointed by the "two houses" to investigate the frauds in St. Martin, you would find out more than this, and besides that, we would prove all the above statements.

I remain, sir, yours most respectfully,

(Signed) ALEX. R. FRANCOIS.

Hon. A. R. Francois states, on oath, that he is a citizen of the State of Louisiana and Senator from the Fourteenth District, parishes of St. Martin, Iberville and West Baton Rouge. Deponent obtained leave of absence from the Senate and went to St. Martin; where he arrived on the 20th of September, 1868. A Republican meeting was held in St. Martinsville for the purpose of receiving him; deponent was nominated President of the meeting; Hon. Mr. McCarthy addressed the meeting. While he was speaking, deponent was informed that the Democrats had armed themselves and were coming for the purpose of disturbing the meeting. Deponent also learned from reliable sources that the Democrats were arming themselves by taking arms from stores, and every place where they could procure them. He sent three persons to the Mayor to inform him of these facts, and also to tell him that the Republicans were peaceable citizens, assembled to express their political sentiments, and they relied upon him to keep peace and order. The meeting was not disturbed. After the meeting was dismissed the delegations left in different directions; one delegation attempted to pass through the town, but was prevented from doing so by the Democrats who were armed in regular military style. They also prevented Republicans from cheering for Grant and Colfax. The Mayor of the town was at the head of the Democrats; he was seconded by V. Fournèt, who seemed to have control over all the Democrats. The Republican delegation attempted to pass through the line of the Democrats; who aimed their guns at them, evidently with the intention of firing. The Republicans then procured arms the best way they could, and as they passed the line of Democrats they still had their guns aimed at them, and threatened to take their lives; at the same time insulting and abusing them, evidently for the purpose of creating a riot. The delegation then passed without resenting their insults and abuse, and proceeded to their homes; after which, the Democrats surrounded the town, and blockaded all the main roads, preventing every Republican from going in or out of the town. They circulated a report that the Republicans intended to burn the town and murder all the Democrats in the place. This report was circulated for the purpose of defending themselves in their actions. They continued to guard the town until Thursday, when a detachment of Federal troops arrived, and compelled them to leave the main roads, and ordered them to go to their homes, but they did not; they were camped in companies on nearly all the plantations in the vicinity of St. Martinsville, when deponent left on Sunday at 12 o'clock, 27th of September, 1868.

"The Courier of the Têche" says:

On election day, all the negroes in this parish, except about fifty, were actively engaged in picking cotton, chopping wood, cutting cane, and attending to other work. The freedmen of this parish pretend that they have had enough to do with politics, and are not going to meddle with them any more, and that they have had too much to do with Radicalism, and will fight out the horrid monster if ever it dares to show its ugly head among them hereafter. They have completely recovered their senses. They now truly understand what is to their best interest and advantage, and appear determined to let the white man rule the country. They want peace, but not such peace as Grant is willing to grant.

"The Negroes' Votes.—If the whites had been willing to urge on the negroes of this parish to vote the Democratic ticket, our majority would have been increased by at least two hundred. But we deem it a bad precedent to advise and induce the negro to vote on either side. If he votes now Democratic, he may vote with the Radicals the next time, if he has a chance; and it will be with exceeding bad grace that we should then go to him and tell him 'that he has no right to vote; it were much better for them to remain at home, attend to their work, and let the white man take care of the politics of the country.' It is better, much better for ourselves, and for those poor deluded people to tell them the truth at once; we know that it is neither our interest nor theirs that they should continue to enjoy the sacred privilege of suffrage. Let us not therefore endeavor to make pliant tools of them now, for we know not how sharp against us may be that tool in the future."

The Freedmen.—"We are glad to announce that in the parish of St. Martin the Freedmen and colored population have understood their position, and how much they have been deceived by scallawags and radicals generally.

"They have in this last election either voted the Democratic ticket or abstained from voting, though our Sheriff had appointed and posted deputies at nearly every point with special instructions to protect all, whether black or white, going to, and returning from, the polls. The freedmen have, with very few exceptions, willingly expressed their determination not yet to exercise a privilege robbed, seemingly, for their advantage, by political adventurers, who have used them as instruments, and who have by day and by night taught them that it was a duty they owed to the government, to burn and destroy the property, and to murder the wives and children of those who fed and clothed them. Were it not for the counsels of moderation given them by our white population, the freedmen would have certainly punished, and in a severe way, their coward leaders."

The following is an official statement of Wm. Baker, Chairman of the Board of Registrars, as to the conduct of the election of November 3, 1868:

"In the parish of St. Martin the Registrars report that 'the registration itself was not free, for armed bands of men prevented colored men from going to register; several of their leaders were killed.' The chairman reports that he knows nothing about the returns, as they were not made to him. Other persons took possession of the returns from the Commissioners of Election, and he was not allowed to see or compile them as required by law."

ST. MARTIN PARISH—SUMMARY.

Number killed, positively sworn to	2
Number maltreated, positively sworn to	4
Illegal Democratic votes cast at the November election	100
Republican voters illegally excluded from voting	250

PARISH OF ST. HELENA.

Charles H. James states, on oath, that he arrived at Amite City on Wednesday, October 28, the night appointed by General Sypher to speak at Tangipahoe, and found a large assemblage of people addressed by one Dr. White (Democrat); about forty of them were armed, and remarked that they were waiting for General Sypher, "that G—d d—d son of a b—h; that G—d d—d carpet bagger, Sypher, why don't he come up with a carpet bag full of revolvers and a dirty shirt." Constantly heard the cry, "When is that G—d d—d Sypher going to arrive." Same night witness went to Tangipahoe, and arrived about 12 o'clock at night; between 12 and 1 a band of armed men (mounted), about forty-two in number, came into the town; their horses as well as themselves covered with white sheets, *en masque*, making inquiries for J. H. Sypher. They took a colored man named John Kempt out of his house and carried him about three hundred yards where they completely riddled him with buckshot. They also went into a store at Tangipahoe and demanded forty-two drinks and four bottles of whiskey, with revolvers pointed at the proprietor's head; after getting which they took all the money in the store and left. In Franklinton the same party carried off a colored man who has not since been heard from. On November 2 the same party visited the Board of Supervisors of Registration—D. Hennessy and Charles Benedict—and told them that if they distributed any Republican tickets in that parish they would take their lives. They then left and proceeded toward a negro settlement in that vicinity; they also visited the house of a colored man named Butler, and demanded of his wife his whereabouts. She came out and recognized the following men: Dunbar Lemons, B. Davidson, of Amite, and Wm. Bell, of Tangipahoe. Butler, who was concealed under the floor of his house, heard them threaten that if he voted the Republican ticket they would kill him. They also inquired for General Sypher, and said they wanted to "kill the G—d d—d son of a b—h." Captain Warren, Deputy Collector of Internal Revenue, left Amite in company with a member of the Board of Registrars for Franklinton, on the morning of the 2d, with Republican tickets, where they arrived at 10 P. M. in safety. On the way back they met three men disguised, when they concealed themselves in the woods, after dismounting and turning their horses loose. While there, a band of forty mounted men, armed, passed; after they passed they resumed their way, and were informed by the negroes along the road that these men threatened to murder any man who voted the Republican ticket. On their arrival at Amite the people generally expressed their astonishment at seeing them alive. Captain Warren's friends informed him that bands of armed men had gone out in all directions to assassinate him; that he was one of "Sypher's pets," and they "would get the d—d son of a b—h out of the way." Dr. Taylor, of Amite, ordered his overseer to discharge every man who voted the Republican ticket. During the six days witness remained in Amite general inquiries were made as to who and what he was. On leaving, on the 3d, two men, armed, (and so buried up in overcoats that it was impossible to recognize them,) approached him when he was getting on the train, and remarked: "There goes a carpet-bagger; I would like to kill the d—d son of a b—h; he is one of Sypher's pets." Witness saw the ballot box opened, and the ballots counted at 3:45 P. M., in Amite.

Luella Ellis states, on oath, that she resides in New Orleans, Louisiana; that she was teaching a colored school of boys and girls on the 23d and 24th of October, 1868, at Greensburg, St. Helena parish. One day a white man by the name of J. Wheat came to her house and tried to get in, but when she refused to open the door he came on the gallery and remarked, "I'll break open this d——d shanty and get them out of there." He used other bad language, and fired a pistol three times from the gallery; one Charles Kempt came on the gallery to assist him. They both tried to break open the door but did not succeed. Some one called them away. Witness being much afraid of losing her life removed to the city of New Orleans. She heard these men say that she should not teach a colored school any more in this parish. She taught school in Greensburg about six weeks; the school was supported by voluntary subscription; she had been a teacher previous to this. On Wednesday, October 21, 1868, some white men, unknown to her, went to her school-house and broke up the furniture and threw it down the well, frightening the children away from the school-house. On Saturday, October 24,

1868, about 5 P. M., a white man named Jerry Kemp, beat a colored man and compelled him to put on a Democratic badge. On the 17th day of October, 1868, two white men named Charles Kempt and H. J. Wheat, beat a colored man named Alick Wheelan in a very unmerciful manner; these men after beating him went down town and beat another colored man. The civil authorities made no endeavor to stop this, but rather encouraged the men to do it.

John Hart states, on oath, that he is a citizen of the State of Louisiana; that he resides in St. Helena parish; he left said parish on account of the way the white Democrats were and are treating the colored people. An old colored man named Joe Thomas, has been hiding in the swamp for the past two weeks, being threatened for having made Republican speeches. The Democrats have been for some time shooting and cutting colored women as well as men. The Ku Klux led by Henry Wormack, Levi McGhee, and one Thompson, with their faces disguised, and horses covered with white sheets, go about to different colored people's houses, and after frightening them, they go into the house and break up furniture and dishes, and sometimes threaten to burn the houses; they did to deponent's knowledge, burn up two colored churches. A day or two before he came away, he was met by one Allen, who told him to give him his revolver, as he would not allow Radicals to carry fire arms; witness gave it to him. The colored people were not allowed to vote the Radical ticket, but all those that did not go to the swamps were made to go to the polls and vote the Democratic ticket. Witness does not know of one colored person that voted the Republican ticket. He saw one old colored man lying in a ditch pierced with six balls; he was killed because he was a prominent Republican. Another colored man was shot in the side, and was confined to his house until election day, when three of the Ku Klux went to his house and forced him to the polls to vote the Democratic ticket, although he was hardly able to walk. A colored man named Mumford McCoy, left the parish, his life having been threatened on account of his politics; after he left a party of Ku Klux visited his house, and threatened to kill his wife if she did not tell where he was. An old white man by the name of Gill, had to hide her in his house to keep the Ku Klux from killing her.

Mumford McCoy states, on oath, that he is a resident of Greensburg, St. Helena parish, La. On or about the 15th of October, Guy Raynall, Mehaley Carter, Jeff Thompson, Peter G. Quin, Charley Kempt, Alonzo Delahoussay, Bob Hodge, and Tom Huss, all armed with pistols and bowie knives, came to witness' shop, and called him to the door, saying they wanted to speak to him; Mehaley Carter said: "I come to tell you what you may expect; we understand you are the representative of your color in this parish, and you are leading them wrong; if a drop of white blood is spilled in the parish, your head will come off, and all the rest of the leaders' heads, yours in particular." Witness replied: "gentlemen, I am for peace, and have been advising my colored friends, in my addresses, to keep the peace, and you know it; but the way the white men are beating and knocking the colored men about, would cause fights between some of them, and if blood should flow in such cases, would it be right for me to be killed for it?" To which they replied, shaking their fingers at him the while, "it makes no difference how it is done, your head comes off. Now we have told you what you can depend upon." They then turned and went towards the court house.

On Saturday, October 17, 1868, Hezekiah Wheat and Charles Kempt hired a colored man named Jerry Fletcher to go down to witness' shop to pick a quarrel with him in order to have an excuse for taking his life. When he arrived at the shop witness was absent; Wheat and Kempt followed Fletcher to the shop, and sent him to witness' house for him; witness met him on the way, when the following conversation ensued:

Question by Witness.—"Were you going to my house to see me?"

Answer.—"Yes."

Q.—"What for?"

A.—"I heard you have been talking about me because I am a Democrat."

Q.—"Who told you so?"

A.—"Them men," (pointing to Wheat and Kempt.)

Q.—"Do you believe it?"

A.—"No, I do not. I have known you ever since you came to the country, and never knew anything wrong about you. I am a man after your own heart. My name is on the Democratic paper, but I am going to vote the same ticket you do; but them men (pointing to Wheat & Kempt) made me come."

Kempt and Wheat then passed. Witness then said, "let us go

down to the shop." Which they did, Kemp and Wheat following them. Wheat followed witness into the shop and asked him if he had any water. He answered "yes; I will get some cool," going to the well about ten steps distant. When witness returned, Wheat asked him to drink; he declined. Wheat pressed him, and said he must. He declined several times, Wheat still pressing him to drink. Wheat then said, "I believe you are afraid I am going to kill you." Witness answered, "I reckon not; what are you going to kill me for?" Kempt, Wheat and Fletcher then went and each took a drink out of a bottle they had, and took some water out of the bucket. Wheat then came into witness' shop, in a threatening manner, when his cousin John Wheat ran in and took him away. The whole party, including the two Wheats, Kempt, and Fletcher, all of whom were armed, then went to the court house; Nelson Vaughn and Bill Wheeler (colored) were at this time passing said court House, on their way to witness' shop, when Kempt, assisted by Wheat, knocked Wheeler down, beat him most brutally, and gouged his eyes out. D. W. Thompson (brother of Senator Thompson) interposed and took them off. They then said to Wheeler: "God d—n you, go down to your friend, your protector," meaning witness. Wheeler then went to witness' shop in company with several others, but witness, fearing the white men would create some disturbance with him for having them in his shop persuaded them to go home and returned to his own house, sending his wife to close the shop.

Kempt and Wheat then proceeded to Gill's store, accompanied by George McGehee and about eight or ten other men, and told some colored men there, that they would either make good Democrats out of them or kill them. They repeated the same in Coles' store, adding that they would pin Seymour badges on them, and if they did not wear them continually they would kill them; if they caught them once without them they would kill them. They took Ned Rayford (colored) out of Gill's store, and another colored man out of Coles' store, and beat them most brutally, so that their lives are despaired of. Witness was compelled to leave home on or about the 20th of October, because a party of armed men came to his house, and inquired of his wife where he was, and said they would have him that night; they would wait there until they got him, that they intended to kill him. In consequence of these threats witness was compelled to hide in the woods to save his life. The next day (Sunday) during funeral service at Day's church (colored), about seven miles from Greensburg, about eighteen white men rode up with clubs and pistols, saying that they would "kill all the colored preachers." The congregation being very large, the colored men and boys went and cut clubs to protect the preachers, and as the services closed they guarded them (there were three preachers there that day) out of danger. The congregation was so large the white men seemed afraid to attack them. Four colored men, going in a different direction from that which the major part of the congregation took, were overtaken by these white men and one, Buckly Ishman (one of those who had a badge put on him at the store the evening before), was asked by one Geo. McGehee where his badge was. He replied "I have left it at home." McGehee then struck at him with a stick, but missed him, and Ishman made his escape in the swamp. They pursued but could not catch him. Returning to the road they said "Now we will get old Mark Lee," but he had escaped in the swamp. They then started after Isaac Hunter, who was riding a mule; overtaking him George McGehee struck him with a club, cutting his head badly. McGehee struck at him again and grazed his shoulder and thigh. He fell from his mule and taking to the swamp escaped from his pursuers. The same day witness learned at church, that a resolution had been passed at the Democratic club the day before to take him to the court house and make a Democrat out of him. Street Thompson (white Democrat) told Jerry Horn that witness would not come out of the court house alive, and witness' friends and wife requested him to leave and save his life, and report the troubles in the city, which he did, leaving on Sunday. On Monday the white Democrats went to witness' house twice, and three times to the shop, looking for him, and when going away from the house the last time they were overheard to say "it's a bad, rainy night, he will be sure to come in, and we'll get him." Since leaving, witness has learned that these same people have broken up the colored school, taught by Miss Ellis, of Jefferson City, and threatened that if she ever attempted to teach another colored child in the parish they would cut both her ears off close to her head. They have burned two churches belonging to the colored people, saying to them "we do this to let you know that we, the white people, intend to do what we please in this country; that we intend to rule this country, and to show you that the Yankees and carpet-baggers can do you no good. They never have done anything for you they promised. *We* are your friends, and you see to whom you have to look. Now if you will sign with your own hands that you will never have anything to do with the Yankees and carpet-baggers and hold no more club meetings we will build your churches again."

Deponent farther states, that on the 29th day of October, 1868, the "Ku Klux," composed of about forty (40) men completely disguised, having their faces masked with skulls, and white caps about three feet long on their heads, and their horses covered with white sheets, went to the house of John Kempt, who was the coroner of the parish of St. Helena, broke down the fence that surrounded his house, broke his front door down with an axe, and after forcing an entrance into his house, they began rushing through the house for Mr. Kempt, who had left his bed on hearing the noise to see what was the matter. On finding him they throttled him and dragged him out of the house by the throat, and on arriving in the street, they said, "G—d d—n you, now we are going to give you a chance to die a Radical. You said that you intended to die a Radical, now we are going to give you a chance to die one." They then fell back a few feet and riddled his body with buck shot and balls. They then went back to his house and demanded his money and papers, including notes. After being terribly beaten, his (Kempt's) wife gave them the papers. After killing Mr. Kempt this band went to Warner Hall's, (who lives four (4) miles from this place), to kill him, and not finding him or his wife at home, they asked their little boy, whom they found in bed, where his father was; he said he did not know. They then said in a savage manner, "If you do not tell us, we will kill you." The boy still said he did not know. They then pulled him out of bed, and knocked him down, then making him get up, they knocked him down again. During the melee, other members of the band broke open old man Hall's trunk and took all the money he had put there for safe-keeping, besides taking his receipt for four (4) bales of cotten that he had let James Cochran have, and also took his registration papers. While they were occupied in seeing what they could steal out of the trunk, the boy slipped away, thereby saving his life. These same men found Mr. Hall on election day, and giving him a Democratic ticket, said, "Vote that ticket or we will kill you," which he did to save his life. While these men were in Mr. Hall's house they threatened to burn it, and would have done so had it not been for one of the number, who objected; nevertheless they destroyed all the bedding.

On Thursday, the 29th day of same month, this same band went to a colored man's house named Sam Hutchinson, and took him out of his bed and dragged him out doors, and told him they were going to kill him, and when he begged them not to do it, they said "G—d d—n you you need not beg, we intend to do it." As they were dragging him along he broke away from them and run a few feet, when they fired, bringing him to the ground, where they left him, thinking him dead. After they had left, his wife went to him and found him alive, but terribly wounded with buckshot and balls. This band then went to another colored man's house, (Nelson Vaughn) and seeing him running from his house, they fired at him and felled him to the ground, thinking him dead they left. The same night that Mr. Kempt was murdered, this same band burned the colored Methodist church. Witness also states that they have no cause to seek his life, except that he is a Radical and President of a colored Club in Greensburg, and the colored people look to him as a leader, but that he has always given them good advice, to attend faithfully to their contracts and to their work, and to be quiet and peaceable; yet witness has always advised them to vote the Radical ticket as he believes that to be right.

On Saturday, October 17, witness was invited into the office of Mr. Pipkin, a lawyer, who told him that he wished to have a talk with him, saying, "I should have done so before, as you are in a very dangerous condition. You are looked upon as the leader of the Radical freedmen here, and your life is threatened unless you join the Democrats and change your principles. They are ready to raise any sum you ask if you will only join the Democratic party—and I tell you Mumford, I believe they will kill you." Witness replied that he did not think it was right to be forced to change his principles, and asked him if they had any charge against him—if he had been accused of doing anything wrong? He replied, "No, Mumford, they have nothing against you, only that you are a Radical, and they think that if you can be changed they can control the balance of the colored people in the parish." He also advised witness to join the Democratic party to save his life. Witness said, "Mr. Pipkin, if I am to be killed for standing to my principles, it must be so, but I cannot change them, though I be killed for not doing it." He then replied, "I would not be in your fix for all the parish, for you are sure to be shot or killed." Witness always looked upon Mr. Pipkin as a friend, and believes that he told him what he really thought was the truth.

CROSS QUESTIONED.

Question—What can you say as to the feeling of the white people in the parish toward the colored people?

Answer—It is bad; they say they intend and are determined to kill every Radical, white or black.

Q.—Do you consider this bitter feeling to be against the colored people as a race, or against the Radical party, white or black.

A.—It is against both white and black Radicals, for they went to the houses of Judge George and Doctor Yerks, both white Radicals, on the same night that they shot Kempt, but they both becoming alarmed had left, and were in the woods. They passed a resolution at the Democratic Club, that no employment should be given by their party to Radicals; that no Doctor should attend on their families, and that no Lawyer should defend the cases of Radicals in court.

Q.—Do they allow colored Democrats to carry weapons of any kind?

A.—Yes; they allow them to carry pistols and knives, and if they cannot get them themselves, the white people give weapons to them.

Q.—Do they allow colored Radicals to carry such arms?

A.—No sir; they do not, and if any weapons are found upon a colored Radical he is severely punished by the white Democrats.

Witness was afraid to go to the polls to vote the Republican ticket as these men had threatened to kill all the colored men who would not vote the Democratic ticket, or who would vote the Republican ticket. The colored men who voted the Democratic ticket were compelled to vote it, or were threatened with death. On or about the 28th of October, Turner's chapel was burned by a mob, who remarked that they did it just to show the niggers what they could do; that if the niggers wanted any friends they would be compelled to accept them, and do as they pleased, and not rely on the yankees or carpet-baggers. Witness dares not return to his house, believing if he did his life would be taken, as a price is put upon his head; three hundred ($300) dollars is offered by Jeff Thompson and another man.

Richard Lee states, on oath, that a band of armed white men went to his brother's house which is situated ten miles from Amite City, parish of St. He na, on the Jackson railroad; they shot his brother dead, his body was found completely riddled with bullets. Deponent further states that his brother Daniel was elected coroner of St. Helena, but had to resign the position as the white men told him that they would kill him if he did not do so; on one occasion he had to run from his house to save his life. Deponent's brother was killed on the 30th of October, 1868. They took from him one hundred and ten dollars in gold, sixty dollars in silver and twenty dollars in greenbacks, and also a revolver, valued at twenty dollars.

The following is an official statement of Wm. Baker, Chairman of the Board of Registrars, as to the conduct of the election of the 3d of November, 1868, in the parish of St. Helena:

"The Registrars of the parish of St. Helena report that 'during the time they were engaged in registering, such an amount of intimidation existed in the parish as to prevent many from registering, and many who had registered were prevented from voting, while a large number who would have voted the Republican ticket voted the Democratic ticket through fear of personal violence; that just previous to the election an organization known as the Ku Klux Klan, in disguise, and threatening manner paraded about the parish for the purpose of intimidating the peaceably disposed of the Republican party. At Tangipahoa, one of the voting precincts in the parish, one John Kemp, a prominent Republican, was murdered by this band, and another citizen was wounded. After due deliberation the Supervisors concluded it was not safe for them to disperse themselves at the various polls on the day of election.' They conclude: 'In our judgment the election was unfair, and should be deemed void.'"

ST. HELENA—SUMMARY.

Number killed, positively sworn to	4
Number shot, positively sworn to	3
Number maltreated, positively sworn to	26

PARISH OF VERMILLION.

Romar Andus states, on oath, that between the hours of 1 and 2 o'clock on the night of October 16, 1868, he heard firing at his mother's house, which is situated a few rods from his, two miles from the town of Lafayette, parish of Vermillion; he immediately dressed himself and went over to her house to see what was the matter. On approaching the house he saw about one hundred white men, four of them who had their faces blackened, he recognized Alcide Bernard, Douglas Cochran, Oland and Eugene Durio; they are all planters and well to do in the world. As he was about to enter his mother's house he was stopped by these men, who asked him "what he wanted." He replied, "I heard the alarm over here and I came to see what was the matter." One of the men then jerked his pistol away from him and said, "let's kill him, too." Deponent then ran to the woods to save his life; they fired a shot at him as he started, but it missed him. After these men had left his mother's house he returned to it. Finding the house in darkness he went to a neighbor's house and borrowed a light. On opening the door of his mother's house he found her lying dead across the door way; at the opposite door he saw his brother, a man of forty years of age, lying dead. Upon examination he found that his mother had been shot in the breast, and his brother through the breast and thigh. Deponent got Sheriff Furniss Martin to go to the house and see the dead bodies of his mother and brother and gave him the names of the parties whom he recognized; the sheriff arrested three of the four named and lodged them in jail, but no witness appearing against them, they were released. The only reason that deponent can give for the murder of his brother is, that he had attended a Republican meeting at St. Martin's about two weeks before the murder, and when the meeting broke up his brother led the colored men through the town to their homes, contrary to the wishes of the white citizens.

The following is an official statement of Wm. Baker, Chairman of the Board of Registrars, as to the conduct of the election of the 3d of November, 1868, in the parish of Vermillion:

"From the parish of Vermillion I have a report from the Registrar which sets forth, among other things, 'that for two or three months prior to the election an armed band of men, under the guise of a vigilance patrol, took charge of the town of Abbeville and its environs, threatening every one who was not prepared to express Democratic sentiments. The Registrar's life has been more than once threatened; messages sent to him to 'shut up his Republican mouth, or a hole would be bored in him,' 'no one would dare vote the Republican ticket.' The club room was guarded so as to keep Republicans from meeting. Considering the above facts, and many others not mentioned, I, as supervisor of registration, do not and can not consider the election of the third instant as a fair and honest expression of the will and wishes of the people; that it is not only unfair, but that it was conducted in its incipient canvass by the force of Democratic powder and lead. I therefore enter this my solemn protest, against any Democratic majority that may be claimed.'"

VERMILLION—SUMMARY.

Number killed, positively sworn to 2
Number maltreated.. 1

PARISH OF DE SOTO.

Stephen Umphries states, on oath, that he is a member of the State Legislature, and that a few days before the April election, he was standing in the door of Terrel's coffee house, opposite the court house, at Mansfield, when he was approached by Mr. Chas. Reynolds, a planter, who said to him, "I understand you are going to run for the State Legislature." Deponent replied, "they say so." As he said this Reynolds took one of three bricks which he had in his hand and attempted to strike deponent in the face with it; deponent raised his arm to protect his face, thereby receiving a severe blow on his arm. Reynolds fired another brick at his head, which missed it, and striking the door was shattered to pieces. Deponent went over to the court house and informed Judge Wormack what Reynolds had done. The Judge promised to arrest the said Reynolds, but failed to do so. A few nights after this outrage, while deponent was at home, a black man came to his gate and called to him to come out; he paid no attention to the summons. At this time a colored friend of deponent's was approaching his house, and answered this stranger at the gate; said stranger taking this colored friend for deponent, fired at him, but did not hit him. Deponent learned afterwards from good authority that this strange black man had been sent to his house to kill him by Captain Hawkins, a storekeeper in the town of Mansfield. Deponent lived on the edge of town; after he had been elected Representative his life was daily threatened; the white people told him that they would kill him if they caught him in town. His family are now living in Mansfield, but he does not dare to go to them. He has been informed by several parties that have left Mansfield since he took his departure, that the white people have determined to kill him if he should return to the parish. Deponent further states, that he can give no better evidence of the intimidation of the colored people in his parish than by referring to the late Presidential election, where it will be seen that out of about two thousand qualified colored voters, not one vote was cast by them for the Republican candidates.

George Washington states, on oath, that he is a citizen of the State of Louisiana, and has resided in the parish of DeSoto since the spring of 1865. He was elected a Justice of the Peace for the Fourth Ward of said parish at the election of April, 1868, and received his commission from the Governor on the 6th day of December of said year. On the following day witness took the oath of office before Hurd McDonnel, Clerk of the Parish Court; after which he walked over to the store of Perry Williams, and while trying on a pair of shoes, Mr. Longmire, a keeper of a livery stable in the town of Mansfield, came in with one hand on his revolver, and a cowhide in the other, and asked him what he came to town for; witness answered, "I come to town;" he continued asking him "why?" and witness continued to answer as before. When looking at him very hard he said he would "either whip me with his cowhide or kill me with his pistol;" when witness saw his determination he told him he would rather take a whipping than to be killed; whereupon he gave him from thirty to forty lashes with the cowhide, cutting through a heavy overcoat, an undercoat, and taking a piece of flesh out of his little finger, and severely injuring his right wrist; the rim of his hat was also cut off by the descending blows. While he was whipping witness he never took his hand off of his revolver, it being his intention to shoot him if he made any resistance; witness was sitting all this time on a trunk, not daring to get up; after he had finished the whipping, he said that "he would kill me if I indicted him." Witness made no answer, and he walked away. Soon after witness walked away (the best way his wounds would permit) to the house of a friend, a colored man named William Jones; he had not been in the house more than ten minutes when John Easton (a tinner) and Mr. Pates (a grocery keeper) came in, and Easton said: "I am looking for a colored man named Poleon Hope," and looking at witness said: "Washington, you had better go with me to the court house and resign, for if you don't you will surely be killed if you remain in this parish."

Witness told him he would not go, as Mr. Longmire was out there with a pistol and would kill him. Easton then cocked his pistol and called witness a G—d d—n rascal, and said he could blow him to *hell* in a minute, and catching hold of him dragged him to the gate. Witness caught hold of a post, and breaking away from him, returned to the house and found Mr. Woodham (partner of Perry Williams) and Mr. Whitworth (planter) standing by the door. Whitworth commenced cursing witness, and told him he would certainly be killed if he tried to assume the duties of the office, and that he had better get out of the parish. These four men then went to a coffee-house to get a drink, and when he saw them coming back he got out of the back window, and went to the house of a Union white lady, by the name of Mrs. Collus, where he remained secreted until night. He then went to a colored friend's house, where he remained all night, and returned to Mrs. Collus' house in the morning before day. He lived at these two houses until he left Mansfield for New Orleans via Shreveport. Mr. Longmire told witness that if he said anything to the authorities in New Orleans in regard to the whipping that he (Longmire) had given him, that there were a thousand men in the parish that were of the same mind that he was, and any one of them would kill him if he (Longmire) did not.

A few hours after witness had been whipped, Mr. Longmire met witness' brother at Dr. Tate's drug store, near the court house, and said, "I whipped George to-day," referring to witness; witness' brother asked him "what right he had to do it;" Longmire answered, "I will whip you, too," and made a thrust at him with a large dirk knife, which was warded off by Dr. Tate, who then shoved witness' brother into the back room of the store, and shut the door; Dr. Tate was formerly the owner of witness' brother; Longmire then went away, and returned, bringing a large crowd of white men with him, some having handcuffs and ropes, and all armed with arms of every description. About an hour after dark, while witness was sitting in Mrs. Collus' house, he heard firing about the college; Mrs. Collus looked out of her back door, and told him that from the noise over at the college there must be a great many persons there, and that it would not be safe for him to remain at her house, as they might suspect his being there. He then took to the field and made his way to the house of an old colored man named Cæsar, where he remained all night. The following morning Mrs. Collus told witness that the firing the night before was at his brother as he was making his escape from the drug store to the ravine, but it was so dark that he escaped unhurt, except a blow which he received from Longmire as he was running. There are about two thousand legal colored voters in the parish of DeSoto, and with one or two exceptions they would all have voted for Grant and

Colfax if they had been permitted to do so by the white men; but not a vote to witness' knowledge was cast for these candidates in that parish; colored men were forced to vote the Democratic ticket. Mr. James McClanahan, one of the editors of the Mansfield Times, pointed a pistol at a colored man named Henry Crosby, and told him that he must vote the Democratic ticket; Crosby succeeded in making his escape while they were on their way to the polls. Bowling Williams, ex-Sheriff of DeSoto parish, rode around town with the said J. McClanahan on the day of election—November 3, 1868—and made every colored man that they could get hold of go to the polls and vote the Democratic ticket. On the day of election news came into Mansfield that the colored people would not vote the Democratic ticket at Kingston, a precinct about twelve miles from the court house, when about sixty armed white men went out there immediately; the colored men had all left the polls when these men arrived, but overtaking some of them on the road they made them return to the polls and vote the Democratic ticket with pistols pointed at their heads.

Sunday night, a short time before the election, a colored man by the name of Charles Meeks went to the colored church during service, while it was filled with women and children, and firing his pistol just outside the door, then entered, and commenced cursing and said "he wanted to kill some Radical niggers;" this man Meeks had gone over to the Democrats, and was put up to commit this outrage by Mr. Longmire, with whom he lives and works.

The next day witness laid these facts before Judge Wormack, justice of the peace for the fourth ward at Mansfield, but nothing was done about it; Longmire came over to the court house and said, "Meeks was one of his men, and would do just what he wanted him to do." The white people of the parish were all under arms and for some time before the election would ride all over the parish, frightening the colored people, giving them to understand that they (the white men) were prepared and determined to see that the colored men voted as *they* did. There was a Republican meeting held in Mansfield about one week before the April election. Many colored men that attended it were fined twenty-five cents for every hour that they were away from their work, by Judge Wormack. A colored man by the name of Henry Crosby refused to accede to these terms, at the last election, and the consequence was that he was killed on the 11th of December, by a white man named Sarey (for whom he worked), at his plantation, about seven miles from Mansfield, on Augusta road. This was done in the day time, and in the presence of Dr. Roach, Jim and Bob Hollingsworth. The same night a body of twenty-five armed men went to the house of a colored man, named Henry Alexander, and shot him dead, and wounded his little son by a shot through his mouth; said Alexander had a fine crop, and it was believed by all his friends that he was killed in order that the white people could get his crop.

DE SOTO—SUMMARY.

Number killed, positively sworn to 2
Number shot, positively sworn to.............................1
Number maltreated, positively sworn to.........................4
Number of Republicans illegally deprived of voting.. 2000

PARISH OF MOREHOUSE.

W. A. Moulton states, on oath, that he was Chairman of the Board of Supervisors of Registration for the parish of Morehouse; on the night previous to the election some unknown parties came to his gate and called for him. When he opened the door they inquired if that was Moulton. He answered "yes." They then called to him to come out to the gate, saying that they wanted to speak to him. He replied that he was going to bed and could not come out. Nothing more was said, when they immediately shot at him. On the next morning he proceeded to the court house to see that the polls were opened and properly organized, and after openly voting the only Republican ticket voted in that parish, he left the polls. During his absence, from his residence, he was told that a party of colored men, lead by four white men, came there and asked for him. The landlady told them that Moulton was not in; and they being satisfied that he was not there, then left. The names of three of these white men were Boatner, Higman and Pugh. He was told that some parties were intending to make a raid on him the night of the election, and he prepared to defend himself in case of any attack, but there was nothing done that night. Witness saw indications of violence in every place where he travelled in the parish to complete registration, more particularly against himself. Previous to his departure from the parish he received a notice warning him to leave the parish, signed by the K. K. K.

MOREHOUSE—SUMMARY.

Number maltreated..1

PARISH OF ORLEANS.

A. P. Dumas states, on oath, that he is a citizen of the State of Louisiana, and a duly registered voter; that on the 12th of September, 1868, at 8 o'clock P. M., he illuminated his house—it being the night of the Republican torchlight procession—and placed the portraits of Grant and Colfax in front of his house on the balcony; some white men passed the house, in squads of ten and twenty, at different times before the procession came along, hallooing for "Seymour and Blair," and making insulting remarks, which witness did not wish to answer, as his family and some lady friends were present on the gallery. After the procession had passed witness took down all the transparencies and pictures, so that his family and friends might not be insulted by these squads of white men; every day since the procession, witness has been insulted and threatened by members of the Democratic party; these men pass his house every night and remark, "this is the house (meaning witness' house); we must have the white nigger Radical; you (witness) must never put the pictures of Grant and Colfax out on your gallery again, and not illuminate your house again for the nigger procession." On the night of September 22, 1868, witness again illuminated his house and put the pictures of Grant and Colfax on his gallery, believing that he had as good a right to do so as any one else. When he put out said pictures, the Democrats cheered for Seymour and Blair. These white men, who are unknown to deponent, then went into the middle of the street and said: "Look at the picture; we know the place well now; we'll pass it again to-night;" meaning that they would insult or injure him. Witness was all the evening on his balcony; the procession commenced passing his house at about quarter past 10; the clubs halted in front a few moments and gave him three cheers, and he answered by cheering for "Grant and Colfax," firing off rockets at the same time. The procession passed on very quietly, and at half-past 11 o'clock his house was closed and all the transparencies, etc., taken in; witness was in his parlor with a party of friends, when he heard quite a noise in front of his house, and looking through the blinds he saw from fifty to one hundred men standing outside, armed with guns and pistols; they called for witness, but he did not go out; they tried to break into the house, and said they wanted to kill every one in the house; he remained very quiet, and sent a man out by the back gate to bring the police to protect him, but the man found so many men on the street that he could not pass, and returned to the house; the crowd outside threatened to make an attack, and remained about the house until half-past 1 o'clock, when they left. Some time after a squad of men came back and remarked, "we have a chance to kill him;" witness and the others in the house remained very quiet, and this squad also left. Between 11 and 12 o'clock witness heard a number of shots fired, and people running in every direction; he did not go out, fearing that the Democrats would kill him or burn his house. Since this time many threats have been made against him. On the morning of September 23, 1868, when Mr. Forrest was killed by Guerin, some white men came in front of witness' house with revolvers and guns, pointing their weapons at the house; they had just supplied themselves with these weapons from the gunsmith's near his house. They continued coming all day until 9 o'clock P. M. Colored men also came to purchase arms, but the gunsmith refused to sell them any; the white Democrats being there and preventing him. At 5 o'clock P. M. witness went with Mr. Joubert to the office of the Chief of Police; he related to him all the facts, and the Chief of Police told him, "never mind; all will be right; I will take notice of what you say."

Captain E. Davis states, on oath, that he was marshal of the Colfax Defenders (a Republican club) on the night of September 22, 1868; as his club was passing the corner of Customhouse street, going down Rampart, between 10 and 11 o'clock, P. M., the cry was given to "fall back." He was on horseback and immediately rode up to Canal street, to see what was the matter; when near the corner of Canal and Burgundy streets, he was fired at by a policeman. Witness pursued the man, but he escaped. Witness then rallied all the men from the Republican clubs that he could, and started down Rampart street; when passing between Customhouse and Bienville streets, several shots were fired at the club from a house on the south side of the street. Members of the club rushed across to enter the house, but witness prevented them from doing so, and marched them down Rampart to Orleans street, where he met a crowd of policemen and citizens, who told him that some persons were firing from a house on the corner of Rampart and St. Ann streets. Witness went by the house, but the firing had ceased. He then marched his club to their club room and dismissed them.

Louis Coregano states, on oath, that on the night of September 22, 1868, he was a deputy marshal of the "Warmoth Guards" (a Republican club). As they were marching along Canal street, at the corner of Bourbon street, between the hours of ten and eleven o'clock P. M., he saw a white man fire two shots at the club from the gallery of Dumonteil's confectionery; he had heard no shots fired previous to these.

William M. Batchelor, and J. B. Cooper state on oath, that they were seated in a Rampart and Dauphine street car, at their starting place on Canal street, waiting for the car to start, on the night of Sept. 22, 1868, between ten and eleven o'clock. They saw the clubs passing on Canal street, and supposed without observing closely, that they were Democratic clubs. They saw a man on the balcony of Dumonteil's confectionery (corner of Bourbon and Canal streets) fire five shots at the procession, and immediately after several shots were fired from the side-walk, and from other directions, at the procession, which immediately scattered in every direction; immediately after a Democratic club came cheering and shouting from St. Charles street, and pursued and fired inio the other procession.

Previous to this, deponents had been listening to a speech being made to these Democratic clubs at the St. Charles Hotel.

Homére Bouthé states on oath, that on the night of September 22, 1868, he was a deputy marshal of the "Warmoth Guards." When the club was passing the corner of Bourbon street, on Canal, a person standing on the corner in front of Dumonteil's confectionery called out "three cheers for Rollins," which was responded to by the clubs by three cheers for "Grant and Colfax." The Grand Marshal told them to keep quiet; the man ran into Dumonteil's. A policeman told the club that he would have the man arrested. At this time a shot was fired from the gallery of the confectionery. This seemed to be a preconcerted signal, for in a moment the firing became general, from the sidewalks and galleries, on each side of canal street. The club dispersed as speedily as possible.

James Gibney states, on oath, that he is a sergeant of police, that on the evening of Sept. 22, 1868, he was on duty, and during the time the Republican clubs were passing out Canal street, he was standing on the corner of Royal and Canal; as the last club was passing the corner of Bourbon, he heard the noise of a disturbance from that quarter, and immediately ran that way. He found severel members of the club on the sidewalk. He saw them breaking the windows with their torches. With the aid of other policemen he cleared the sidewalk. As the members of the club were retreating from under the balcony of Dumonteil's confectionery; a man appeared above *on* the balcony, and fired into the procession, and the firing then became general along the street; the clubs immediately dispersed. Witness, with a detail, accompanied them as far as "Congo Square," down Rampart street. The members of the clubs went quietly to their homes.

C. C. A. Stevens states, on oath, that he is a policeman, and on the night of Sept. 22, 1868, he was detailed as corporal in charge of a "squad," to accompany a Republican club called "The Grant Invincibles," for the purpose of preserving order. While they were passing the corner of Bienville and Rampart streets, some three or four shots were fired at the procession; some of the members of the club ran away, and others stood to see what was the cause of the firing. Witness blew his whistle to call together his "squad," for the purpose of keeping the peace. The procession then proceeded down Rampart street, and at the corner of St. Anne street eight shots were fired into the procession from the upper part of the building, occupied as a coffee house. Other shots were fired from a car which was passing; witness followed the car, and called to the driver to stop, but no attention was paid to him; from that time everything was quiet.

E. Alix states, on oath, that on the night of September 22, 1868, he, with his Club (the Warmoth Guards), was passing out Canal street, by the corner of Bourbon, between 10 and 11 o'clock. As they were passing Dumonteil's confectionery, a person on the sidewalk commenced cheering loudly for Rollins, a noted colored Democrat, and for Seymour and Blair, to which the members of the Club responded, by cheering for Grant and Colfax; a policeman, fearing that this might cause a disturbance, spoke to the man on the sidewalk, admonishing him to be quiet; some of his companions then shoved him into Dumonteil's saloon, and the doors were closed; at this time some person appeared at the railing of the gallery overhead, and fired into the Club; some members of the Club attempted to enter the saloon, but finding the door closed, broke in the windows; witness endeavored to stop them—at this time shooting had commenced from all directions at the Clubs, and the men dispersed and scattered for home.

Julins Lanabére, also a member of the "Warmoth Guards," fully corroborates the above testimony.

Richard Fortune states, on oath, that as a member of the "Pinchback Zouaves;" he was in the Republican procession on the night of September 22, 1868; at the time of the commencement of the disturbance on Canal street, he was on Rampart street, near Customhouse, a crowd of white men gathered on the sidewalk, yelling and firing into the procession; shots were also fired from the house on the left hand corner of Rampart and Bienville, going down. After this excitement was over, as wiiness was standing on the corner of Conti and Trémé streets, a crowd of white men came up, headed by a man named John Henry, who threatened him, and was about to attack him, but the better counsel of his friends prevailed; soon after witness saw another crowd who carried with them a white flag, on which was displayed the words, "No Quarters;" they were all armed with pistols and knives.

A. T. Selover states, on oath, that he was Vice President of the 5th Ward Radical Republican club, during the recent political canvas. On or about the 22d of September, 1868, at 8 o'clock in the evening, he went with his Club to the house of the Hon. Octave Belot, on Claiborne street, for the purpose of witnessing a presentation of a flag to his Club. After the presentation was over, deponent marched with his club, in company with some other Republican clubs, through some of the principal streets in the 2d District of the city. Every thing went off peaceably and quietly until said clubs reached Canal street, and had passed down said street until the head of the column had passed down Rampart street, for the purpose of quietly dispersing, when suddenly and unexpectedly the rear of the column was fired upon by parties about Dumonteil's confectionery, which is located at the corner of Canal and Bourbon streets. Not anticipating any trouble, most of those in the procession were unarmed, and consequently a stampede was immediately created throughout the column, the boys crying out: "we are attacked, we are attacked." The Zouave Club, just ahead of deponent's, cried out: "rally, boys, rally," and rushed back to the rear of the column to resist the attack. Word came back, "all is quiet, boys, return to your clubs," when immediately a promiscuous attack was made on the entire column, from Bourbon to Basin street, from banquettes and windows, completely breaking up the whole column. At this time Mr. R. H. Shelly was arm in arm with deponent, and they were advised by the boys to "run for their lives." Deponent then crossed over to the south side of Canal street, and while quietly walking on said street a person dressed in light uniform came running furiously behind him, and while passing gave deponent a desperate thrust with a sharp instrument, cutting through his coat, vest and shirt, inflicting a wound on his breast (6) six inches in length. The force of said blow threw his arm in lock with deponent's, and in his drawing away from him the instrument inflicted a severe and very dangerous wound across the centre of deponent's arm, just escaping the main artery. After deponent had been cut, the would-be assassin turned around, looked him in the face, and ran rapidly away. Deponent was advised to go to the hospital and see Dr. Smith, and ascertain the extent of his wounds; on his way there he met some of his Democratic friends, and showed them his wounds; they remarked that it was "a shameful affair." He also met several of his colored friends, who were much agitated in consequence of being attacked, and having been plundered of their torch lights, banners, flags, musical instruments, and their friends left dead on the streets. Several of his friends advised him to go home, as his life was in danger. After the general excitement was over deponent heard hackmen making brags how many "niggers" they had cut, at the same time displaying long knives, and saying "that they were not through with the black sons of b——s yet." The day after the riot deponent heard some "Dagos" remark, as he was passing along, where they were delivering oysters, that "they made the damned niggers fly last night." Deponent heard one say that he "wanted to kill ten more niggers, and would not be satisfied until he did." During this time it was dangerous for a Republican to be seen on the streets, even in the day time. The streets were thronged with men, business paralyzed, parties at every corner secretly consulting, and strangers in passing them would be subjected to the strictest scrutiny. Every man seemed to be armed, and the gun shops were doing the best business in town. The shops were thronged daily with customers buying revolvers, shot guns, and the latest improved rifles. The poor negroes were discharged, and thrown out of employment on account of their politics. The officers of steamboats furnished the colored men with Democratic certificates, giving them protection from their party, and promising them employment if they would vote the Democratic ticket. The gun shops refused to sell fire arms to the colored people. A colored man took his revolver to a gun-smith on Dryades street, above Poydras, to be repaired, but was not able to get it back until the riots were over, and then only obtained it through the agency of Mr. Henry, a school teacher. This is only one case, however, out of a hundred.

About the last of October deponent, while talking with some friends at the Customhouse, saw immediately opposite, in front of a coffeehouse, a fierce looking man with a Spencer rifle in his hand, looking into the coffeehouse in a very suspicious manner; he got into position to fire, but did not. Several police officers were on the corner of Canal street, and although they saw this man's movements, made no effort to arrest him. This man passed up Canal street unmolested by said police officers. Deponent is favorably known by both the Radicals and Democrats, and was advised by the latter to look out for himself, as he was "spotted;" he was also invited by some of them to come to their houses and live. Some of the leading Republicans, were frequently obliged to change their abode, in consequence of having been threatened and attacked. During the late riots, and a few days before the Presidential election, bands of armed men, visited Republican club rooms and sacked them of every thing that was of use to them in processions, such as banners, etc. The Republicans about this time held a public meeting in "Congo Square," Second District. While Mr. Thomas W. Conway was addressing the meeting a rough looking man approached the stand, and in a loud and yelling way denounced Mr. Conway and his party as "a set of G—d d—d carpet-baggers, scallawags and robbers," and that "they would catch it soon." Mr. Conway, to avoid trouble called for a police officer and had the fellow taken away, at the same time advising his audience to take no notice of him. When the meeting was about to break up, some colored men came running toward the stand crying out that they were "killing all of their people up on Canal street." Some of the clubs (Republican) were attacked while peaceably parading. Mr. Conway advised the different clubs to keep back of Rampart street, as the enemy were in force on Canal street. They did so, but in dispersing, they were attacked, shot at and plundered of their banners, and had to run to save their lives. Dr. Clark and deponent walked up Canal street towards the river and over the ground where the scene had happened; the dead and dying were strewn by the way, lamps and oil were scattered in every direction. They saw no negroes; while making this inspection, about fifty men passed us in one squad yelling over their victory, and cursing the "d—d negroes and d—d Yankees," at the same time discharging their fire-arms at any one that they thought did not belong to their party. This was done in front of General Rousseau's headquarters.

Gabriel Paholy states, on oath, that on the night of September 22, 1868, as a member of the "Pinchback Zouaves" he was in the Republican procession. His club had begun to pass down Rampart street at the time of the commencement of the disturbance at the corner of Canal and Bourbon streets. A crowd of white persons gathered on the sidewalk between Canal and Customhouse streets and commenced yelling and firing into the club; other shots were fired from the houses, and he particularly noticed from a white house on the south side of Rampart street. He proceeded with the club to the corner of Claiborne and St. Ann streets. As he was returning he saw a person on Villere street carrying a white flag, on which was displayed the words "*No quarter.*" Nearly every person whom he saw on the streets at this time was hurrahing for "Seymour and Blair;" most of them were "Sicilians." He, finding it unsafe to proceed, turned back and remained all night at the house of a friend.

Raphael Santana states, on oath, that on the night of September 22, 1868, he was marching with his club, the "Pinchback Zouaves." As they were passing down Rampart street, between Canal and Customhouse, parties on the banquette fired into the procession. Shots were also fired from the gallery of a brick house, on the corner of Bienville and Rampart. The procession proceeded as quietly as possibly down Rampart street, and was again fired into, at the corner of St. Peter. The members of the club, now justly excited, ran to the house, determined to find the assassin, but were dissuaded from carrying out their purpose by the police, who promised to search for him. The club then dispersed.

Octave Rey states, on oath, that on the night of September 22, 1868, he was Grand Marshal of the "Warmoth Guards," and as he, with his club, were passing out Canal street, past the corner of Bourbon, between ten and eleven o'clock, a man standing on the corner, in front of Dumonteil's confectionery, apparently very much excited, commenced cheering in a lond manner for "Willis Rollins," a notorious colored Democrat. Witness sent a policeman to quiet him, fearing that owing to the feeling against said Rollins among the members of the club, the men would become excited. The policeman spoke to the man, who immediately went into Dumonteil's saloon, and the doors of the saloon were closed. Some excited members of the club ran up on the side-walk, when he called all the men to fall into the ranks. At this time he heard some person running on the gallery overhead, and looking up saw a man at the railing, who fired a revolver at the club. This was the first shot fired, and apparently directly at him. He then advised all his men to go home. At this time the firing had become rapid, and to avoid exposure, he being on horseback, rode along under the balcony on the sidewalk to Rampart street, but found that the procession was entirely dispersed.

William R. Mason states, on oath, that on Tuesday night, September 22, 1868, that he was standing opposite Dumonteil's confectionary on the corner of Bourbon and Canal streets, at about half-past ten o'clock, looking at the Republican procession. Thinking he saw Captain Rey saluting some person on the gallery of said confectionery he remarked to a friend, who was with him, "What is the matter *here*, it seems strange that they should salute us from this corner;" his friend replied that he did not understand the movement. Immediately afterward a shot was fired at Captain Rey from the said gallery, a shot was returned from the club, and the firing then became general. Upon the springing of the rattles by the policemen, in the vicinity, the clubs immediately dispersed. As witness was proceeding homeward, he passed, on almost every corner, groups of half a dozen or more of men who are identified with the Democratic party, at this time they were peaceable though excited.

Pierre Edwards states, on oath, that he was in the Republican procession on the night of September 22, 1868; his company was turning from Canal street down Rampart, when the firing commenced on the corner of Bourbon and Canal. That part of the procession, then on Rampart street, was immediately fired upon by a crowd on the opposite corner of Canal and Rampart. They halted the procession and the firing ceased. The procession again started down Rampart street, when some persons in a passing car fired again into them; some members of the club tried to overtake the car, but it was driven too fast, and they did not succeed. Witness left the club, and went home, at the corner of St. Louis and Rampart streets.

Baptiste Barrow fully corroborates the above testimony.

James Johnson states, on oath, that on the night of September 22, 1868, he was with his club, the "Pinckback Zouaves," in the Republican procession. As they were passing Dumonteil's confectionery, corner of Bourbon and Canal streets, shots were fired into the procession by persons on the gallery of said saloon. The club proceeded out to Rampart street, down which they turned; they were again fired upon near the corner of Conti; they were also fired upon, seven times by white men from a passing car. The club proceeded to the corner of Toulouse street, where they were met by the Hon. Messrs. Campbell and Lowell, who persuaded them to go quietly to their homes, and avoid any further difficulty.

William Brown fully corroborates the above testimony.

Edward Linderman states, on oath, that about half-past 10 o'clock on the night of September 22, 1868, he was standing on the corner of Canal and Carondelet streets in front of Kuntz's confectionery; at this time the Republican procession was passing on the opposite side of Canal street, in front of Dumonteil's saloon; when the last club of the procession had arrived at this point he heard considerable yelling and cheering by white men from the sidewalk for "Seymour and Blair," and also for "Rollins." The men in the procession hissed, which caused considerable excitement; a shot was fired at this moment from the gallery of Dumonteil's confectionery, where a number of white men were congregated; after the first shot was fired, he saw distinctly several more shots fired from the said gallery into the procession; some members of the club then commenced smashing the glass in the windows of the saloon, and this was followed by a general retreat of the procession in that vicinity. Witness crossed over and found a pool of blood on the sidewalk where the affray had commenced, and walking on, he found a colored man on Burgundy street, lying apparently dead; the procession had at this time dispersed, and everything seemed to be quiet.

Charles H. Washington states, on oath, that on the night of September 22, 1868, he was on the corner of Canal and Dryades streets, as the Republican procession was passing on the other side of Canal street; he saw the procession fired into from the brick building on the corner of Dauphine and Canal streets; the Republican clubs fell back to Rampart street, when they were again fired into from the building No. 6 Rampart street; he saw a continual firing of pistols in front of Christ Church, on Canal street; the members of these clubs ran in all directions; he saw a colored man running from Bourbon street out Canal, and upon reaching Burgundy street he fell, apparently dead; a crowd of white men started from the corner of Burgundy and Canal, and ran rapidly after the procession to Rampart, firing into the procession continually.

The wounded man referred to above has since died.

Felix Dumonteil states, on oath, that on the evening of September 22, 1868, at about a quarter past 10 o'clock he was walking on Canal street from Claiborne street toward his store on the corner of Bourbon and Canal; he saw a procession coming out Canal street, and soon after heard firing in the direction of said procession, he then ran toward his store; upon reaching it he found the doors on the Canal street side closed; quite a crowd was collected there, mostly of colored people; through the windows he saw his clerks trying to close the doors on the Bourbon street side, resisted by the people outside. He then went down to the kitchen entrance on Bourbon street, and went in to the assistance of his clerks, and succeeded in closing the door; soon after quiet was restored.

Felix Somali states, on oath, that he is employed as a waiter in Dumonteil's confectionery, corner of Canal and Bourbon streets; that on the night of September 22, 1868, there were several gentlemen and ladies on the gallery of the saloon at the time the disturbance commenced; he was in the kitchen filling an order when he heard the report of pistols, and the noise of the smashing of glass; he ran out upon the gallery to see what was the matter, and found that two men who had been sitting apart from the rest had gone; he immediately turned off the gas in the saloon up stairs, and while thus enaged several men rushed up from below, and one of them ran to the railing of the gallery and fired into the procession, and then ran back down stairs. Witness tried to prevent this man from shooting, and requested him not to go out on the gallery, but did not succeed in his endeavors. All the waiters were then called down stairs to aid in closing the doors. Witness and others did not go, being afraid. Soon after this everything became quiet again. During the whole disturbance he saw no member of the clubs in the saloon.

John Connor (policeman) states, on oath, that he was at the Central Police Station on the evening of September 22, 1868, at about 10 o'clock, P. M., and news coming in of a disturbance on Canal street, he immediately went down there; upon reaching the corner of Canal and Rampart streets, he saw about thirty-five members of the Republican procession—they appeared very much excited. Witness labored in vain to pacify them, until after the arrival of the Chief with others, when they were prevailed upon to leave for their homes, and promise not to interfere with any body unless they were first interfered with. Witness was detailed with another policeman to go down with them; on the way down Rampart street he was repeatedly told by the members of the Republican club that they did not wish to interfere with, nor molest any one, but that they had been fired upon on Canal street without any cause or provocation. When deponent had reached St. Peter street with the party he was guarding, he heard two shots fired, which seemed to him from the sound to have been fired from the confectionery building on the corner. The colored men got very much excited and made an attack on the said confectionery, doing some damage to the show window; they said they wanted the man that had fired the shots at them. The Sergeant and policemen told them that they should have justice done them; they then proceeded on their way quietly. There was no further disturbance.

Philip Montani states, on oath, that he is a citizen of the State of Louisiana, and resides at No. 322 Prieur street, New Orleans. On the night of September, 22, 1868, between ten and eleven o'clock, he was passing Dumonteil's confectionery, corner of Bourbon and Canal streets. He saw a white man come out of said confectionery and cheer for Seymour and Blair, remarking, "Get out, you d—d niggers." A man from the procession stepped up on the sidewalk and was immediately pushed back into the street by said white man. A white man then fired a pistol at the procession from the balcony of the saloon, and the proprietors immediately closed the store. Two more shots were then fired from the gallery; the shots were fired through the blinds on said gallery. The procession proceeded out Canal street to Rampart, and stopped; they were there joined by a party from Dauphine street, and all proceeded down Rampart street. The procession was again fired upon from a private house on the corner of Conti street. Witness could not see who fired the shot. He had no weapon with him. After this he went home.

J. J. Williamson, chief of police in New Orleans, states, on oath, that on the night of Sept. 22, 1868, at about half past eleven o'clock, he was in the office of the fire alarm and police telegraph, city hall, receiving reports from different sections of the city, and directing the movements of bodies of police, when Mr. Joseph Ellison came in and in an excited manner said, "who is in charge here? I want the general alarm rung on all of the bells." Witness asked him why; he said "I want the citizens called out to stop and put down the riot." Witness told him that everything was quieted down, and that the colored people had all dispersed for their homes. Mr. Ellison said: "I don't care, I will have the alarm rung and have the people out."

Witness answered him, "we have had enough of riot and bloodshed for once" and although the fire alarm office was not under his control, he would not permit him, or any other person, to ring an alarm from that office that night. Mr. Ellison replied that he did not care for him or his police; he could and would ring an alarm without the use of "that office." Witness told him that his actions were calculated to incite a riot; that if he undertook to carry out his threats, or if he went out of that office with those intentions, he would arrest him and put him in confinement, let the consequences be what they may. Mr. Ellison at once changed his tone, and remarked that he would go to Generals Rousseau and Buchanan, and left the office.

Aid R. L. Bradley, special officer William Walsh, and operator Adams were present during this interview, and fully corroborate the above testimony.

Joseph Ellison states, on oath, that about noon of Sept. 22, 1868, he was called upon by the chief of police, who desired him to use his influence to prevent Democratic clubs from turning out on that evening. Witness complied by writing a note to the "Frank Blair Guards, Jr.," requesting them not to turn out. The chief stated that he had made arrangements with Mr. Landry, Marshal of the First Ward Club (who were to turn out that evening to serenade Colonel

Fuller, at the St. Charles Hotel), which, if carried out, would prevent any collision between the different political clubs. Mr. Landry being absent when these clubs started down the street, Mr. Maxwell and witness came down ahead of the clubs to see that the streets were clear, and that no possibility of a collision could take place; they requested Mr. M. Farrell, then on Canal street, to solicit the marshal of any colored club to avoid St. Charles street, for a few minutes, during the time that the Democratic clubs might be at the St. Charles Hotel. Witness also stationed private police officer McIntyre at the corner of St. Charles and Canal streets, with the same instructions, and to promptly advise him, at the St. Charles Hotel, so that he could induce the Democratic clubs to leave the street prior to the approach of the colored clubs. While there he saw the colored clubs passing out Canal street, and soon after received intelligence of a fight on Canal street. He then, with a view of preventing the Democratic clubs from entering into the trouble, ran down St. Charles street to Canal, and out Canal to Carondelet, calling loudly to the First Ward Club to go back. There was no crowd at Dumonteil's, on the opposite corner, at this time, but there was rapid firing farther out Canal street. He could not distinguish who was doing the firing on account of the darkness. He could find but one man in the Democratic clubs who would acknowledge that he was armed. After this occurrence an excited crowd gathered about the "Clay Statue," whom he endeavored to send home; they demanded that some action should be taken, as people were being butchered in the outskirts of the city. Two gentlemen volunteered to ride down and bring back correct information. On the report of one of them (Deputy Sheriff Dick), about fifteen minutes later, that there was considerable fighting on Esplanade street, witness, accompanied by Mr. Wells, went to the office of the chief of police, and thence to the telegraph office, where, finding said chief (who was receiving a dispatch at the time), asked him what was the news. He stated in reply that there was a devil of a fight in the Third District, and as the police were not sufficient he had sent to General Neil for a company of cavalry. Witness then told the chief that if he could not take care of the people of New Orleans they should be allowed to take care of themselves, and that he ought to ring the alarm bell; his reply was very rough, that no man should touch the alarm, etc., to which witness answered that "if it was necessary to ring the alarm it would be done: that he would ring it himself," and on Williamson's threat to arrest him if he repeated it, he did repeat it, stating at the same time that he had spent an hour in endeavoring to protect the peace, and his officers, and this was a poor return for it. Witness then drove to General Rousseau's residence on Apollo street, near Terpsichore, and awoke the General, who had not been notified that troops had been ordered out, and then proceeded, in company with General Rousseau and Mr. Wells, to the residence of General Buchanan, who was also not aware that troops had been ordered out, who accompanied them to the city hall (this was seven minutes past twelve), and from there to the "Clay Statue," where they found the chief of police, and after a short interview the Generals left. Witness states that his motive in desiring the ringing of the alarm was a necessity of self protection, when the law failed, and he was unwilling to trust the handling of troops to a partisan chief of police, who was evidently incapable of doing his duty, and in whom a mass of the citizens had no confidence.

Jack Evans states, on oath, that he resides in Algiers, parish of Orleans, near the line of Jefferson parish; that on or about Friday, October 23, 1868, during the excitement at Gretna, a party of white men came to his house, broke in the door, and took from the house his *gun*, axe, hatchet, and several other articles of value; they also broke down his fence and his *corn crib*, letting the cattle into the crib. Before leaving they beat an old colored man who was in the house.

Frank Johnson (colored) states, on oath, that on the night of October 24, 1868, he was in the Republican procession with the Eleventh Ward Club; at the corner of Carondelet and Canal streets they met the Democratic "Working Men's Club," who cheered for "Seymour and Blair;" this club answered by cheering for "Grant and Colfax." They then cried out, "You d—d black sons of b—hs, hush up your d—d mouths." They, however, continued cheering as before; when the club was in front of the "Constitution Club Rooms," on Canal street, between Baronne and Dryades streets, a pistol was fired from the sidewalk; the shot was answered from the procession, and a fight immediately commenced; during the fight the policemen on this beat ran away; a colored boy named Antoine was killed in the melee; two colored men and a colored woman were shot dead, and several were wounded.

Samuel Bell and Edward DeCree corroborate the above testimony.

Account of the riot in New Orleans on Saturday night, October 24, 1868, taken from the Republican of October 26, 1868:

An eye witness, whom, we are informed, is a United States officer, states that "when the head of the column (Republican) reached the hall of the Constitution club, the foot still on the north side of Canal, making the form of the letter S, I saw the Democratic Working Men's club approaching on the south side of Canal street from St. Charles at a quick pace, and remarked to my friend that I apprehended trouble, when he replied, 'You are quick to discern the temper of the people,' and scarcely had the words passed his lips ere the white club dashed into the centre of the colored line, when the firing commenced. Being unarmed and in no way prepared for this attack, the colored men fled precipitately, not, however, till several shots had been fired into their ranks, they apparently being unaware of the true nature of their situation. Such yells and hurrahs as accompanied their triumph over four unarmed black men, whom they left in the gutters riddled with bullets, could hardly be exceeded by the warrantable clamor of a victorious army. A mere child, a boy of perhaps ten summers, was struck with a club, breaking his neck and killing him instantly. His corpse was left between those of two colored men, and was by my friend picked up soon after and laid upon the banquette. The white club then turned and marched toward St. Charles street in confused order. That it was an unprovoked assault is certain, the Democratic journals to the contrary notwithstanding. Numerous anxious parties were assembled as near as safety allowed, awaiting the restoration of quiet, and for a half hour I never knew such an excitement. Squads of men were hurrying to and fro firing their pistols, yelling and making night hideous with their wild demonstrations, and while we were gazing upon the result of their demonstration, firing was heard at the corner of Basin and Canal streets, to which point they all ran, crying 'kill 'em, kill 'em,' 'white men to the rescue.' Anxious, of course, to ascertain the true result, I hastened there, but was too late, as a man had been carried from there either killed or wounded,

I could not learn which. At this moment a shot was fired at the corner of Common and Basin streets, and there was a general rush for that point, but I did not go there. Five men in citizens dress then ran back and deliberately fired as many bullets into the lifeless body and again rejoined the 'Seymour Sentinels,' of whom be it said none of them participated in this horrible tragedy.

"Twenty or thirty besides myself drew around the spot, when a policeman came up and ordered the crowd to disperse. Then they set upon him, driving him away and taunting him with, 'Where's your Metropolitans?' 'Where's your Yankee troops?' 'Come back and carry him off.' 'He's your brother,' and such like jeering."

We have another verson of the affair near the corner of Canal and Franklin streets.

A policeman stated that "when the Democrats in uniform were passing along on the north side of Canal street, near Franklin, and cheering for Seymour and Blair, a colored man, barefooted and not in uniform, who had just come up Franklin from Customhouse street, stood on the Corner and cheered for Grant and Colfax. Men on the opposite side then shouted, 'Kill the black son of a b—h ; let's go for him.' Then the colored man in the neutral ground was shot as described.

"The body of the murdered man, whose name is Henry Clay, was conveyed to the Trémé Station and delivered to his friends yesterday. Edward Crosby, another colored man, died at the Marine Hospital this morning of wounds received Saturday evening. Coroner Roche will hold an inquest on Wednesday morning and investigate all the circumstances connected with this most unfortunate tragedy."

Dr. D. Mackay states, on oath, that he is a commissioned surgeon of the Metropolitan Police of this city; that on the night of October 24, 1868, he was called upon to visit a colored man at the First District, main station. He found him severely wounded about the head and face, as if with a hatchet, and a gun shot wound in the right thigh. Deponent ordered the patient to be taken to the Charity Hospital, after he had dressed his wounds. He was lying without any covering in the hall of the station, shivering with cold. This was after eleven o'clock P. M. Superintendent of Police J. J.

Williamson said, "he could not be bothered sending a nigger to the hospital that time of night." The wounded man was a discharged United States soldier. Deponent then had him covered with blankets. The patient remained in the station until morning, when he was removed to his home. Deponent visited him at his home a few hours afterwards and extracted a ball from the upper and back part of his head, which had entered the brain. He died on Monday, October 26, 1868. On Sunday morning, October 25, about two hours after deponent had dressed the wounds of said colored man, there were brought in dead to the main station three (3) colored men and one (1) boy, some of them with four gun shot wounds in their bodies, and their heads and faces severely lacerated. The boy's neck was dislocated and his body covered with contused wounds, as if kicked or stamped upon. Deponent believes he was taken by the heels and swung against a wall or post. On the 17th day of September deponent was called upon to attend a wounded (white) police officer, at two o'clock A. M., at the Fourth District station. He had an incised wound between the eighth and ninth ribs, producing internal hemorrhage, which caused his death about five hours afterwards. The officer's name was Butler. He was a member of the Tenth Ward Radical Republican Club. He was stabbed by a man that said, "he would get rid of one d—d Radical son of a b—h." Deponent visited four (4) other colored men who were suffering from gun shot wounds received on Saturday, October 24, 1868; three of them still have bullets in their bodies. One deponent extracted which had gone clear through the upper part of the left lung, and the man is probably disabled for life. Deponent is known in his district as a Republican, and has been assaulted while quietly walking the streets. He would not vote during the day of election because the same ferocious crowd surrounded the polls who had been the cause of all the troubles in this city that have taken place since the massacre at the Mechanics' Institute, on the 30th day of July, 1866. Deponent firmly believes that if the Democratic clubs had supposed that the military would have been used to suppress any violence that they might have committed, no Republicans would have been molested; but, on the contrary, they reckoned on the affiliation of the First United States infantry, under the command of Generals Rousseau and Buchanan. Deponent has repeatedly seen colored men insulted and abused by members of that regiment. He knows numerous cases where colored men have been discharged from employment because they were members of Republican clubs and would not join the Democratic organizations. Some Captains of vessels and stevedores before employing colored men, would require from them a certificate from some one of the presidents of the Democratic ward clubs. The club house of the Tenth Ward Republican Club, of which deponent was president, was sacked on or about the 27th day of October, 1868, by a band of men known as the "Innocents." The man that struck deponent was a member of the Blair Guards.

Question (by Mr. Campbell)—State, if you please, all that occurred in an interview between General Rousseau and the Chief of Police and some Democratic citizens of Algiers, with reference to a request of the latter to be allowed to patrol the streets of their town, which interview took place on or about the 28th day of October, 1868.

Answer—I entered the Chief's office at the same time with the citizens referred to and heard the request, made to General Rousseau, that they should be allowed to patrol the city. The General answered, "Well, I can see no objection for any citizen to do that." I then asked the General "if he meant by any citizen, colored men also;" when one of the Algiers deputation said, "Oh, we would take care of the colored men." The General then said, looking at deponent haughtily, "What need is there for both parties patrolling the city? I do not think this is the proper time to start such a question, and it is just such men as you are that create disturbance." Deponent replied, "General, no one desires peace more than I and my party do; but I would be better protected by a patrol of colored men than by one formed of such men as these," pointing to the deputation from Algiers. Superintendent Williamson then ordered him out of his office, although he was there and spoke merely as a citizen like the rest present. Deponent further states, that out of all the colored men that were killed and wounded on the night of the 24th of October, 1868, not one of them were armed. Deponent repeatedly heard Democrats while in the cars, and who knew him to be a Republican, threaten his life and other "white niggers," as they called the prominent Republicans; furthermore, he firmly believes that if General Mower, with his few colored troops, had been brought over to this city from Ship Island, no disturbance whatever would have arisen from political causes.

William Richardson states, on oath, that on Saturday evening, October 24, 1868, while he was with his club passing the corner of Baronne and Canal streets, a shot was fired from the window of a house on the southeast corner of said street; a second shot was fired from the sidewalk by a white man, the firing then became general and the members of the club scattered and ran.

William Lewis states, on oath, that on Saturday night, October 24, 1868, he was with his club, First Ward Club; they were quietly marching along Canal street, past the corner of Baronne, when firing commenced from the building occupied by the "Constitution Club." The firing was so heavy that he ran away to the corner of Erato and Bacchus streets, here he, with some others, met a Democratic club coming down Bacchus street; members of this club commenced chasing them and yelling "Kill the d——d scallawags." He managed to escape in safety.

Emile Oliver states, on oath, that he is a citizen of Louisiana, that on the night of October 24, 1868, between the hours of ten and eleven o'clock, a colored man named Alfred Garner came to his house, No. 359 Camp street, and said to him, "Oliver, I'm shot;" witness examined him, and found that he was shot in the breast; he asked him who shot him, he answered, "I was shot at the corner of Erato and Camp streets, coming home, when some unknown white men came along and shot me." He got into witness' bed, and in half an hour he died. Mr. Garner was a member of the Grant Guards, and was out parading with the club; he was a true Republican.

Peter Joseph states, on oath, that on Saturday evening, about eight or nine o'clock, October 24, 1868, he was passing on Josephine street, near the corner of Fulton; the Working Men's Democratic Club was passing down Josephine street toward Magazine street; at the corner of Annunciation street, some member of the club fired a shot at some colored people who were quietly standing on the sidewalk. Witness afterwards reported at the Rousseau street police station, and received orders to call in his men, as there was a riot on Canal street. He met two men in the uniform of the above named club, and heard one of them remark, "I'll bet you that the Radicals will be short of some voters to-morrow morning." Witness continued his course to the corner of Dryades street, where he saw two colored men wounded. One James Williams, who was shot in the head, has since died. He afterwards heard a call whistle, and running in the direction he found near the corner of St. Mary and Religious streets, officer Kline lying with his throat and leg cut, and officer Wolfram badly beaten. There were two caps belonging to members of the "Working Men's Club" lying in the vicinity; he did not succeed in ascertaining who were the perpetrators of this outrage. On Sunday morning, October 25, 1868, he, with Corporal Kline, of the Metropolitan Police force, were threatened and abused by armed white men at the Jackson street ferry landing, they were six in number, two of them came into the street and drew their revolvers, one of them levelled his at witness and Kline, saying, "Shall I shoot the son of a b—h," the other said, "let him off," the former replied. "I want to try it on a Metropolitan Policeman, any way," but he did not fire. As witness and Kline, soon after, were passing the station, these men commenced to abuse them by saying, "You half white sons of b—hs, and all you Metropolitan Police." On Monday, October 26, 1868, a colored woman notified witness that she overheard some white men say in a grocery on Jackson street, "We will have to go for that half white son of a b—h that lives on Philip street (meaning witness), he's on the Metropolitan Police, we'll get a sly crack at him." On the following day, about noon, a squad of about thirty white men, armed with shot guns, revolvers, etc., came to the corner in search of witness, but not finding his house, went away.

Simon Jones states, on oath, that on or about the 24th day of October, 1868, as he was coming out of the Post Office he heard a party of men who were there congregated, remark: "There goes that d—d Radical son of a b—h; let's make a row with him and kill him." To avoid the crowd, witness went into the private office of the Deputy Postmaster; a few minutes afterward a man came into the office and said that on a previous occasion he had asked

Charles Smith and witness whether they would allow their daughters or sisters to marry a "nigger," and that they had replied in the affirmative; witness then replied that it was untrue, and that he would leave the matter with Charles Smith to settle; this man then said that *he had* said so, and that he was "a d—d nigger loving son of a b—h, and ought to be killed." Witness then seeing that the excitement was increasing in the street, went up stairs into the Custom House, and from there he went to his room Having heard that one Winn Rogers had laid a plot to assassinate him at 1 o'clock that night, he remained at the house of a friend; when he returned to the house a few days afterward, the ladies of the house told him that a party came there the first night that he was away, and swore that they would shoot him; they did not, however, make any attempt to enter the house. They came again on the following night at about 12 o'clock, and swore they would "go through the house, ladies and all, if witness was not produced; that they had sufficient men to do the work, and his blood should be spilled that night." At about this time Walter Rogers, brother of this man, Winn Rogers, came to the door of his house, on the opposite side of the street, and called his brother in; no further demonstration was made after that. Witness has been told that it was unsafe for him to go about that locality, as they were fully determined to murder him.

Eugene Staes states, on oath, that on Monday, October 26, 1868, during the night a body of armed men came to his house, corner of Claiborne and St. Philip streets; they attempted to break open the door, threatening to kill him, but were prevented from doing so by some more quiet members of the party; they, however, left, threatening to return and kill him if they caught him. They returned the following night, and again attempted to break into the house, but were prevented by some parties unknown to witness. They have since called for him, but he, with his family, have remained away from home at night.

Edward Giff states, on oath, that on the morning of October 2,6 1868, about 12 o'clock, he was standing on the corner of Toulouse and Rampart streets, as a night watchman, when seven white men came to the opposite corner and called to him and another policeman named Nicholls, who was with him, to halt, and then asked them who they were. At this time these men discovered that they were policemen, and one of them, who was on horseback, called out to the others to "come on, now we have got them," and one of them fired at policeman Nicholls, and the man on horseback fired at witness. Witness then ran for his life, they continuing to fire at him. He turned and fired one shot at them. He succeeded in escaping to the Station house, and found that Nicholls had been wounded by one of the shots fired at them by the aforesaid party (which consisted of seven men on foot and one on horseback). Witness took Nicholls home and remained with him until morning.

J. Lanabère states, on oath, that on Monday morning, October 26, 1868, some time before 4 o'clock, about twenty unknown white men came to his coffee house, corner of St. Peter and Basin streets, broke into the house, destroyed the billiard table and all the furniture, and took in cash about one thousand dollars; also three gold watches and his books, besides other property. The Sicilians had previously threatened to kill the owner of the house "and every d—d nigger in it." The bar-keeper told them that they could kill him if they wanted to do so. They replied, "never mind, we will come back another time." These men came around the house every day, using bad language and abusing the colored people. On October 27, 1868, a number of these men were standing on the corner in front of his coffee house with pistols in their hands, not allowing any person to approach the bar-room. Mr. Gustave Arnheim, his bar-keeper, was coming at the time and these men shot at him three times, preventing him from coming to the house. Witness knows of no reason for this persecution. He is a Captain in the "Warmoth Guards."

James Wilson st[illegible] [illegible] oath, that on Monday evening, October 26, 1868. a number of white men, twenty or thirty, many of whom wore the uniforms of Democratic clubs, some with red caps, white capes and black pants, came rushing into the house were he lives, corner of Triton Walk and Dryades street, and called loudly "Where is the d——d son of b——h who fired that pistol at us." Witness said he did not know of a shot having been fired. They held him and searched his room for arms, saying, if they found any weapons they would kill him on the spot; they found no weapons, but found and took his watch and coat, a box of carpenter's tools, and a pocket book, containing about ten dollars; they also took from his wife's hand her pocket-book containing about nine dollars and a half. Witness is now without house or home, and is afraid to go back to get his bed and bedding, as parties lurking around there say they will shoot him if he shows himself.

Celestin Oliver states, on oath, that on Monday morning, October 26, 1868, about one o'clock, a party of about forty armed white men came into his neighorhood, near the corner of Franklin and St. Philip streets, and inquired of a lady named Mrs. Bryan where he lived, and offered her twenty-five dollars to tell them; she told them that she did not know any such person, fearing that they would kill him. On Wednesday evening, October 28, as he was going home he was met by a young colored boy who told him not to go home, as he had heard a party of white men say that they "wanted to put his light out," because he had been a captain in one of the colored clubs; he remained away from home for five nights until the excitement was over.

Richard Johnson states, on oath, that on the 26th day of October, 1868, at nine o'clock, a party of about forty white men came to his house, No. 197 Franklin street, all armed with shot guns, revolvers, etc. They knocked at the door and ordered him to open it, which he did; one of them demanded weapons from him; he told them he had none; they said he was a d—d liar, and asked if there were any more men in the house; he told them there were four, when six of these white men went to them and demanded their arms, but they did not have any. They then searched the house and took the registration certificates away from two of the men in the house. They told all of the men in the house that if they went to the polls to vote they would kill them. They also threatened to kill witness on the spot if he did not give them his certificate of registration, at the same time presenting a pistol to his head and drawing a knife on him. Witness told them that they would have to kill him, as he did not have any. They then left, ordering him to put out the lights after they got away.

William Nicholl states, on oath, that on the night of October 26, 1868, he was on duty as a policeman, on the corner of Toulouse and Rampart street, a party of white men appeared on the opposite corner and fired several shots at him, one of which took effect in his back, where it still remains. Their intention evidently was to kill him, but he succeeded in making his escape to the stationhouse. Another policeman named "Giff" was also fired upon about the same time and in the same vicinity; he, however, escaped unhurt.

John G. Seldon states, on oath, that he is a citizen of the State of Louisiana; that on the 26th day of October, 1868, between 3 and 4 o'clock P. M., he was at the corner of Toulouse and Burgundy streets, in the presence of L. D. Larene and A. Dourd, when one Alphonse Picou came up to him without any provocation, and presented a pistol to his face, asking him if he was armed; he answered "no;" Picou then said that he was a Democrat; that he was hunting Belot and all the leading men of the Republican party; witness answered that he was a Republican, and fully determined to sustain it; he then left him; an hour afterward, when in company with his daughter, he met the same man—A. Picou—on the corner of Claiborne and St. Ann streets; he saw the said Alphonse Picou draw a revolver from his pocket and shoot a colored man, who then ran away; witness then went away with his daughter to avoid the difficulty. On the 28th day of October, 1868, about 11 o'clock P. M., some twenty unknown white men attempted to break open his door, saying, "this is John G. Seldon's house, the leader of the Republican party;" some one of them remarked that he was a Creole, "let him be; we will see him after awhile;" these men then went away.

Augustin Maurice states, on oath, that on Monday evening, October 26, 1868, he saw a party of white men break into the Eighth Ward Republican Club room, from which they took a banner and an American flag; the party numbered about one hundred men, and were armed with shot guns and revolvers. They destroyed all the furniture and transparencies, and everything that was in the room. These men called themselves "wide-awakes;" they said they would kill all the officers of the said club before the week was out. On Tuesday, October 27, 1868, from about eleven o'clock P. M. until four o'clock the following morning, about fifty white men surrounded witness' house, armed with guns, pistols, etc.; they knocked at his door but he did not answer; they concluded he was not in, and said that they would wait for him; they, however, left finally, and went to his neighbor's (Mr. Foucher), broke into his house, broke his furniture, and took away clothing and about ninety dollars in money; they left, saying that they were going to burn the colored church on Poet street.

William Murrel states, on oath, that on Monday night, October 26, 1868, he attended the meeting of the "Guiding Star Benevolent Association" on Terpsichore street, between Carondelet and St. Charles streets; while there about twenty "Innocents" (a noted Democratic club) in uniform broke into the room and drove all from it, and threatened to kill the ladies who were there unless they should show where the arms were concealed; the ladies informed them that there were no arms in the place. They destroyed a United States flag, and took sixty dollars from the colored woman who resided in the house, and took away and destroyed all her furniture and everything she possessed. They also broke into the Second Ward Republican Club room, and destroyed whatever they could lay their hands on; they also broke into a barber shop, belonging to a colored man named Stephen Strange. They shot at every colored man whom they met, and by mistake shot and killed one of their own men, supposing him to be a colored man. On the following morning he saw these same men displaying the trophies (money and other articles of value) which they had taken from the colored people the night previous, and boasting of what they had done.

John Little states, on oath, that on the night of October 26, 1868, a party of about one hundred armed white men came to his house and demanded to know if the body of the colored man named James Williams (who was killed on the night of October 24 in the riot on

Canal street), was in the house; if it was, they would burn the "d—d son of a b—h," and that they would not permit the body to be buried. Witness is afraid to stay in his house at night, as this crowd of men (all of whom he believes are armed) said they wanted to get him, and he is afraid they would kill him if he remained.

P. M. Williams states, on oath, that he resides at No. 300 Gravier street; that on the nights of October 26 and 27, 1868, a body of armed men, some of whom were mounted, came to his house and demanded admittance. The gentleman of the house told them that he would not open the door. They then broke open the door, and one of them said "strike a light boys, we will get that d—d son of a b—h that spoke to us from the gallery." After obtaining a light they went up stairs and commenced breaking open trunks, armoirs, bureaus, etc., and taking the contents—two hundred and twenty-five dollars in greenbacks, eighty dollars in city money, three hundred and nineteen dollars in bonds, also watches, jewelry, chains, etc., and all the valuables that could be carried away, and breaking the crockery, glass-ware and other valuable property that was in the trunks, belonging to different individuals. They broke the furniture, took the bedding from the beds, and placed everything in confusion. They opened a closet and took liquor and cigars and everything that they could use. They destroyed and carried away property to the amount of twelve hundred dollars National currency.

Captain Eugene Staes states, on oath, that he is a citizen of the State of Louisiana, and minute clerk of the House of Representatives.

Question—By Mr. Campbell.—Captain, please state all that was said in any conversation between yourself and General Rousseau on or about the 27th day of October, 1868, when you applied to him for protection, in company with Mr. William Vigers, Chief Clerk of the House of Representatives?

Answer—On or about the 27th day of October, 1868, I went, in company with Mr. William Vigers, chief clerk of the House of Representatives, to the Headquarters of General Rousseau, to demand protection, my home having been attacked, and my life threatened the night before by a band of men who were, to the best of my knowledge and belief, white Democrats, the General said "he was willing to extend protection to any one, but could not detail his troops on guard to every one that came and asked of him protection, but would do all he could to keep quiet in the city, and that it would take twenty thousand men to do that." Upon stating to the General what position Mr. Vigers and myself held, he said "it was probably on that account that we were the object of the hatred of the opposing party," and added, "that the State officials were obnoxious to the people, and if they were to resign their positions, that quiet would be restored immediately; that in the present excited condition of affairs he was unwilling to have his men killed for the purpose of maintaining in position men who were obnoxious to the people." The same night of the interview a band of men came to my house for the purpose of destroying it, to the best of my belief, as threats had been made to that effect, but they were prevented by some one, I do not know who.

Captain William Vigers, chief clerk of the House of Representatives, being duly sworn, corroborates the foregoing statement of Captain Eugene Staes, and also states that *his* house was entered on or about the night of October, 27, 1868, or the morning of October 28, 1868, by a party or parties unknown, while he and his family were absent, who destroyed furniture to the amount of seventy-five dollars.

On account of threats offered deponent absented himself from his home for the space of fifteen days, not thinking his life would be safe if he should return during that time.

The following appears in the Republican, of October 27, 1868:

"On Friday evening last a large number of Democratic citizens waited on Mayor Conway, at his residence, and urged him to appoint an entirely new police force, including the Chief, and to disregard the Metropolitan District Police law. Mr. Conway was disinclined to act upon their suggestions, and gave them his views of the effect of such a movement on the prospects of the Democratic party at the North.

"His constituents were not satisfied with his reasoning, and told him, in substance, that they would give him till 5 o'clock Saturday evening to consider the matter, declaring that if he would not act they would take the matter into their own hands. On Saturday evening others or the same citizens visited the Mayor at his residence, but it is not believed that they succeeded in persuading Mr. Conway that it was prudent to disregard a State law.

"Last evening delegations from Democratic clubs, many of the men armed with muskets, estimated by one of the morning papers to number six hundred in all, patroled the streets, and at length approached the City Hall.

"They marched up St. Charles and Carondelet streets in detachments of from twenty to fifty; some of the squads halting at Hawkins' Branch and at Cassidy's to fortify their courage with old Bourbon or other stimulants.

"They gathered in front of the City Hall, and success seemed about to crown their movements until Major Keeler or Captain De Russy appeared, and accompanied Sheriff Maxwell to the Mayor's parlor, where a number of citizens had assembled, offering assistance.

"It being considered certain that the military authorities would sustain the Superintendent of the Police, and order the self-constituted guardians of the peace to disperse, prominent Democrats were called upon or volunteered to address the assemblage.

"The Mayor was not convinced of the necessity of establishing a citizen's police, and could not be won over to its support.

"The first to address the multitude of armed citizens from the front of the City Hall was General Steedman, who, according to the Times, spoke as follows:

"'To-day has been one of excitement. In obedience to the call of the Mayor, six hundred men have reported here for duty. The Mayor says there will be no need for your services here to-night; I therefore advise you to go quietly to your homes. He has been advised that the chief Executive of the State had informed General Rousseau that he was willing to turn over his authority to the military commander. Gen. Rousseau had refused to receive it. The Democracy were a people of law and order. If the party in power could not run the machine, let them get off of it—let them turn the power over to the people to whom it rightfully belongs.

"'Go now quietly to your homes, with the assurance that good news is in store for you, for I have intelligence that Horatio Seymour now is on the stump, and is producing among the people of the

North great changes. The American eagle will yet overshadow this land; the Goddess of Freedom will kneel and not beg in vain for human rights. I beg, then, of you, as men engaged in the great struggle for human rights, to go now to your homes.'

"Mayor Conway being called upon, said that he was ready to indorse every word that had fallen from the lips of General Steedman. He believed that General Rousseau was doing everything in his power to show himself the friend of the city. He begged the crowd, as peaceable citizens, to disperse and go peaceably to their homes."

General Harry T. Hays next spoke thus, according to the same report:

"I came here to say to-night that if your liberties were imperilled, I would be the first to shoulder a musket. I wish to give you some advice as one of you—as one of the poorest of you: I went to the Chief of Police to find out precisely how the police stands, and I tell you that the Chief of Police has bearded the Commissioners, and told them that while they were sitting that they should not put a negro policeman on duty. This much praise is his due. At the time he spoke there was not one negro policeman on duty."

He gave them, in conclusion, the same advice as that given by preceding speakers.

Senator Ogden was the next speaker, and said:

"I have no praises (referring to an interruption) to give to any but the citizens of New Orleans. I am proud to have been born a citizen of the place, and I tell you, gentlemen, that we have stood on the brink of a volcano—one of the greatest political convulsions that the world has ever witnessed. It is the cause of law and order, the cause of our wives and sisters, that has united us to-night. All that we now ask is that their lives and our property shall be protected. When, therefore, the chief executive comes to you and begs you to disperse, will you not hearken to his appeal? Will you not go, like good citizens, to your homes? When the Governor of this State comes to you and tells you that he cannot control the storm he has raised—that the dissensions which he has occasioned have sprung into armed men, General Rousseau did right to refuse to shoulder his responsibility. This action of General Rousseau it is now the duty of the people to sustain. The speaker begged his audience to retire quietly and be contented with the present situation."

Sheriff Maxwell also addressed the armed people and advised them to retire from the scene and go to their quiet homes. When these speeches were ended some of the club delegations left, but not all. The Mayor went over to the office of the superintendent of police, and between these officials there became a good understanding. After the Mayor's return to his parlor, there being still quite a crowd remaining in front of the city hall, Lieutenant Spaulding appeared in uniform, and informed the people that it was his duty, in obedience to military orders, to request them to disperse. His request was heeded without much delay, as he appeared to be backed up by soldiers to enforce any orders he might be compelled to execute.

W. B. Gray states, on oath, that on Tuesday, October 27, 1868, between the hours of eleven and twelve o'clock P. M., he was aroused by some unknown persons knocking at his door. He got out of bed and opened the door, and saw about twenty-five men armed with shot guns, pistols, etc. One of these men, designated by his companions as "Major," asked him if his name was Gray. He answered yes. These men then asked him if he was marshal of any "nigger club." He answered that he had been a marshal of a Republican club. Several of these men then remarked, "You are the very G—d d—d Radical son of a b—h," and told him to "come out there." He remonstrated with them. The Major told them to wait until he asked some questions. He then asked witness if he had any arms. He answered that he had a revolver. He then asked if he knew "where any other leading nigger Radicals lived like himself." Witness was afraid to tell them, fearing that they would go and kill them; he answered "No." They then asked him if the niggers had any arms. He answered that he did not know. Afterwards these men took hold of witness and pulled him into the street. He was in his night shirt. Some of them said, "Let us shoot him." Others said, "Let us hang him to the lamp post." The Major said, "If we make too much noise, all these niggers back of town will come out and make it too hot for us; we are too far from the rest of our men to do this; we will let it go until another time; but we must have his arms." The Major then commanded witness to go into the house with them to deliver his revolver. Several of them followed him into his room, where his wife and children were. His pistol was lying on the table near his bed. They seeing it said, "G—d d—n you, give us that pistol;" at the same time several pistols were presented to his head. He gave them his pistol, thinking it was the best. They then went into his parlor and broke some furniture and crockery. They then left his house saying, "We will come again for you, you d—d nigger son of a b—h!" They then crossed the street to a house where Mr. Payne lived (formerly a candidate for Representative for that district). They demanded of Mr. Payne his arms. Witness was informed that these men were coming to pay him another visit, and, believing that they would come and kill him, he moved his family away. He was informed that these men came to his house the following night, but found that he had left.

Noah Douglas states, on oath, that he was shot at on Orleans street by a party of white men on Tuesday, October 27, 1868.

Hon. D. Douglas, late a member of the Constitutional Convention, states, on oath, that on Tuesday, October 27, 1868, between the hours of twelve and two at night, he was passing down Rampart street, accompanied by a friend. Arriving at the corner of St. Ann street they were attacked by a party of white men, who said, "There are some of Warmoth's thieves!" These men followed them and shot his friend, who fell, and witness was compelled to fly for his life.

Napoleon Richardson states, on oath, that on the night of October 27, 1868, a white man named Flanders Clark came to his house, No. 110 Prytannia street, and broke open the door. He was accompanied by six other armed white men. They demanded his guns. He told them he had none. They then searched the house, but found none.

Edward Mead states, on oath, that he is a citizen of Louisiana; that on Tuesday, October 27, 1868, between the hours of eleven and twelve o'clock at night, a body of armed white men came to his house, on First street, between Liberty and Franklin, and finding him up in the loft called out to him to come down, and wanted to know what he was doing up there. He told them that he heard them coming and went up there to hide, as he was afraid of them. The leader of the gang then wanted to know if he had any fire arms. Witness answered that he had a gun. The leader said, "Then give it up to me, as the cavalry are coming." The gang then took witness' gun from his bedroom, his pocket-book (containing six dollars and thirty-five cents, all the money he had in the world for his daily support), from under his pillow, and said, "Give up your fire arms and we will not hurt you, but if you don't we will kill you."

John Campbell states, on oath, that on Tuesday night, October 27, 1868, he saw a crowd of white men standing on the corner of Third and St. Patrick streets, at about twelve o'clock. They went to his house and broke in and searched for him, for the purpose of killing him; they did not succeed, however, in finding him. They broke into the Eleventh Ward Republican Club room, and destroyed the United States flag and all the furniture in the room.

Charles Grandpre states, on oath, that on the 27th day of October, 1868, at about 7 or 8 o'clock in the evening, as he was standing in the cigar store, at the corner of Orleans and Rampart streets, he saw a party of white men shooting and creating a disturbance; he shut his door and kept very quiet, fearing an attack; the same thing occurred again at about 9 o'clock; he afterward heard that some colored men were shot. On Saturday, October 24, 1868, while the Democratic procession was passing his place, some party fired into his store.

Reuben Johnson states, on oath, that on Tuesday night, between 11 and 12 o'clock, October 27, 1868, a party of white men, one of whom had a large knife in his hand, came to his residence and searched the house—as they pretended—for weapons; they ransacked the house generally, and took from him a double barrelled shot gun; they opened all the drawers and upset everything in the house; they afterward entered the house of a neighbor.

Charles Collins states, on oath, that he resides at No. 62 Franklin street, that on Tuesday, October 27, 1868, at about 9 o'clock P. M., a crowd of white men entered his house and stabbed him in the back and shoulder with a bowie knife; they asked him if he had any arms concealed in the house; he told them that he had none; they searched the house for arms; not finding anything, they left without committing any further outrage.

Alfred Taylor (colored) states, on oath, that on the night of October 27, 1868, a party of ten or more white men entered his residence on Calliope street, between Baronne and Carondolet, and took forcible possession of his registration certificate.

Warwick King, (colored) states, on oath, that on the same night aforesaid, a party of twelve or more white men, entered his residence, No. 153 Calliope street, and robbed him of his registration certificate, a pistol and a hatchet.

Robert Jones (colored) states, on oath, that on the same night, a party of about eight white men came to his residence, No. 207, Calliope street, and took from him his certificate of registration.

William C. Brewer states, on oath that on the 28th day of October, 1868, at about 2 or 3 o'clock P. M., he was on Roman street, and saw a crowd of white men running toward Prieur and St. Ann streets; he inquired what was the matter, and learned that these white men had tied a colored man up as a target and shot at him; they killed said colored man, and pursued others to treat them similarly. Witness was compelled to leave his house with his family, as threats had been made against his life.

J. P. Martin states, on oath, that on the 28th day of October, 1868, he was at the corner of Urquart and Mandeville streets, between the hours of eleven and twelve P. M. He saw a crowd of about fifty white men on the corner headed by a man named "Jacobs," they went to a house on Spain street, belonging to a man named "Antoine." They broke the furniture and everything in the house, Mr. Antoine and his family being absent at the time; having been threatened, they had left to save their lives. These men took from Mr. Antoine's house about eighty-five dollars ($85), and afterwards broke into the house adjacent and took therefrom a considerable amount of clothing.

Benjamin Scott states, on oath, that on Thursday evening, October 29, 1868, about four or five o'clock, a crowd of about twenty white men were congregated at the corner of Conti and Marais streets, they were in pursuit of Mr. Wickliffe, the Auditor of the State, to kill him, but it being day light, they did not attack. The people living in the house did not dare to remain there during the night. Witness has also been compelled to move from fear of being murdered.

J. P. Martin states, on oath, that on Thursday, October 29, 1868, at about 11 o'clock, P. M., a Democratic club called the "Wide Awakes," broke into the hall of the "Young Friends' Association," and broke the benches and all other furniture and articles in the place; they pretended to be in search of arms. On Monday, October 26, witness saw a band of white men, armed with guns and pistols, parading the streets in the Third District.

Henry L. Tanzin states, on oath, that he is clerk of the Board of Supervisors of Registration of the Fifth Ward; that owing to threats of violence, he was compelled to suspend his work on Thursday and Friday, October 29 and 30, 1868. The Chairman of the Board was assaulted at his own residence on the night of the 30th, and has been compelled to leave the city for safety.

Peter Johnson (colored) states, on oath, that on the night of October 30, 1868, at about half past nine o'clock, three white men came to his house, and ordered him to let them in, or they would break in the door. He opened the door and they demanded of him his registration certificate, and those of two other colored men who were with him. Witness told these men that their papers had already been taken away by the Democrats, whereupon they left, saying "we can get nothing here, let us go somewhere else."

The Times of Friday, October 30, 1868, has the following account:

"The Second District yesterday morning, was, comparatively speaking, quiet. The station and court building was guarded during the night with fifty soldiers. Two places were entered by bodies of armed men, and the contents of the buildings more or less injured. Economy Hall, on Ursuline street, between Villeré and Robinson streets, was sacked. It was at one time a registration office, and is a place of great resort for negroes residing in the faubourg Trémé.

"The origin of the unfortunate difficulty of Tuesday noon is yet an inexplicable mystery, and would probably require days of searching investigation to ascertain all the particulars. The following are those known to be killed or wounded:

"Joseph Punch, colored, residing at the corner of St. Anthony street and the Mexican Gulf Railway, was wounded at No. 255 Dauphine street, it is thought dangerously, and sent to the Charity Hospital.

"A colored man, stabbed and killed at the corner of St. Ann and Bourbon streets. His body was taken to the Second District Station, afterward sent to the graveyard. The colored man, George Allen, wounded on Crossman street Tuesday morning has since died.

"Deputy Coroner Espinola, we hear, has held an inquest on the body of a colored man, unknown, found dead a few squares from the Laharp Street Station House, Third District.

"Mr. Sanches, who was shot in the left side going home Monday night, we hear, is doing well.

"The police report a colored man wounded at the corner of St. Ann and Derbigny streets.

"The lower portion of the city was patrolled Tuesday night by the citizens. They report everything quiet in the Seventh and Eighth Wards.

"The colored man found dead at the corner of St. Ann and Rampart streets was taken to Trémé Station.

"Accounts were brought to the station of one or two political assaults made in the rear portion of the city, and of houses being broken open and entered. About midnight a half dozen shots were fired out on Johnson street, between New Basin and Common streets, and two other shots were fired in the same quarter some time after. Shots were heard in the neighborhood of Claiborne Market, and a good many on Common street, about daybreak.

"A man by the name of Nugent, who is said to have made himself unpopular with laborers, is reported to have been chased and fired at.

"About 10 o'clock Tuesday night a party of about a dozen men entered the club room of the "First Ward Grant and Colfax Club," on Terpsichore street, between St. Charles and Carondelet. No persons but women and children were in the place, and they were not molested; but the flags, uniform caps, lamps and other paraphernalia of the club were carried off, except what was destroyed and thrown in the streets. During the time occupied in 'cleaning out' the establishment, sentinels were posted at the street corners, and all passers halted.

"So quietly was the affair conducted that many residents in the immediate vicinity were not aroused from their slumbers. One or two shots were fired near the corner of Terpsichore, on St. Charles street, but we cannot learn that any one was injured."

The following paragraph appeared in the New Orleans Bee, in connection with the state of lawlessness in the Second District:

"At twelve o'clock yesterday a negro was shot in the head and killed at the corner of Bourbon and St. Ann streets, and another was subsequently found dead at the corner of St. Ann and Rampart streets. They are reported by the police to have been killed by some of the armed men going through the streets. A third negro was killed near the house 225 Dauphin street."

Police Reports.—George Allen, colored, was shot on Crossman street yesterday.

The following appeared in the New Orleans Bee of October 31, 1868:

"There was a large meeting of the 'Innocent' club last night at their hall on Orleans street, where Gen. Rousseau appeared and addressed them in acknowledgement of the serenade tendered to him at his headquarters, which happened, he said, while he was absent. He spoke but briefly, giving them good advice, which was received with the heartiest applause, and will no doubt be faithfully observed. He said he was satisfied that offenses of which they were not guilty had been charged upon them, that they did not look like men who were either cruel or ferocious, and hoped that no more disturbances would occur, and that all persons entitled to vote would be allowed and encouraged to do so."

Joseph Neele (colored) states, on oath, that he is employed on the ferry boat called the "Belle Lee," commanded by Capt. Wiley. On the 31st day of October, 1868, said Capt. Wiley came up to him and said, "Joe, mind what I tell you, if you vote the Republican ticket on the 3d of November, I will shoot you and throw you in the river; no one will know it. The niggers make me mad, and I hate every nigger." Witness, therefore, did not dare to vote on the day of election.

A. T. Selover states, on oath, that he was commissioner of election in New Orleans, during the election held November 3, 1868, at Poll No. 3, Precinct 10, 5th Ward. From the opening of the polls until about noon, the white voters had complete possession of the polls. At noon they, finding there were being no Republican votes polled, started around in bands, in search of colored voters and offered them money, and in some cases threatened them, to induce them to vote. They told many that they would protect them and see that they should vote as they might choose. Several white men attempted to vote twice; they were, however, detected and prevented. Contrary to orders the deputy sheriffs took charge of the ballot box, after the counting was over, and took it to the sheriff's office. The sheriff had given them orders to "stick to it until hell froze over."

W. B. Phillips states, on oath, that on the morning of November 3, 1868, he went to the poll near the corner of Claiborne and Common streets, and while there he saw three young white men approach a colored man and tell him "if he did not want his brains blowed out, he had better vote for Seymour and Blair."

D. W. Brandon states, on oath, that on November 3, 1868, the day of the election, he went to the poll corner of Josephine and Laurel streets, with thirty three (33) colored men, to vote, and when there was threatened by a crowd of white men there congregated, who remarked, "here come the d——d nigger sons of b—s, and a white Radical with them, to vote the damned Radical ticket." Witness advised the colored men to return home; while they were returning some one in the Democratic ranks said, "if those d——d niggers had voted, and had *not* voted as we wanted them to they would never have seen another day."

Joseph Mintan states, on oath, that he served in the federal army during the late war, and for having done so he has been repeatedly threatened, some telling him "you will pay for it when Seymour and Blair are elected" On the day of the election, November 3, 1868, he was walking along quietly, when he was seized by a party of seven or eight white men, who wore the badge of the "Broom Rangers," and who told him that he must vote. He told them that he had not his registration certificate with him; that he did not wish to vote. He told them this because he believed it to be unsafe to vote the Republican ticket. He finally made his escape from them.

Leander Collins states, on oath, that on the 3d of November, 1868, he was standing on the corner of St. Louis and Trémé streets; he saw a colored man coming down Trémé street and saw two white men shoot at him, but without hitting him. They then arrested the colored man and took him to the Parish prison.

Thomas Washington, George W. Washington, Edward Johnson and Stephen Rag state, on oath, that during the election of November 3, 1868, they went to poll number three, precinct twenty, Tenth Ward, corner of Laurel and Josephine streets, to vote; when within a few steps of the polls a man in the crowd (which numbered about forty), who wore a red ribbon badge, marked deputy sheriff, said, "there comes that same white d—d Radical son of a b—h that was at Jackson street poll this morning with some d—d Radical niggers here to see if he can vote them at this poll, but I'll be d—d if he does, except they vote for Seymour and Blair." Hearing these threats used by the deputy sheriff, they concluded to go home. Had it not been for this intimidation they would have voted the regular Republican ticket.

Daniel Hollins, Patrick Johnson, James Williams, James Page, Washington Green, Jordan Mulligan, S. C. Criber and William Leonard (all colored) state, on oath, that on November 3, 1868, the day of election, they went to poll number two, precinct twenty, Engine house number twenty-two, on Tchoupitoulas street, for the purpose of voting, and when near said poll, a white man came up to them and asked if they were going to vote. They replied "yes." He then asked what ticket they were going to vote. They answered the Republican ticket. The white man then said, "You d—d sons of b—s, you don't vote no such d—d ticket at this poll." They asked him if they didn't vote at that poll. He replied "Yes, but you have got to vote for Seymour and Blair, or not vote at all." They immediately turned from the poll and went home. Had it not been for this intimidation they would have voted the regular Republican ticket.

Edward DeCree, Pierre Grant, Charles Ennis, Samuel Campbell, David Fisher, Samuel Bell and Samuel Basil (colored) state, on oath, that they are registered voters in New Orleans, Louisiana, in the Tenth Ward; that on November 3, 1868, during the late election, they went to poll number one, precinct twenty, on Jackson street, for the purpose of voting, when within a short distance of the poll (around which a crowd of about two hundred white men were congregated) they heard some person in the crowd remark, "here comes the d—d black Radical sons of b—s, and a d—d white Radical with them, to vote the d—d Radical ticket." They then believing it to be impossible for them to vote, started to leave the polls. As they were leaving the same man said, "it is better for you d—d niggers to go home, for if you had voted the d—d Radical ticket, your G—d d—d heads would have been blown off." Witnesses further state that had they not been thus intimidated they would have voted the regular Republican ticket.

The following is an official statement of Wm. Baker, Chairman of the Board of Registrars, as to the conduct of the election of the 3d of November, 1868:

"There is not a ward in the city in which threats of violence have not been made to the Supervisors of Registration in the performance of their duties. Many of them for some time prior to the election were afraid to sleep in their own houses at night. Others were threatened, and in one instance one of the newspapers called upon the people to 'hang the Registrars to the nearest lamp post.' Is it any wonder that they resigned rather than perform their duties at so much personal risk? In the First Ward one of the Registrars was hung in effigy in front of his own door. Since then, as a matter of personal safety, he has sold out his place of business at great loss, and moved to another portion of the city.

"One Registration office (the Sixth Ward) was broken into and all the furniture and stationery destroyed, fortunately the records were deposited elsewhere for safe keeping. The First Ward Registration office was broken into and the whole records destroyed. It is believed it was done for the purpose of destroying the evidence which the Registrars had been collecting, respecting the breaking into the house of colored men, and with pistols at their heads and threats of instant death if they resisted, robbing them of their registration papers. I am in possession of many affidavits setting forth these facts. Many club rooms were broken into and sacked, the furniture and everything destroyed.

"So far had these threats of violence, intimidation and murder been carried that when the Registrars came to that part of their duty requiring them to appoint Commissioners of Election, that in not one ward in this city could be found Republicans who were ready to incur the risk of serving as Commissioners of Election, showing most conslusively the reign of terror which had been inaugurated and which but too truly made "the election a farce," the "tragedy" having preceded it.

"The consequences of the intimidation just referred to, is no where more perceptible than in the city of New Orleans. With more than eighteen thousand (18,000) registered colored voters in this city, and certainly not less than six thousand white Republicans, it appears that less than three hundred persons voted the Republican ticket. Why the Republicans did not vote, is easily explained, by taking a glance at the weekly mortuary report of the Secretary to the Board of Health, which shows that three white men and ten colored came by their death, either by gunshot or other wound, in one week in this city, during which time such a state of anarchy or mob law existed that the ordinary police authorities were powerless, and the streets at night were patrolled by bands of self-appointed men, armed with all kinds of dangerous weapons, during which time no colored man or known Republican dared show themselves on the streets after dark."

John Dennis states, on oath, that on the 3d day of November, 1868, he saw Judge Gastinel and Mr. Rousseleau make three colored men vote the Democratic ticket at the poll on St. Philip street, between Marais and Trémé streets; these men did not wish to vote, but did so, being afraid that they would be killed if they did not. (The said Rousseleau is a member of the "Innocent Club.") Mr. Rousseleau's brother-in-law was there, and made colored men vote the Democratic ticket. At the corner of Rampart and Ursuline streets, Mr. Trémé and John Henry, members of the "Innocent Club," stopped witness and asked him to vote the Democratic ticket, when he refused to do so; they told him he must vote that ticket; he left them; between 11 and 12 o'clock these men came to his house for him, but he was out, they then went to his uncle's, Mr. Johnson Dennis's house, and made him leave his sick bed and vote the Democratic ticket; one of these men was named Lieutenant Joe Jacobs, of the Third District Station. At No. 14 Engine House witness saw white men point their revolvers at colored men's heads, and make them vote the Democratic ticket; he saw Judge Gastinel point his revolver at colored men's heads at the engine house of Pelican 1, Hook and Ladder No. 4 and make them vote the Democratic ticket; Judge Montamat and Arthur Guerin were, together at Poll No. 21 and forced colored men to vote the Democratic ticket. Witness further states that he saw Judge Gastinel, Mr. Sambola, and another man—all having badges on—with others, one night, in the latter part of October, go to Economy Hall, on Ursuline street, and destroy all the blanks for the registration of voters, and all the furniture in the room. The Supervisors of Registration held their office there. Witness intends leaving the State for fear of being killed; his life being openly threatened by one Oscar Blasco, Marshal of the "Innocent Club."

CROSS-EXAMINED.

Question (by Mr. Campbell)—Do you know Judge Gastinel?

Answer—I know Judge Gastinel by name, sight, and by reputation. I was raised with him all my life.

Question—You state that you saw Judge Gastinel make three (3) colored men vote the Democratic ticket, because they were afraid they would be killed; how do you know this?

Answer—I heard the threats, I heard Rousseleau say, "We will go in your bed and get you out, and you will be sorry for it; you had better vote my ticket." Judge Gastinel told them to vote; he would fix it all right with them; "they must vote his ticket." A young man by the name of Henry, who was along with me, witnessed this at the Engine house of Pelican Hook and Ladder, No. 4.

Q.—How close were you to the parties?

A.—About fifteen (15) feet.

Q.—Are you sure that it was Judge Gastinel?

A.—I am, for I know him very well.

Q.—You state that you saw Judge Gastinel and Mr. Sambola, with thirty or fifty other men, on the night of October 23, 1868, go to Economy Hall, and destroy blanks, furniture, and so on?

A.—I did.

Q.—Are you personally acquainted with Mr. Sambola?

A.—Not personally; I know him by name and sight; I used to go to his house before the war; I have known him for about twenty-five years.

Q.—State how close you were to those parties on that night, and if you are positive that they were the parties.

A.—I live a quarter of a block from Economy Hall. I was standing on the top of my gate, looking over at them. They were about fifty feet off. The moon was shining; it was a clear night; you could pick up a pin in the street. I recognized the parties plainly. While I was looking at them they went into the Hall. I heard the breaking of the things, and through the windows saw the breaking of the glass. After it was done they came out with a new banner in their hands, and passed right before my door; there were about thirty or fifty of them. A young colored man named Henry saw this beside myself.

Charles J. Fogarty states, on oath, that on the 3d day of November, 1868, he visited the polls in the Eleventh Ward, six in number. A Republican could not express his political sentiments without endangering his life. Nearly all the white men, (and they were numerous about each poll,) were armed with revolvers; Republicans were in the greatest danger, and probably would have been killed had they attempted to vote. Few Republicans voted, and upon inquiring of the negroes why they did not vote, they answered that they would not go to the polls because they believed that if they did they would be killed. Republicans, appointed as commissioners of election, refused to serve for the same reasons, and others were appointed.

Joseph Lee states, on oath, that he resides on Dryades street, between Common and Gravier streets; that on November 6, 1868, he was standing on the corner of Common and Dryades streets, at about half past ten o'clock A. M., when he saw a white man run out of a house and assault a negro, hitting him three or four times, and then drew his revolver and pointed it at said negro and said, "I am going to shoot that G—d d—d nigger." A policeman came up to interfere, when said white man pointed his revolver at said policeman, who turned and walked away.

James McDonald corroborates the above testimony.

The Committee append to the testimony from this parish the following evidence, in relation to a secret semi-military and political society, styled in its ritual "The Knights of the White Camelia."

The evidence shows that this organization extends throughout all the Southern States, and also has auxiliary branches in many of the Northern States, and particularly in New York city and Washington.

It is also in evidence, that this is the same organization which, under the common name of the "Ku Klux Klan," has committed so many crimes and spread such terror throughout the South for the past two years, and whose existence and operations have been reported to the War Department by Major General Thomas and Brevet Major General Reynolds, and which have also been exposed by Governor Clayton, of Arkansas.

The evidence before the Committee has come from persons within the order, and from different parts of the State and of the Union.

The evidence to the facts herein presented is signed and sworn to; the names of the witnesses are, for obvious reasons, withheld. The Committee are also in possession of much information of the local operations of the order in this State, which it is not deemed expedient now to publish.

—— states, on oath, that he is a member of the order of "Knights of the White Camelia," commonly known as the Ku Klux Klan, and that when seeing a special meeting called, which was done by inserting the following in the New Orleans Times: "K. W. C., No. —, important," he attended. He has also visited the following Councils of the K. W. C.'s, viz:

Council No. 11, Poydras and Carondolet streets.
Council No. 14, Magazine and Phillip streets.
Council No. 13, at the Fair Grounds.
Council No. 10, at the School of Medicine, Common street.
Council No. 9, Eagle Hall, Prytania street and Felicity road.
Council No. 4, corner Bienville street and Exchange Alley.
Council No. 8, corner Canal and Rampart streets.

The K. W. C. is a secret organization composed entirely of white men who are opposed to granting to any other race, or class of men, rights or privileges that did not belong to them before the late war. Before any person can become a member of this secret order his name must be presented by some member of the order, and balloted for at least one week before he can become a member; the person whose name is before the order is supposed not to know that fact, not even of the existence of the organization. One black ball is sufficient to reject—in that event he is never to know the fact. But if he is accepted, then the brother who proposed him may, (in as guarded a manner as possible) make himself acquainted with his views upon the matter of permitting the negro or African race to have any voice in the political affairs of this country, or of granting that race any rights or privileges that they did not *have or enjoy before the commencement of the rebellion.* If the applicant is found to be all right, or in other words, if he is unconditionally opposed to the African race having any control whatever of our political affairs, and also opposed to "Scallawags," or white men who believe that all men are born equal and entitled to equal rights and privileges upon this continent, and if he is willing to consider the last named class as enemies of the white race, he may be brought to the council room for examination, under oath. Before the candidate is permitted to enter the council room he must take the following oath, which is administered by the person known to the order as the "Grand Conductor."

You solemnly swear, in presence of these witnesses, that you will never, by word, act, or sign, or by any other means whatever, divulge or make known, to any person or persons, the existence of this order, its objects, its places of meeting, or the name of any person or persons you may see here, or anything you do now, or may hereafter see here, or suspect concerning this order. You further swear that you will make true and faithful answer to all questions that may be put to you by those who are authorized by this order to ask such questions, so help you God. For the faithful keeping and performance of this oath, you pledge your life and sacred honor.

The candidates are blindfolded and taken into the council room in charge of the Grand Conductor. As soon as they have entered they are challenged by the person who is at the head of the council, and known as Grand Commander, viz:

By Grand Commander: Who comes there?

Answer by Grand Conductor: Friends of our race.

Q.—What do they want?

A.—Peace and order and the observance of the laws of God and the maintenance of the constitution framed by our forefathers in 1776.

Q.—To do that what must we do?

A.—We must be joined together as brothers and united as are the flowers that grow upon the same stem.

Q.—Are they willing to join us?

A.—They are here to answer for themselves under oath.

The candidates are then seated and addressed by the Grand Commander as follows:

By Grand Commander: My friends, it becomes my duty to propound to you certain questions which you must answer truthfully. Your admission into this order depends upon your reply:

Q.--Do you belong to the white race?

A.—I do.

Q.—Do you believe in the superiority of the white race?

A.—I do.

Q.—Did you ever marry any woman that did not or does not belong to your race?

A.—No.

Q.—Will you promise never to marry any woman unless she belongs wholly to the white race?

A.—I will.

Q.—Are you opposed to allowing the political affairs of this county to go, in whole or in part, into the hands of the negro or African race?

A.—I am.

Q.—Will you do everything in your power to prevent its going into the hands of any inferior race, and especially that of the African race?

A.—Yes.

Q.—Will you promise, under oath, never to fail to cast your vote at any election for a white man attached to our principles, when he is opposed by a negro or one attached to negro principles, unless prevented by severe illness or other disability?

A.—I will.

Q.—Will you promise to defend and maintain the principles of this order against all enemies, and at all times and places to observe a marked difference between the white and the negro or African races?

A.—I will.

By the Grand Commander: You have answered the questions satisfactorily. It now becomes my duty to administer to you the oath that we have all taken.

The Oath.—You solemnly swear in the presence of these witnesses that henceforth you will maintain and defend the superiority of the white race upon this Continent, and at all times observe a marked difference between the white and negro or African races; that you *will do all in your power* to prevent the political affairs of this country, *in whole or in part*, passing into the hands of negroes or other inferior race; that you will never fail to cast your vote against a person opposed to our principles, who may be a candidate at any election for any office of honor, profit or trust, unless prevented by severe illness or other disability; that you will never marry any woman that does not belong to the white race; that you will *obey the orders of those who by our statutes have a right to give orders;* that you will at all times and in all places respond, if at the peril of your life, to a sign of distress or cry of alarm coming from any fellow member of this order, and that you will defend and protect them, and will do all in your power to assist them through life; that you will never reveal to any one, without authority, the existence of this order or its signs of recognition, its pass word, its signal of alarm or distress, or the name or names of any of its members or anything whatever that you may see, hear or know concerning this order; you further swear that you will always cherish those grand principles and use your influence, your intelligence and power to instil the same into the minds and hearts of others. For the faithful keeping and performance of this oath you pledge your life and sacred honor.

By virtue of the power in me vested, I now pronounce you "Knights of the White Camelia."

At this point the newly initiated are turned over to the Lieutenant Commander, who proceeds to instruct them in the secrets of the order, viz:

The sign of recognition is made by carelessly drawing the index finger of the left hand across the left eye, (all the other fingers of that hand closed). If the person addressed be a member of that order he will respond in like manner. If either party have any doubts he will ask the question, "Where were you born?" The answer is, "On Mount Caucasus." *Q.*—"Are you free?" *A.*—"I am." *Q.*—"Were your ancestors free?" *A.*—"They were." *Q.*—"Are you attached to any order?" *A.*—"I am." *Q.*—"To what order?" *A.*—"To the order of the Knights of the White Camelia." *Q.*—"Where does it grow?" *A.*—"On Mount Caucasus."

The order has a signal of alarm, which is given by four raps with the hand upon the door of the council for entrance. The same number of raps are given upon the bells for a grand alarm.

There were in August last fifteen (15) Councils of K. W. C.'s in the Parish of Orleans, but they now number eighteen (18), one of which is the Grand Council for the Parish of Orleans and State of Louisiana. The Grand Council is composed of three members.

The Grand Commander and the Grand Lieutenant of a council are allowed to sit with the Grand Council while transacting the business of their immediate Council, and at no other time, so that the Grand Commander and Grand Lieutenant of each Council take their turn sitting with the Grand Council. Each Council reports to the Grand Council once in each week; the Grand Commander and the Grand Lieutenant take the report of their Council to the Grand Council and sit with them while receiving the report and transacting the business of this Council and retire with the verbal orders from the Grand Council, which they deliver verbally to their Council, thus making the number present, while transacting the business of any particular Council, five (5).

The city of New Orleans, Algiers, and Jefferson are divided into military districts, with a Grand Military Commander for the State, and subordinate officers for the districts.

The Grand Military Commander for the State of Louisiana is ——.

The organization comprises principally ex-rebel soldiers, although any youth of eighteen and upwards can become a member, whether a citizen of the United States or not. All the banished and transported desperadoes now in New Orleans are members of the K. W. C.'s or K. K. K.'s.

The reckless, disappointed, Democratic politicians are all members. Many merchants, clerks, and brokers, have been drawn into the order under the pretence of uniting to redeem the State from the so-called negro rule. These men are withdrawing from the order as they discover its criminal designs. Every foreigner, whether he had been in the State a week or no, that could be made to promise that he would vote the Democratic ticket was brought to the Democratic Committee, and they (the committee) would give the friend of the foreigner who brought him a note to the Democratic Judge of the court, who would give said foreigner naturalization papers, so that he could register and vote; thousands of names were registered in this way. Every member of the order who could not procure a revolver was supplied with one by the Councils; the members subscribing according to their means. Muskets were procured also, and armories established where the members (K. W. C.) drilled.

In case the order and signal was given for a general massacre of the loyal whites (scallawags and carpet baggers, as they call them) and blacks, all the members of the order (K. W. C.) could go to the gun stores, or places where arms were sold, and take them, and the

Council would afterwards pay for them. In case of a massacre, if the military interfered they would fight them too, and they openly boasted that they could "clean the military out in fifteen minutes."

The house of every prominent Republican was watched, and the hours that each kept, so that in case of a massacre they would know where and when to find their victims. In October, 1868, they concluded to break up the Metropolitan Police force, under the pretence that "they were not a lawful force, and were not capable of preserving the peace," notwithstanding the K. K. K.'s were the only ones that did disturb the peace, and to arrest one of them would have been the means of calling out twenty thousand armed men.

During the disturbance in Jefferson and Gretna, six black men were murdered in Gretna and their bodies thrown in the Mississippi river by members of the K. W. C's. It was the intention of the K. K. K.'s to kill enough Republicans before the election to intimidate the rest from coming to the polls; they said they had no hopes of Seymour's election, but they were determined to redeem the State of Louisiana from negro and Radical rule.

The murders committed in the State of Louisiana, in the different parishes, were committed by the K. K. K's. The braves [members] would boast among themselves of killing, saying, "I took two niggers down" and "I took one down," etc.

Their mode of assassination was as follows, to wit: When any Republican becomes prominent in the carrying out of the reconstruction laws of Congress, or by his expressing a desire to allow the black man his equal rights before the law, or in keeping company with black men and instructing them in their political rights, such Republican becomes hateful to them, and they wish to get rid of him in any way; they call it "attending to him;" and when a member wants a man killed he will say in the Council of which he is a member to the Grand Comanander, and those present "I want ———," (giving the man's name and address in full), "attended to," then gives the reason why he wants him attended to. When it is put to a vote of all the members present, and if a majority of votes cast are in favor of the proposition, it is granted; but if a majority of votes are not in favor of it, then nothing is done; but if it should be carried and granted, they then elect a member to carry out the designs. If any one is proposed by another he stands up, and if the members think him a fit person he is elected, but if not he is rejected, for the reason that they do not consider the brother a fit person to participate in the work on hand. If a brother is elected to perform any work, and rises up to excuse himself as being sick, etc., a doctor is called—a member of the order—and if pronounced well and in good health, he is then branded as a coward and not permitted to enter the Council in future, and is again sworn to secrecy as to what he knows.

In cases where a man is to be "attended to," reckless desperadoes are always proposed and elected. When a man is to be killed in a district, word is sent to another district and a member is sent to do the work, giving the members in the district where the victim lives due notice of the time it is to take place, when they are on hand in waiting, and if the brother gets into trouble the members in waiting assist him to their utmost ability. In the country parishes they send word to an adjoining parish, and that council elects a brother to do the work, who immediately notifies the brothers of the council in the parish where the victim lives, and they are about at the time specified, when if the brother gives a sign of distress, they rush forward and assist him. The K. K. K. members boast that the Legislature—*i. e.* the present body—will never be allowed to meet here again.

This order exists in all the Southern States; but in some to a greater extent than in others; in the States of Louisiana, Mississippi, Arkansas, Georgia, Tennessee and Texas to a greater extent than in the others. The members of the order say "they will remain united as long as a black man holds office;" but a black man can vote free provided he does not vote the Republican ticket. Witness further states that he has the names, residences, and business of the wealthier members of the order, and of the prominent men in the councils. They talk of reorganizing the order, altering the constitution, and changing the signs and pass words. It is asserted by members of the Ku-Klux that they are glad the Radical Legislature are moving their quarters from the Mechanics Institute to the old Louisiana Bank, as they did not want to see the Institute burned down, which would be the case if said Legislature continued to occupy it, and that it is very doubtful whether the Legislature meet in January or not. Bets have already been made that the Legislature will not meet. One man said on Canal street on Sunday that every man who had a white heart was a walking arsenal, and by two words he could have Canal street in an uproar. He said that the military forces would not last five minutes—besides, he knew the military authorities sympathized with the white people of New Orleans, and that it was, and is the determination of the whites to remain united until the last Radical and nigger is out of office.

The following is a continuous narrative of some of the secret proceedings of this organization in New Orleans for the two months preceding the election:

SEPTEMBER 15, 1868.

The city is laid out in military districts, and every member is required to arm himself.

OCTOBER 2, 1868.

——— states, on oath, if a member is able to walk he must go to the place armed and ready for action; in no case must a member provoke a quarrel; if he does, he will get no assistance, even if he is killed, so long as he commences the disturbance and is to blame for it.

They are determined to resort to violence in case Grant is elected; they propose to raise all over the South.

They call it slow poison to have a black man to rule over them.

They also say that in case of a disturbance that no man under General Rousseau will shoot at a white man.

OCTOBER, 1868.

The members at No. 9 met last night at —————, up stairs.

They appointed a patrol of one hundred men divided into groups of ten each, who have a chief, and they all under a grand chief, ———. They are to meet every night at 7 o'clock in case they should be needed; as matters now stand they will not patrol except called out.

The G. C. said last night: "Brothers, all of you that can come to drill, do so; the armory is up stairs."

A supply of arms has arrived here lately; it is stated that the order now numbers sixteen thousand (16,000) in the parish of Orleans, La.

There is a move on foot in the city (October 29, 1868) to put Judge Ong, of St. Bernard, out of the way. The orders come from St. Bernard parish.

OCTOBER 10, 1868.

Council No. 4 met at the fair-grounds. Nearly all the members are foreigners. The meeting was a special one, called by order of the

Grand Council. Resolutions were passed urging every man of foreign birth to go forward and procure naturalization papers, and to see that every man did so, whether he belongs to the order or not. It was also stated that there would be no trouble in getting papers, even if the applicant was only three days in the country, as the Democratic Committee had matters arranged with the Courts about giving men papers. Resolutions were also passed forbidding Democrats to employ a colored man, except that he could get his services for a less price than that of a white man; also prohibiting members from talking or associating with white Republicans, or even to do business with them, when it could be possibly avoided.

OCTOBER 25, 1868.

Council No. 15. On Friday there were two colored men killed, and in the evening there were five colored men killed, by members of Council No. 15 and some members of the "Wide Awake Club." The bodies were thrown in the river. (Some of the members of No. 15 say that there were six colored men killed and thrown in the river.)

There are about twenty United States soldiers in Gretna; they are drinking whiskey with the Democrats, and say that they (the soldiers) do not care a d—d how many "niggers" are killed. Yesterday (24), the Democrats or K. K. K. pointed their pistols in the faces of the Metropolitan police and made them march down to the river.

Orders have been issued to all the Councils to hold themselves in readiness until election, and to carry their arms with them.

The "Innocents" will march to-morrow evening (2500 strong) through those portions of the city that are the most thickly settled with colored people.

JEFFERSON, OCTOBER 26, 1868.

The authorities of Jefferson had nine men in custody last evening, seven of them members of the Metropolitan police and two suspected spies, who gave some signs of the K. K. K., but could not carry them out.

On Saturday five men were arrested as spies, because they could not show all the signs and pass-words; but afterwards, proving that they belonged to Council No. 12, they were released.

Twenty men have been detailed from each Council, to remain in Jefferson and do picket-duty, until the police matter is settled. Large numbers of the K. K. K. have come to Jefferson from adjoining parishes; they are armed with shot-guns; every man is well armed.

OCTOBER 28, 1868.

There were one thousand Manhattan revolvers received on Friday by one of the commanders of the "Braves," expressly for the members, to whom they have since been distributed. The revolvers have six chambers and a six-inch barrel. On Friday and Saturday night the "Braves" had mounted pickets about the outskirts of the city, none inside of Claiborne street. These pickets were to see if any crowds of colored men assembled. They had a lariat or lasso, and pretended to be catching stock. The outskirts of the town were watched because the major part of the colored people lived there.

OCTOBER 26, 1868.

It was announced in the Councils of the K. K. K. some nights ago, that if any disturbance took place all the members who had no arms could go to the gun store—the proprietor of which was a member of the order—and get all the arms they wanted, and the order would pay the bill.

The Democratic Central Committee granted permission to the "Innocents" to parade, the object being to intimidate and frighten the colored people. They rejoice in the belief that they have that accomplished already.

A large attendance was had at every Council last evening. No business was transacted; the members were merely present for the purpose of being on hand in case of a disturbance. Extra patrols and pickets were out last night from every Council.

Some of the members are very uneasy and anxious to kill certain Radicals. They say that unless an example is made of some one, they will not leave nor will they keep away from here and let the black man alone. They boast of having the Radicals, both white and black, cowed down.

Large numbers of the K. K. K. moved about in groups in the back part of the city. About one hundred of the Wide Awakes and Innocents carried muskets and shot guns; every man was armed with one or two revolvers and knives.

A supply of arms having arrived, the different Councils are now furnishing them to those who have none.

OCTOBER 27, 1868.

If a disturbance takes place in Jefferson there will be one started in Algiers, so that the colored men living over there, and who it is thought would go to Jefferson on hearing of a disturbance, will be kept across the river. Council No. 15 is in Algiers; the K. K. K. care nothing about the military, as they say that the military cannot get around fast enough for the kind of fighting they will do. The K. K. K. will not commence a disturbance, but will give cause to be attacked in some manner, when they will call all members to action by their signs and signals.

OCTOBER 30, 1868.

Council No. 9, seventy-two (72) members present, met last night over ————, Camp street; they went up into the third story to drill, those who had been in the Confederate army declined to drill, stating that they were perfect in drill. About thirty (30) men then drilled for about fifteen or twenty (15 or 20) minutes. The room is a bad one, and it is the intention to get another in the Second Ward, which the Council represents. There were about one hundred new muskets there, and it is believed that they were brought there since last Wednesday night. The Chief of the hundred patrol knows where the arms are stored.

OCTOBER 31, 1868.

Council No. 10 met Saturday evening. The Grand Commander requested all the members to go to the polls armed, but under no circumstances to try to keep any colored man or white Radical away from the polls, as the Democrats were certain of carrying the State; that matters had gone too far already, and that the Radicals would take advantage of what had occurred.

NOVEMBER 13, 1868.

Council No. 9 met last night; twenty-five new members were admitted; violent speeches were made by ——— and ——— to the effect that the organization had acted on the defensive too long; that the Radical party had been the aggressors for the last six months, plundering the people, etc.

They spoke very bitterly against Lieutenant Governor Dunn, saying, "here is a negro that could be bought for fifteen hundred dollars ($1500) seven years ago, now the Lieutenant Governor of the State and President of the Police Board—how long are we to put up with it?" They also complained about the Radical Press getting to know too much about them.

NOVEMBER 18, 1868.

Council No. 14 met last night; a letter was received and read from the Tammany Hall (N. Y.) Vigilance Committee, recommending four (4) men to the "tender mercies" of the K. K. K.

These men are noted Radicals, and they will be watched; the letter will be sent to every Council in the city.

NOVEMBER 26, 1868.

They talked of revising the whole Constitution, and reorganizing the order, and excluding a certain class of members, who they say never ought to be admitted, viz: Loafers.

DECEMBER 3, 1868.

One man said that they had been outraged, the G. C. replied "Yes, and the eyes of twenty thousand indignant men will watch the traitor, he need not think that he will escape, he will be found sooner or later." In Council No. 4, they think that it is one of their members who has betrayed them, and in No. 14, they strongly suspect ———.

COUNCIL NO. 14, DECEMBER 9, 1868.

The Grand Conductor said that they might as well throw the doors open and admit everybody, as there was no secret about the order now. He also spoke of the benefit derived from the organization, and the great necessity for keeping it together, saying that it was the fear of the order that kept the Radicals in the Legislature from passing several extreme measures; he also told the members that nothing had been received from the Grand Council yet. The members, in speaking of the Legislature, say that it will not be allowed to meet. They also say that they will positively kill every black man that is put on the police. Some say that when the Legislature meets there will be a committee to wait upon the Governor and first request him to urge the repeal of certain acts, and if he refuse, they will then demand their repeal. The notices in the Times calling special meetings are for effect, merely to make people believe that they are not affected by the exposure of their signs, etc.

There are a number of the members of Council No. 10 who drill every night at ———, Canal street. They drill with muskets—the muskets are always found in the drill room when they meet. Only one hundred drill at one time, as that is all the muskets they have there. Council No. 9, meet and drill in the room over ——— on Camp street. Each Council has a drill room; each Council also details a certain number of men armed with revolvers—most of them the Manhattan revolvers—that were received from New York for distribution, and which have been referred to at earlier dates. During the riots these armed men patrolled the city, and when they met a colored man they would assault, rob, and sometimes kill him. This patrolling party broke up the Republican Club rooms. This patrolling party was divided into groups of ten men each, with a chief, and the whole under a grand chief. When these groups met a policeman they would assault or kill him.

—— —— states, on oath, that on or about the twenty-sixth day of October, 1868, he was in the Merchants' Bank, on Camp street, and while there saw several gentlemen come into said bank and go into the back room, where they were met by some officers of the bank, who delivered to them money or a check, and ordered the bookkeeper to make the entry of money paid to purchase arms to keep the peace.

ORLEANS—SUMMARY.

Number killed	63
Number shot	11
Number maltreated	87
Total victims of massacre	161

APPENDIX.

The following affidavits and statements were received too late to be compiled in the body of the Report, and are here inserted as an Appendix:

PARISH OF ST. LANDRY.

F. J. D'Avy states, on oath, that he is a citizen of the State of Louisiana, and a resident of the parish of St. Landry; that on Monday, September 28, 1868, he was informed that Emerson Bently had just been killed at his school house. He proceeded immediately to the school house, and meeting Bently about one block from the school house, he learned from him (Bently) what had just transpired; that the Seymour Knights had called upon him and administered to him a caning, because of an article published in the "Progress" about a meeting held at Washington. Witness is of the opinion that Mr. Bently's editorial report of that meeting was moderate and entirely truthful. While Bently and witness were proceeding together they met B. R. Gantt, a member of the Democratic Committee, when witness informed him of what had transpired and asked him what he had done in the case, and what steps he had taken towards having the assaulting parties arrested. He replied that "he had nothing to do with it." Witness then referred him to the treaty which had been made by joint committee of both parties the week previous guaranteeing the preservation of peace and order during the campaign (Gantt was a member of that committee). Gantt replied "D—n you and the treaty. If you are not satisfied with it, tear it up and go to h—ll." Witness then left, and soon meeting several Republicans, related all that had transpired—the conversation with Bently and Gantt—and while doing so he noticed a great stir around the court house, some twenty or thirty men riding to and fro at full speed. Witness then left these parties and went towards the court house, where he met Dr. James Ray, a member of the peace committee and asked him what was meant by the excitement. He answered that "it was nothing; in a few moments it would subside."

Two or three minutes after, the court house bell rang, when witness saw men coming from all directions—some mounted and some on foot—armed with shot guns and revolvers. Witness then met P. L. Hebrard, a Democrat, who advised him to go home. He said the excitement would subside after a little, but he would advise him (witness) to keep out of sight, as he being the leader of the Republicans, and being on the street at that time of night, might tend to excite the feelings of the people more. Witness then started to go home, and when nearing the "Progress" office he met a company of the Seymour Knights mounted and armed with shot guns and revolvers, commanded by one Ned Lewis. As they passed witness some one of them remarked "Where are your niggers now, God d—n you." Witness then went in the "Progress" office and found Mr. Bently in bed with a high fever. Mr. Donato and others having sent to witness to know what steps it was best to take, witness replied that "the only thing to be done was to telegraph to the Governor." They agreeing with witness, he sent for a courier while he wrote the dispatch. While witness was writing the dispatch near the window up stairs in his house he saw his rebel uncle, Yoes D'Avy, with a shot gun going towards the Catholic church; at the same time August Perodin passed him on horseback armed also, and asked him where he was going. He (Yoes D'Avy) replied "on picket." By the time half of the telegram was written, witness was informed that they were fighting at Paillet's plantation. He started immediately down town, and on reaching the "Progress" office saw several companies of armed white men coming up the street, stopping all colored men, beating some and searching others. Witness called Linden Bently and informed him of the fact and told him to close the "Progress" office and get away with his brother as soon as possible, as he (witness) anticipated very serious trouble. Witness then went to Felix Lessassier's grocery, where he met Gustave Donato, and while talking with him was told by a colored man that "several companies were coming up town after them, and to get out of the way as quick as they could." Witness proposed to these gentlemen to come home with him. They hesitated, and he proceeded home alone and remained in his garden until after dark and then went to get his supper. While he was at supper he was informed that everything was becoming quiet and there would be no danger. He retired to bed sometime after supper, and about 10 or 11 o'clock he was awakened by his aunt saying, "My son, they are after you." She opened a clothes press and shoved him into it. Some of these men knocked at the door, saying, "We want D'Avy, we will not hurt you, do not be afraid." She refusing to open the door, they procured some instrument (witness thinks it was an axe) and was about to break open the press when his aunt opened it, and witness stepped out saying, "here I am gentlemen, I am but one man." Witness then heard the same remark that he had heard during the evening, viz: "Where are your niggers now, God d—n you." Witness recognized Ned Lewis as the commander of the company. A great many hands then laid hold of witness and dragged him into the street, where he received a blow with the butt of a gun, near his arm pit, knocking his shoulder out of place, and at the same time he was shot on the right side of his head, the bullet glancing on the cheek bone below the temple; the force of the powder stunning him and causing him to fall, he feigned death until his enemies departed. This company halted a short distance from the house, when another company, of horsemen, rode up, crying out, "What is the matter here?" and receiving the reply from the former party "it is nothing, it is D'Avy who is killed;" they answered "bully for that." They also indulged in hearty laughter after passing witness. Witness seeing several men coming back with shot guns he arose and ran through the house. A volley was fired at him, but he escaped. On passing through the parish, witness found the public roads guarded; he was halted once by pickets and was once captured, but escaped with an ankle out of place. Witness could state some other incidents in this connection, but will not, as it would endanger the lives of his friends. He was eighty days on the way from Opelousas to New Orleans, having left Opelousas on the 28th day of September and arrived in New Orleans December 17, 1868. During this time he was concealed and traveling through fields, woods and swamps; he had several opportunities of conversing with some of the bitterest Democrats, who expressed themselves freely to him, not knowing who he was. These parties said that the State now being in the Union, no one or two companies of Yankees could come there and rule them as they had done heretofore; and if they attempted such a thing, they would "give them the worst thrashing they ever had;" and no "carpet-bagger" or scallawag could ever come and live in that parish again. Now they had the upper hand of the Radical negroes, they intended to keep it. These parties told witness that they had destroyed the nigger paper, or "black swan," the Progress, and that they had killed between three hundred and fifty and four hundred Radical niggers, about the majority the Radicals had over them. It is the opinion of the witness that no Union or loyal man can live with safety in the parish of St. Landry, and that no redress can be obtained by them through the present civil officers of the parish. Deputy sheriffs and other leading citizens were at the head of companies, committing depredations, arresting peaceful citizens and lodging them in jail. These prisoners would disappear before morning. The bloody work was carried on with enthusiasm, even women exulting in these deeds. Witness estimates the number killed during the riot in St. Landry parish between four and five hundred, there being from five to ten persons killed every night from the 28th day of September until the 3d day of November, 1868, about which time the murders ceased.

Stephen Jones states, on oath, that on the 29th day of September, 1868, he was in the town of Opelousas, parish of St. Landry, and while returning from his work on said day, he was approached by Mr. Francois Richard and about 25 other white men, all armed with revolvers, etc. They accused deponent of shooting Dallas Hays on Saturday night; deponent told them that he was not guilty of the act; they said he should never shoot at another man, and ordered him to walk before them to the road. The leader of these men, Francois Richard, sent one of his men to Opelousas to ask Solomon Loeb, the President of the "Seymour Knights," what they should do with him. F. Perodin, Deputy Sheriff, returned with the messenger; he remarked, "boy, walk on before me," which witness did, going towards Opelousas. When they arrived on the outskirts of the town F. Perodin ordered him to enter the woods, which he did; he then told him to enter some brush; deponent, thinking they were going to kill him, ran; while running, a white man named Henry Quatreveaux shot him in the arm, the ball passing through his muscle; another passed through his thigh. In this condition he took refuge in the field of Enos Parrots, where he remained until night, when he went to his home, and putting on his shoes left for Washington and New Orleans; he was five weeks in making the journey. Deponent has left his family in destitute circumstances, and states that his life would be in great danger if he should attempt to return.

PARISH OF EAST BATON ROUGE.

Jacob Church states, on oath, that he has lived in the city of Baton Rouge, parish of East Baton Rouge, for the last forty-eight years; that on or about the 10th day of October, 1868, several colored men presented themselves at the registration office, at the court house, for the purpose of getting registered; while they were quietly waiting their turn, Thomas Brady, the City Marshal, came to the door where said colored men were standing, and said, "they must stand back;" a colored man answered, "that they had as good a right to get registered as any body;" Brady then said, "If you don't stand back, I will shoot your head off;" the colored man told him "to shoot;" Mr. Brady then turned and went off. There were from two to three hundred colored men that would have registered at the court house if they had not been prevented from doing so by white men, armed with all kinds of fire arms, who would press them out of their positions in such a manner that they would not be so foolish as to attempt to register, knowing that if they were not shot or clubbed on the spot, that they would be "marked men," and subject, sooner or later, to the maltreatment of the Democrats. Deponent was prevailed upon to call on the Mayor, Hon. James E. Elam, and put these facts before him; in reply, the Mayor said: "He could not help it; that it was done by the order of Sheriff Bird." Deponent then left and went to the court house and told his friends what the Mayor had said; they said: "Very well; there is no use to try to register, then; the way they are pushing and jerking us about plainly tell us that they do not mean to let us." On the 3d day of November, 1868, between the hours of 2 and 3 o'clock P. M., deponent went to the poll at the court house to vote; after he got there he saw the impossibility of doing so; policemen demanded the colored people to show them their tickets, which demand being refused, the colored men were forcibly pushed away from the polls by said policemen; deponent saw at least twenty or thirty treated in that manner; there were some colored men that voted, but they had to vote the Democratic ticket. About 4 o'clock P. M. about fifty deputy sheriffs and policemen, with revolvers in their hands, fell in line outside of the court house, by order of Edward Cheatam, Deputy Sheriff. The colored men seeing this warlike demonstration, walked and ran away; Cheatam and Mayor Elam called upon them to come back, that they would not be hurt, but the colored people were filled with terror, and could not be persuaded to come back. The streets were patroled by bands of armed white men day and night. Deponent firmly believes that no less than two or three hundred colored men were frightened away from the polls at East Baton Rouge on the 3d day of November, 1868.

PARISH OF ST. BERNARD.

John B. Jacques states, on oath, that he was commissioned a Metropolitan policeman on the 19th day of October last, and reported the same day to the Lieutenant of Police, Third District, for duty, and was directed by him to go to the court house in St. Bernard Parish, and report to Corporal Taylor, of the Metropolitan police force. He arrived at the court house on the following day, and reported himself according to his instructions; he was put immediately on duty. The next day he was told by several colored women passing by, that he had better not walk far from the court house, as the white people said "they were going to kill all the Metropolitan policemen." While deponent was at his house on the 30th day of October last, two white men, one Tanas and Robert Ducreaux, went there at 5 o'clock P. M., with a colored man named Wm. Gofney, who was their prisoner; the white men were armed. Gofney called to deponent to "come out," which he did; the white men said: "you are our prisoner." Deponent asked them "why?" they answered, "were you not with William Godchaux, to kill Mr. A. Mararo at his plantation?" (Battle ground plantation). Deponent said, "no sir;" but seeing that they were determined to take him prisoner, asked permission to return to the house and get his coat, (he was in his shirt sleeves). Ducreaux replied, "no, I will shoot you if you do; get some one to bring out your coat, but you cannot go in the house." Deponent's little boy brought him his coat. He was then taken, in company with the colored man Gofney, to the parish prison, in New Orleans, by Mr. Ducreaux, Mr. A. Mararo, and Mr. Challiere, the Sheriff of St. Bernard. He was confined in prison from Friday at 8 o'clock P. M., until Sunday morning at 7 o'clock, when he was released and taken back to the parish of St. Bernard by Sheriff Challiere, Mr. Dublanc and Felix Poke (all of St. Bernard) and confined in the court house jail, where he was confined eight days. The same day that he was released, Mr. Marard told him that he had been imprisoned because it was reported about that he had been down on his plantation to do him some harm; but he believed he was innocent of the charge, and got the Sheriff to set him at liberty. Deponent told him that he was innocent, and that he had not been down to his place. There were eight or nine other colored men confined in jail at the same time that deponent was, and released with him; but they were innocent of any crime, as proved before Judge Toker at the court house.

The following letter was received by the Hon. Thomas Ong:

PARISH ST. BERNARD, December 19, 1868.

MR. THOMAS ONG:

DEAR SIR—I called on Judge Thornton to make the affidavit I spoke to you about, and he refused to arrest the parties. He states that the freedmen could get no justice in that parish, and if he arrested the parties it would be at the risk of his life. I saw General Lee yesterday, and he thinks Judge Thornton is right, as for the present it would be impossible to convict those parties in St. Bernard. * * * * * * * *

Yours truly,

(Signed) H. M. WHITTEMORE.

Mr. Whittemore is agent of the Freedmen's Bureau, and the parties spoken of are accused of having committed certain murders and outrages in the parish of St. Bernard on the 26th, 27th and 28th days of October, 1868; and the above agent was ordered to make affidavit by General Hatch, Assistant Agent Freedmen's Bureau for this State.

——— states, on oath, that there were from thirty-five to fifty colored people killed during the recent riot in St. Bernard parish. One woman was shot in the abdomen, while she was lying in the gutter pleading for mercy. A colored man was shot near her, and afterwards cut to pieces with a knife. These two persons were killed within half a mile of where the United States troops were stationed. It is believed that at least one-half of all those killed in the riot were killed after the arrival of the troops. Colored men say that the white people said to them, "I suppose you think the soldiers came down here to protect you, 'niggers,' but you will find out that they came here to protect us, white people, before they go away."

About one week before the riot commenced it was stated by Michael Curtis, the Metropolitan policeman who was murdered during said riot, that it would not be safe for any Metropolitan policeman to go by the house of Pablo Fillieu, as he had threatened to "kill every Metropolitan policeman that passed there." This man Pablo Fillieu was said to have been a very passionate and vindictive man; the colored people generally were afraid of him. It is stated that Pablo Fillieu fired the first shot the night that he was killed, and that the colored people demanded an entrance to his house, it was presumed to get whiskey, as he had been in the habit of selling them liquor.

——— ——— states, on oath, that a party of white men named Julien Cerpas and his son Oscar, Philip Gautier, Victor Stopena, Victor Besant, Pepi Stave, and his son Joseph, Leona Stopena and his son Raphael, and Raphael Vaillon—all planters, went to Jules Dirkins plantation, in sight of the court house, on Monday the 26th day of October last, at 3 o'clock, P. M., and surrounding the colored people's quarters, commenced an indiscriminate fire upon them, killing a colored man named Pierre Gaulet and wounding three men and one woman through both breasts. These men took twenty dollars in greenbacks from George Washington and three dollars and a razor from another colored man, both hands on the place; they also broke down the door to witness' cabin. The white men of the parish made all the colored men vote the Democratic ticket at the late election, giving them to understand that they would all be killed if they should vote the Radical ticket. The only reason that the above named white men gave for killing and wounding the said colored people was, using their own words, "We want to kill all the Radical niggers in the quarters." They would have shot more, but all that could ran for the cane, where they hid until the slaughter was over. Another squad of armed white men went to the plantation of Mr. Oliver the same day, and took four colored men from their quarters and shot them dead. The day after the

Presidential election a squad of white men went to the plantation of Mr. Cofield, about 3 o'clock, P. M., and took a colored man from the field; they asked him "how he had voted." He replied, "like the rest of the colored men." Not being satisfied with this answer, they took him to a ditch and cut him to pieces and left him there. A white man in the parish by the name of Pablo Fillieu had been in the habit of making threats against the colored people if they should vote the Radical ticket. At a Democratic meeting held at his house on the 25th day of October last, he laid plans with the white people present to go that night to the houses of the colored people and shoot them down as they presented themselves at the door. Witness heard that the said Pablo Fillieu fired the first shot the Sunday night that he was killed.

PARISH OF ST. MARY.

C. H. Alden states, on oath, that the recent election in the parish of St. Mary was a perfect farce; that he has been living in said parish since January last, and that all was quiet until three or four months prior to said election, when the Democrats commenced making all kinds of threats, denouncing all who did not favor and acknowledge themselves Democrats, and that they also intended to kill all who did not support Seymour and Blair." Deponent was told after the election that if he did not leave the Radical party he would share the same fate as all the leading Republicans; which was, that he would be put out of the way so soon as they (the Democrats) should gain sufficient strength; this was said in a threatening manner, by an old citizen of the parish, two or three months before the election. The Republicans have a large majority in the parish of St. Mary, but they are colored people, and easily intimidated by the white Democrats. The colored Republicans had their clubs well organized throughout the parish, but these clubs were broken up on several occasions by the brutal treatment of the Democrats; notwithstanding this, they remained firm up to the time of the assassination of Col. Pope and Judge Chase. On the same night, all the homes of the leading colored Republicans of the town of Franklin were searched, but the occupants were not found, as they had that day attended a Republican meeting in the upper portion of the parish, and did not return, hearing of the murder of the said Pope and Chase, and that their own lives were threatened, and knowing full well that they, too, would be killed if they should return to their homes. The following day (Sunday) all the Democrats of Franklin were on the streets armed with guns and pistols; deponent, not understanding the meaning of this demonstration, left town. Mr. Snear, a member of the board of supervisors, left at the same time. They had searched Snear's boarding house for him the night before; he made his escape out the back way and came to the city, where he remained. Deponent remained with a friend that night, down the Bayou, and learning the following day that all was quiet at Franklin, returned to said place, as he was Chairman of the Board of Supervisors, and considered it his duty to go back and complete the business appertaining to the office, although his life had been threatened by such remarks as "you are the only white Radical in the parish now, and we will get you." The supervisors of each board had all left except deponent, and Capt. Abe Smith, who had just returned from the city, with extra blanks for the office. Deponent tried to get Republicans to assist him in the business of registration, but failed; he was therefore compelled to appoint Democrats as supervisors. From the time that Col. Pope and Judge Chase were assassinated the streets of Franklin, and in fact the entire parish, was under patrol. The last week of registration passed off quietly; there were very few colored men registered during this time, in consequence of the great excitement prevailing, and they knowing that the roads were well guarded where they would have to pass. On the following Saturday the office was closed and deponent left for the city, as he had been told by a friend that he was not safe one moment after the closing of the office of registration. Deponent returned to Franklin a few days before the election for the purpose of appointing Commissioners of Election. He was compelled to appoint Democrats, Republicans being afraid to act; while performing this duty he was again notified to leave, with others, and did so the day previous to the election. Deponent has been informed by some of those who were present on the day of election that there was much fraud practiced by the Democrats. On the night of the 18th of October, 1868, the office of the "Attakapas Register" was broken open, and the contents, consisting of a portion of the press and type, taken out and thrown into the river.

PARISH OF TENSAS.

St. Joseph, La., Parish of Tensas, December 15, 1868.

Colonel—Inclosed find the Coroner's report of a murder committed in this parish shortly before the late election. With the exception of this unfortunate affair, I am happy to say that good order has prevailed in this parish, and the citizens, black and white, voted as their own wishes dictated, which accounts for the large majorities we gave for Grant. Very respectfully,

(Signed) H. R. STEELE, Parish Judge.

Colonel Hugh J. Campbell, Chairman Committee on Condition of Peace and Order in the State.

The testimony inclosed corroborates the testimony before published under the head of the parish of Tensas.

PARISH OF CADDO.

The following is the copy of a telegram received by Governor Warmoth:

"Shreveport, December 19, 1868.

"To his Excellency, Governor Warmoth:

"William Pittman and Heuly, under sentence of imprisonment for life, pronounced this morning, for murder of Bob Watson, a colored man, were rescued by an armed crowd from the custody of the Sheriff on their way to the jail after sentence. The excitement here about it is intense. The police jury offer one thousand dollars reward. Will the State offer five thousand dollars, or how much?

"JOHN J. HOPE, Sheriff Caddo parish."

PARISH OF MADISON.

Hon. Curtis Pollard states, on oath, that he is a citizen of the State of Louisiana and a duly registered voter. Last Saturday night about fifteen armed white men, four of whom were disguised by having white sheets thrown over them (about ten of these men were on horseback), came to my house in Madison parish, which is situated opposite to Vicksburg, about an hour after dark. I had heard a few days before this visitation that men were coming to kill me, and consequently was on the lookout for them. About the time they arrived I had ten guards about my place. These men in white sheets approached my house, and seeing them, my friends and self fired at them, they then run away. I do not know whether any of them were hit or not. The following night these same men went to the house of Mr. John McDonald, sheriff of the parish, elected on the Republican ticket at the spring election, and made an attempt to assassinate him. Mr. McDonald also had some friends with him in his house to protect his life, and seeing these men, fired at them, but do not know whether any of the shots took effect or not. On the 29th of December the said sheriff's house was visited again by the same party, who made another attempt to kill him, but were discovered in time to be prevented in their design. The white citizens of the parish are continually abusing the colored people on account of the little crops they have raised; they say they are going to take their crops away from them, also their stock and money, or else take their lives. About four weeks ago a claim agent, who was telling colored men (ex-United States soldiers) in the parish how to get their bounty, was taken from his house at 12 o'clock by eleven or twelve Ku Klux (hand cuffed) to Milliken's bend, tied to a tree and whipped with a cowhide, and told to leave the parish immediately, which he did by the first boat that night.

The colored people in the parish live in a great state of terror from the threats made against them and outrages committed by the white people, so much so that they are afraid to rent or work land on their own account. The white people say that they will not rent any land to colored people that voted for General Grant unless they pay them twelve dollars an acre rent for the land, and then they must pay them half cash down. The white people know very well that the colored people are not able to make any such arrangement, thereby depriving them of doing anything for themselves. The colored people are very anxious to rent or buy land upon the same terms as are offered to white people, which is from two dollars and a half to three dollars per acre. Colored people in many portions of the parish were made to vote the Democratic ticket by the Ku Klux. Many of the colored people were deprived of the right to register in consequence of the threats made against the Supervisors by the Ku Klux, which prevented them from visiting certain portions of the parish.

PARISH OF ST. HELENA.

Samuel H. Houston states, on oath, that during the Presidential election in the parish of St. Helena, there was a perfect reign of terror. The so-called Democratic party of this parish beat and miamed several negroes, because they were Republicans, and in some cases murder was committed. John Kempt, a mulatto, coroner of said parish, was taken from his house and brutally murdered by an armed mob, about forty in number, who went over the parish and committed other murders. The black people were run into the woods, and in many cases the women were cruelly whipped. The planters read a resolution to the negroes (that had been adopted by the Democratic clubs throughout the parish) informing them that they *must* vote the Democratic ticket, otherwise they would run them out of the country. The negroes on Abram Wormack's plantation relate the facts as above stated.

Witness was a registrar under General Buchanan, in this parish, and while acting in said capacity he was very kindly treated by the people, but when he returned during the campaign his life, and that of General Sypher, was threatened, and he believes that they would have been murdered had they visited Tangipahoe, as they were advertised to do. The house in which he resided was entered by a mob, who came for the purpose of murdering him, but having been notified of the danger, he had previously left. Had the election been a fair one the Republican ticket would have had from two to three thousand majority. Witness was informed by a Democrat of truth and veracity that at least one hundred and fifty negroes were murdered between Carline Bluffs and Shreveport, in a few days preceding the late Presidential election.

The following is an official statement of William Baker, Chairman of the Board of Registrars, as to the conduct of the election of the 3d of November, 1868, in the following parishes:

PARISH OF JEFFERSON.

In the parish of Jefferson the riot and murder of a number of colored citizens was but another link in the chain with which loyal citizens were to be bound and deprived of the right of exercising the franchise, except at the risk of their lives. One of the most intelligent and useful of the Registrars was threatened and told that his life was to be the price of his daring to continue in the performance of his duties; his family was also visited and threatened. Under these circumstances he resigned.

In this parish (Jefferson), on the day of election, one of the Commissioners reports "that three or four gangs, numbering some two hundred men each, went to Kennerville on cars or special trains provided by the Jackson Railroad. They were apparently organized bodies and all armed." These rowdies demanded that the returns should be made out in their presence, "and even went so far as to enter the private apartments of the Commissioners and with drawn revolvers and every conceivable kind of weapon forced the Commissioners to make the returns at once," "and owing to threats and intimidations the tickets were forced to be thrown under the table and destroyed against their will."

One thing with reference to the vote in the parish of Jefferson I forgot to mention. It is this:

There are registered in Carrollton, Kennerville, Gretna and the Glassworks, Precincts 2, 3, 4 and 5		3461
Whites	1061	
Colored	2400	—3461
Democratic vote in the four precincts........	995	
Republican vote in the four precincts.......	658	
Total number voting..................		1653
Registered whites not voting...............	66	
Colored men not voting....................	1742	
Total not voting......................		1808

Thus showing that considerably less than half of the registered voters voted.

PARISH OF ST. BERNARD.

In the parish of St. Bernard, such was the state of things that two of the registrars had to take to the swamp for safety, and wait for the excitement to abate. One of the registrars came to this city and has not been heard of up to the present time. No commissioners of election were legally appointed, and no legal election was held in the parish, so the registrars report to this office.

PARISH OF ST. LANDRY.

The registrars of the parish of St. Landry report that for nearly two months before the election a state of anarchy existed in the parish, and that over two hundred colored men were murdered during that time. Of the election they say such was the state of things at that time that no one would have dared vote any but the Democratic ticket, except at the risk of his life.

PARISH OF WASHINGTON.

In the parish of Washington, the registrars had to go armed night and day, and were frequently threatened and insulted. Colored men were beaten and obliged either to vote as directed, or not at all. So outrageous were these acts of violence, so far was it from being a fair election, that the registrars refused to certify to the returns, "regarding the election in this parish as carried by the knife and revolver."

PARISH OF PLAQUEMINES.

The registrars for the parish of Plaquemines report that legal voters were refused the right of voting; others were permitted to vote on old registration papers; some who were not residents of the parish were allowed to vote, while many, from the murders in the city of New Orleans and the adjoining parish of St. Bernard, were so intimidated that they were afraid to vote. In one precinct an election was held by unauthorized parties, and should not be regarded at all, under any circumstances. But for these influences the registrars report that the Republican ticket would have had six hundred more votes in the parish.

PARISH OF ST. MARY.

The parish of St. Mary, add what has transpired there during the time the Board of Registration has been in existence, is too well known for any one to contend for a moment that anything like a fair election has been held in the parish. I have no other comments to make; I merely submit a copy of a report by the registrars of the parish:

NEW ORLEANS, November 6, 1868.

WILLIAM BAKER, Esq.,
Chairman Board of Registration:

SIR—The undersigned, Supervisors of Registration for the parish of St. Mary, would respectfully represent that the returns of the election from said parish have been duly sent in; but, under the existing circumstances, we have seen proper to make this further statement:

The chairman of this Board, a resident of the said parish of St. Mary, was compelled by threats to leave the upper end of the parish, and other members of the Board were driven out of Franklin several days before the election. Such an amount of violence and intimidation was used before the election and on the day of election, that we are satisfied that the election in the parish was not an expression of the will of the people, and we believe the returns from all the precincts, except Brashear and Pattersonville, should not be counted.

Not fully knowing our powers under these peculiar circumstances, we have signed and sent in the returns accompanied with this further statement of the facts.

Very respectfully.

Signed by the Supervisors of Registration of the parish of St. Mary.

PARISH OF EAST BATON ROUGE.

In the parish of East Baton Rouge the circumstances attending the registration and election, although not accompanied by the same amount of violence as is found in many other parishes, yet the facts show clearly enough that no election such as is contemplated by law was held. The parish being a populous one, two sets of Supervisors were appointed, so that all duly qualified might have an opportunity to register in the short time allowed by law. One Board was to be located in the city of Baton Rouge, the other was to move from point to point in the parish. When the moving Board came to Manchac, they found it impossible to get accommodation of any kind; they were unable to hire any place for an office; no one would supply them board or lodging. They proposed to erect a temporary shed for registering in. Colored men and others were forbidden to work for them. So after traveling a day and night, they had no other alternative but to return to Baton Rouge, where they announced they would be ready to register all who came and were qualified. By this time a large number of colored men were in the city of Baton Rouge waiting to be registered, but had up to that time been unable in consequence of the interference of the Mayor, Sheriff and others, who insisted the Registrars should only register one colored man for every white man registered. As there are about five colored men for every three white men in the parish, this course would necessarily have prevented two fifths of the colored men from registering. The presence of the second Board in the city of Baton Rouge gave the opportunity for these men to register. At this moment Messrs. Fugua, McCollum and others, obtained from the Parish Judge, a writ of injunction prohibiting the second Board from proceeding any further in the work of registration in the parish of East Baton Rouge, thus practically closing the registration office seven days sooner than provided for by law, thereby preventing, it is believed, about twelve hundred colored men from registering, by a base use of the law, and the prostitution of justice, to serve the purposes of those who are legally disfranchised. With respect to the election in East Baton Rouge, the protest of four of the Supervisors of Registration is the best evidence in what light it is to be viewed. The original protest is attached to this communication, so that your Excellency may see for yourself:

Parish of East Baton Rouge, La., Nov. 9, 1868.

To Chairmen and Members of Board of Registration.

Gentlemen—We, the undersigned, Supervisors of Registration of the parish of East Baton Rouge, do solemnly protest against the election held in said parish, on the third day of November, 1868, for the following reasons, viz: That being obstructed by the Parish Court, and want of material, we failed to complete the registration of the parish by about (1200) twelve hundred persons, who would have registered.

The conduct of the police, who were authorized by his Honor, Mayor Elam, and Thompson Bird, Sheriff, to keep the peace, at the Court House, First Precinct, on the day of the election, was outrageous in the extreme, they taking away the ballots of citizens wishing to vote for Republican Electors and Congressmen, and substituting other tickets instead; on their refusing to vote said substituted tickets they would destroy their certificates of registration (This was not done in every case, but in many). In consequence of the threats and intimidations used by said police, about (200) two hundred men left the poll without voting. All other precincts in the parish (with the exception of the first) were conducted in accordance with law. We signed the returns of the election believing it was required by law, otherwise we would not have done so.

We have the honor to be your obedient servants,

(Signed by the Supervisors of the Parish.)

PARISH OF CLAIBORNE.

We append a letter from the Hon. W. Jasper Blackburn, of Claiborne, member of Congress from the Fifth District. Mr. Blackburn being one of the oldest and most respected citizens of the State, with a record as a Union man throughout, and as an editor and citizen *sans peur et sans reproche*, his testimony will deservedly have great weight throughout the Union. The following is his letter:

HOMER, LA., December 15, 1868.

Editor in Chief New Orleans Republican:

MY DEAR FRIEND:—Beside the second destruction of my printing office, there have been many other foul and cowardly outrages committed in this parish since the election. Several freedmen have been shot, and numbers of persons, Republicans, both black and white, have been taken out at night and whipped most unmercifully, and ordered to leave the country. In consequence of such brutal and heathenish conduct as this, many of the best citizens of the parish both Democrats and Republicans, have moved away, and others are constantly leaving. And yet the infamous, rotten, cowardly Rebel press of the country seem to think it strange, "passing strange," that any one should leave so good and so peaceable a land as this! Would you believe it, that the entire press of this section—all Rebel and Tory now, since the brave mobbing of the loyal offices—come out openly and commend and recommend mobocracy, and set assassins and outlaws upon the loyal officials of the land? Such is the plain and naked truth!

To prove this, I will give you just a few sample extracts from these journals, which I trust you will find room for, to the end that their infamy may have the extent of your circulation.

And as "charity begins at home," so will I.

The Claiborne Advocate of the twenty-eighth ultimo, published at this place, and edited by one John Doe and one Richard Roe, has the following article:

ARKANSAS.—This State is cursed beyond all others but Tennessee, in the low and vindictive wretch whom the Radical party have elevated to the position of Governor. He has declared martial law in a considerable portion of the State—is organizing negroes into regiments, and hounding them on to the destruction of the white population. He has started three companies of negro soldiers to find Cullen Baker. If he would head this delectable battalion in person, we would wish him God speed in the object of his expedition. There is no greater good could happen to Arkansas than for Governor Clayton to go in search of Cul. Baker—and find him.

The Southwestern, of the 25th inst., published at Shreveport, speaking on the same subject, has the following:

"ARKANSAS MILITIA IN THE FIELD.—A Little Rock dispatch, of the 9th, says Governor Clayton had sent three companies of negro militia to look for Cullen Baker. We hope they will have a good time of it. Sending negro troops to hunt up Cullen Baker is like sending a small sized male individual in search of a streak of chain lightning. Ugh! Governor Clayton has also ordered the raising of six thousand cavalry throughout the State. Serious trouble is apprehended."

Now, we all know who "Cullen Baker" is—a gentleman in his line, I take it, compared with any editor who would put forth such paragraphs as either of the foregoing, and we also know who Governor Clayton is, and are somewhat acquainted with the condition of Arkansas. We all know something of the outlawry and assassination there, which have compelled Governor Clayton to resort to the stern constitutional means which he has called into requisition to enforce order and bring about peace—precisely the means which will have to be used in Louisiana before murderers and robbers can be made to know their place and feel their just doom, and the sooner the better. None but assassins at heart, and the cowardly aiders and abettors of thieves and robbers will object, under the circumstances, to the employment of such means to enforce the laws.

I will begin at home again, and give another quotation from the Claiborne Advocate. In that sprightly sheet, of the 5th instant, we have this item:

"ANNULLING THE ELECTION.—We understand that Warmoth, Governor, "so-called," has issued a proclamation declaring the election of three Democratic members from this State to Congress a nullity. This action, on the part of his Excellency, which has neither law, precedent or reason for its sanction, is based upon allegations of terror and fraud, which never had any existence except in the Governor's imagination.

"This thing of elections by the people, at least in the South, is rapidly degenerating into a farce.

"We shall not, however, be at all surprised if it eventually ends in tragedy.

"Our people have already endured more from the carpet-bag dynasty, in the way of outrage and oppression, than they would have submitted to but for the peculiar circumstances surrounding them. But endurance has about ceased to be a virtue. We have tried the effect of turf upon these incorrigible rascals in the political apple tree. It is about time to resort to stones."

* * * * * * * * * *

But seriously, if Governor Warmoth should do what the Advocate here seems fearful he will, he will only have done a just and righteous thing. What, tolerate such outrage and infamy as were perpetrated by rebel outlaws and assassins at the late pretended election in this State? Never! It does seem to me that the Governor, with others who had the official counting of the vote, should at once have declared the whole thing null and void. If it is not yet done, either by the Louisiana officials or at Washington, the whole question of voting in this State will have become a farce too contemptible and too corrupt to be tolerated, or at least too much so for any decent, honest man to ever again take any part therein, as they most assuredly were not permitted to do so, in this section, at the late so-called elections. Wipe the whole thing out and let us, in the future, have at least some show of decency and fairness at whatever cost.

I might proceed to give many extracts to show that the rebel-tory press of this section encourages and recommends mobocracy.

The Shreveport Southwestern of the 2d instant, the leading instigator of riot and mobocracy in Northwestern Louisiana, contains the following characteristic item:

"ANOTHER RADICAL PRESS DESTROYED.—The Rapides Tribune, published at Alexandria by W. F. McLean, has gone the way of the Homer Iliad. Some party who had the good of the community at heart, entered the office at night and destroyed the press and type."

And such is the general tone of the Tory press throughout the country.

* * * * * * * * * *

And that pink of decency and chivalry, the Alexandria Democrat, encourages and justifies the mobbers of McLean's office at that place by saying it was the work of himself or some of his friends, thus aping the villainous slanders of certain political nondescripts and reckless liars who had similar remarks to make in regard to the first mobbing of my office. * * * * * * *

Now what does all this prove? Simply that the "public sentiment" of this country is at present manufactured, swayed and directed by influences that are as foul, vicious and corrupting as the very society of hell itself!

Is there any way to remedy this? Or shall the evil be endured forever?

It is useless, worse than folly, to listen to the protestations of peace and good will from those whose past history in this respect prove them as false as the author of lies.

When Mr. Breckinridge—the immortal "John Cataline!"—heard that Mr. Lincoln was assassinated, he simply remarked, using a quotation:

> "If 'twere well done when 'tis done,
> Then 'twere well it was done quickly."

And this is precisely the spirit which still actuates his leading followers. Assassination is a mild remedy with them when a brave and honest man stands in the way of their success.

Indeed, it would seem that the best of them are hardly reliable or to be trusted under the most sacred circumstances. * * * *

I tell you what they will do: They will lick the dust from the feet of General Grant, and the next moment murder a man for voting for him! They are acting in this way constantly. The rebel organs of the South vehemently pleading for a conservative administration and mild terms at the hands of the incoming President, while their debased minions are assassinating every man they can find who voted for him! And this infamous conduct these leading devils indorse. And not only so, they instigate and advise it. They gloat over and glory in it! And shall such men be trusted? Shall they be tolerated?

Shall such editors be fostered and permitted to manufacture and direct "public sentiment," while loyal editors, who sustain the Government and advocate peace under the rule of right and justice, are mobbed with impunity, and robbed of their hard-earned property and forced to leave the country or be murdered or starve? I merely ask for information. * * * * * *

I want it known that I ask no mercy or immunity at the hands of the common foe; and especially do I want my friends to know that, notwithstanding I have been time and again mobbed and hunted down by rogues and rascals and cowardly murderers, "I still live," and am yet man enough to be "just and fear not."

W. JASPER BLACKBURN,
Fifth Congressional District, Louisiana.

As an illustration of Mr. Blackburn's perfect knowledge of the people with whom he has to deal, and of a political foresight and a penetration into the real designs of the conspirators of this State, which it is to be regretted that more persons had not shared before the last election, and to show how subsequent events more than confirmed his first predictions, we reprint a portion of his testimony, as published in our former report. His statements were at that time denounced and branded as false and malicious by the Democratic press and by Democratic members of the General Assembly, with what truth the facts recorded in these pages will show.

Extract from the evidence of the Hon. W. Jasper Blackburn before this committee, published in their report of September 24, 1868:

CLAIBORNE PARISH.

For weeks previous to the late election (of April 1868) parties of armed men with blank book and pencil, perambulated the country, called on freedmen in the fields, at their cabins, or on the highways, wherever they could find them, and by menaces and threats forced them to swear that they would not go to the election, or if they did that they would not vote for the then pending Constitution, or for the Radical State ticket, and after thus procuring the names and pledges of the freedmen, these hostile white men told the freedmen that if they failed to keep their oaths or pledges thus extorted, they would kill them. After this conduct had progressed for some time, certain parties who had been thus misused called at the office of a certain loyal justice of the peace by the name of Wilson Adams and made affidavit to the facts here mentioned. These affidavits were sent to the Sheriff of the parish, who declined to execute them or have anything officially to do therewith, giving as a reason, that he could not do so without the aid of more physical force than he could command. By this means hundreds of freedmen were deterred from going to the polls.

And besides this, armed men appointed by the so-called Democratic party for that purpose, attended the different polls in the parish, challenged votes, browbeat and threatened freedmen, thus deterring many from voting at all who attended the polls to vote the Radical Republican ticket, and forcing others to vote the Democratic ticket. All these facts, and more of a similar character, are patent to the public mind of the parish of Claiborne.

I further testify and swear that pending the ratification of the Constitution it was not advisable or safe in the parish of Claiborne for any man to favor, or advocate on the stump, the adoption of that instrument, nor was it safe for any man, white or black, to vote openly for the adoption of the same on the days of the election. I would state that since the close of the war, and especially for the few months previous to the late election and immediately thereafter, what is termed the ruling public sentiment of the white people, was very hostile toward those termed loyal citizens regardless of color, but more especially toward leading freedmen who had taken a prominent part in elections and political matters, some of whom have been murdered on account of their political sentiments and activity in politics, and many more greatly abused and outrageously tortured, nor do I know of a single instance of any effectual attempt to bring any perpetrators of these outrages to an account before the civil tribunals, or to a proper punishment in any way.

In regard to the late election in the parish of Claiborne and some of the adjoining parishes, I would state that I look upon the whole transaction as a farce and a cheat, and a perfect mockery upon the elective franchise: for instance, at the election for members to the late Constitutional Convention, where there was no brute force used to deter men from voting as they pleased, and when the Democratic party had in the field regular nominees, intelligent and popular gentlemen, and had also induced an independent Republican ticket to run, nevertheless the regular Republican nominees were elected by a majority of about one thousand, whereas, at the recent election, by means of fraud and violence, the Republican ticket was defeated by a vote ranging from four to six hundred majority, whereas, the registered vote shows a majority of about fifty blacks, with several hundred white minority.

I would mention as a sample of the unfairness used, the fact that at the precinct called Terryville, where the registration shows a large Republican majority, there was not a single Republican vote polled. This fact was boasted of by Democrats before the poll was counted, thus showing that they knew by previous concert of action what the result was to be; and this is but a fair exposition of the manner in which the late election was conducted throughout North Louisiana.

I wish to state that during the pendency of the reconstruction measures of Congress, I stood almost alone in their advocacy and defense among the white men of my section.

Prominent freedmen have been taken out at night since the late election and terribly whipped; one in the vicinity of Homer named Scott, and one within the corporate limits of said town, whose name I do not now recollect, but who had been employed about the office of the agent of the Bureau, and who was known to be a prominent Radical.

The main features of this statement I swear to positively, and unhesitatingly assert that there is no feature thereof which is not the current information of the section in which I live. I would not impugn the motives of my political adversaries who are my neighbors, but we differ so much in our notions of right and wrong in such things, that what I would swear to as radically wrong they would swear to as radically right; for instance, many of them hold that it is proper and legitimate for an employer to discharge a freedman if he refuses to vote as he dictates, whereas, I hold that such conduct is wrong and inadmissible, and is prostituting the elective franchise and subversive of liberty.

I give it as my deliberate testimony under oath that, to the best of my knowledge and belief, I do not think it is the purpose or intention of what is termed the secession element in the South—the so-called Democratic party as it now stands organized—including as it does almost the entire white population of the country, I do not think it is the purpose or intention of this element ever to submit quietly to negro suffrage, unless they find they can control it for their own purposes. Whenever they can find a black man whom they can control and who will vote with them, he is all right and a very honest fellow—he must vote; but freedmen who vote the Radical or Republican ticket are great rascals in the fair and impartial estimation of these liberal-minded and constitution-loving Democrats, and ought to die, and frequently do.

The truth is, the ruling Democratic element in my section will not listen to reason or argument on the political issues of the day. If a man says he is a Radical or Republican it is enough, "he is a negro equalitist;" such is their argument and it is folly to waste breath with them.

Nothing, in my estimation, but the election of a true and firm Republican as President of the United States, can restore the country to quiet and peace. If this is not accomplished I fear all is lost.

APPENDIX—SUMMARY.

Number killed	151
Number shot	2
Number maltreated	11
Number of Republicans excluded from registering	300
Number of Republicans excluded from voting	2108

The following affidavits were received after the foregoing had gone to press:

PARISH OF RAPIDES.

B. C. McKinney states, on oath, that he is a citizen of the State of Louisiana, and a registered voter in the parish of Rapides. On the third day of November, 1868, he was appointed and sworn in as Commissioner of election at poll ——, Plainsance Ward. When he arrived at the poll he saw Mr. M. Ryan and Captain J. G. Hoe, and other white men, present. Mr. Ryan objected to their holding the election at that precinct, on the ground that the previous election was held at Mr. Hoe's store. The Commissioners held the first election at Mr. Hogan's, and no objections were made. When they were about to open the polls in the morning Mr. Ryan came in and protested against holding the election at that place, and said it was illegal. Louis Taylor, deputy sheriff, asked Ryan to keep order in the house. Ryan replied that he wanted to put one of the citizens out of the house, and added that he would have Taylor arrested and charged with assault and battery. Mr. W. S. Calhoun said to the Commissioners that if they could not hold a peacable election they had better close the box. Taylor went up to Mr. Ryan and told him if he did not keep order he would be compelled to put him out of the building. Mr. Ryan then left the house and went out into the yard, and remained there with his friends for sometime, and witness heard nothing more from him during the day. He was drunk and very insulting to all in the house. On or about the seventh day of November witness was arrested at W. S. Calhoun's plantation, by Harris, deputy sheriff, on a warrant issued by W. W. Whittington, a justice of the peace in Alexandria, and was carried to the court house before Whittington, and was tried on the charge of holding an illegal election, and found guilty. The affidavit was made by Ryan. Witness was placed under two hundred and fifty ($250) dollars bonds. The court room was crowded with Democrats, who were all armed with revolvers. Mr. Calhoun was grossly insulted by Ryan while a prisoner in the sheriff's office, and was in the court house abused very much by Ryan. Witness and Mr. Calhoun have to appear and stand their trial in the month of May at Alexandria, and if there is no more protection for them than there is now, witness does not think that their lives would be safe. He is positive that had Messrs. Calhoun, Taylor and himself gone to Alexandria unaccompanied by their friends one if not all of them would have been murdered. Witness does not think that a fair election can be held in Rapides parish without the aid of the military.

Hon. W. S. Calhoun states, on oath, that he is a resident of Rapides parish, State of Louisiana, that on the 3d day of November, 1868, he was a commissioner of election at Pleasant's Ward, parish of Rapides. He arrived there at 6 o'clock, A. M., and saw Judge Ryan who was opposed to holding the election. Witness remarked to him that "this was a Democratic trick for the purpose of preventing the commissioners of election from holding the election," and then said to the colored Republicans who were present, "you see the Democrats are your friends, and don't want you to vote." After this remark, J. G. P. Hoe made a Democratic speech to the colored people, telling them that they were free, and to vote for whom they chose, but not to be led by a d—d puppy. The said Hoe was armed with a club and revolver, and had about ten of his company with him, all armed. The commissioners then proceeded to a room to hold the election, and were sworn in by one Lewis Taylor, a deputy sheriff, who delivered the ballot box to them. Judge Ryan went into the room with the commissioners, he being in a beastly state of intoxication, and was so boisterous that they could not proceed with their business; the said Ryan protested against the election, and made threats to arrest the commissioners and send them all to the penitentiary.

Witness told the colored Commissioner, B. C. McKenney, that as they could not hold a peacable election, they had better go home. Ryan finding that the Commissioners were about to do so, ordered the polls to be opened, still using improper language, and threatening witness, that he would report him to Congress; witness remarked that he had better wait until he got there. On or about the 7th day of November, 1868, Deputy Sheriff Harris came to witness' house with a warrant for him to appear forthwith before W. W. Whittington, justice of the peace, at the town of Alexandria, on the charge of holding an illegal election; witness not thinking his life was safe took a friend with him, and accompanied the deputy sheriff to Alexandria, where they arrived on the 8th; the deputy took witness before the Justice; while in charge of said deputy, witness was most grossly insulted by Judge Ryan, and the civil authorities would not protect him. Justice Whittington put witness under five hundred dollar bonds, but Ryan objecting to this, he was allowed to go on his parole to appear at 10 A. M. on the 9th. Witness was notified by his friends to leave the town, as his life was in danger, which he did; but returned the next day and appeared before the justice of the peace; he found much difficulty in securing the services of an attorney on account of his political opinions; but finally did secure the services of Judge Cullum, and stood his trial, was found guilty of the above charges, and put under bonds in the sum of one thousand dollars, to appear before the next term of the District Court; witness immediately left the town, and is certain this plot was laid in order to assassinate him. He is satisfied that no fair election can be held in the parish of Rapides without the protection of military authority.

PARISH OF ST. BERNARD.

J. Lewis Spalding, commanding the United States forces in the parish of St. Bernard, states: "On the 15th day of November, (Sunday) I left Lee's plantation in company with General A. L. Lee, for the city of New Orleans, taking a carriage from his place. I left him in the city and returned myself the next day; I arrived at the court house about dark. After taking dinner, I started on my return, stopping at Ong's plantation to change my horse for a mule; the night was exceedingly dark, and I allowed the mule to take his own way, I being unable to see. About three miles from Ong's in the most lonesome part of the road, I heard the cry *halt*, coming from one or two voices; the mule at once stopped; I demanded the cause of this with some emphasis, at the same time taking my pistol ready for any emergency; almost instantly a light from a dark lantern was thrown into the carriage, the lantern being in the hands of some party on horseback on my right; by this light I could discover two more men on horseback on my left, armed with guns. As soon as it was seen who I was, I heard one of them say to the others in Spanish, that it was the Lieutenant, when one of them rode up and said they expected a friend, and wanted to frighten him. I told them to go on, which they readily did. The following extract from a letter of Lieutenant John Hamilton, will tend to explain the cause of my adventure: * * * * "I was astonished to hear of your adventure last night, it clearly demonstrates the fact that the evil passion of these cut throats have not yet subsided, but I do hope that a day of reckoning is near at hand. * * * * I think it would be well for you to make a statement of the occurrence of last night, and forward it through me to General Neill. I think the intention on the part of these vagabonds was to make an attack on General Lee, or Mr. Ong, had they been in the carriage with you. I think it is but right that the proper authorities should be put in possession of the facts. * * * * * * * I have been in command of the troops in this parish for two months, with the exception of a few days that Lieutenant John Hamilton, first infantry, was here, it is my decided opinion that during the past twelve weeks there have been no less than thirty or forty murders committed in this parish, and I doubt if the annals of crime furnish more brutality than these murders indicate.

It is presumed by some that this is only the sixth day of creation, and that the devil was to be let loose a short time before the end of the creation, which was to be the millenium. If such is the case I am inclined to believe that the "old gentleman" has slipped one or two links, if not the whole chain, in this parish. It is not without reason that history has always been considered as the light of ages, the faithful evidence of truth, and the source of prudence and good counsel. Confined without it the bounds of the age and country wherein the people of this parish live, and shut up within the narrow circle of such branches of knowledge as are peculiar to them, and the limits of their own private reflections, they have continued in a kind of depraved infancy which leaves them strangers to the rest of the world and profoundly ignorant of all that has preceded or even now surrounds them; thus situated they have only sought out all that is infamous and vile, and all that can debase. I have not the time nor the disposition to write of the many acts of villainy they have committed since my stay here and known to myself, and I am glad that I have not the time, for I desire to forget that such a people live; their brutal life and character is fully written in the habits of the Alligator. But I have written more than I intended and will close." * * * * * * * *

General A. L. Lee states, on oath, that he is informed by Lieutenant Spalding, of the United States army, that on or about Sunday, October 25, 1868, the day when Pablo Fillieu, a party of white men armed visited the "Daguin plantation" and there took by force a negro man and cut his "ham-strings," and then forced him to try to walk; after torture these men then shot the negro to death.

THE REPORT OF THE FREEDMEN'S BUREAU.

Through the kindness of Brevet Major General Edward Hatch, Assistant Commissioner, and of Brevet Lieutenant Colonel Lucius H. Warren, Acting Assistant Adjutant General, your committee are enabled to append a full detailed copy of the report of murders and outrages during the months of September, October and November, 1868, made by the Bureau from this State to headquarters at Washington. The report of murders in St. Bernard parish during the massacre of October will be found under a separate heading. Part of the report of the Bureau covers the same ground as that of your committee, but the largest portion of cases specified in the two reports are distinct and separate.

The Bureau also seems not to have completed its reports from all parts of the State; for instance, its report states little in reference to the massacre of St. Landry, of which your committee has a detailed account. On the other hand, the report of the Bureau from Caddo and Claiborne parishes is much fuller than that of the committee, it having been impossible, on account of the frightful lawlessness and terrorism prevailing in those parishes, for your committee to procure testimony from them.

The total number of murders included in the following reports of the Bureau is two hundred and ninety-seven.

Total number of other outrages is one hundred and ninety-two.

List of Murders and Outrages Reported to Headquarters Bureau Refugees, Freedmen and Abandoned Lands, District of Louisiana during the month of September, 1868.

PARISHES.	When Com'ted.	On whom Committed.	By whom Committed.	Nature of Outrage.	Remarks.
St. Landry and Calcasieu.	Not stated	William Johnson, colored	Name not stated, white	Killed	No action reported.
	Not stated	Jacob Johnson, do.	Name not stated, white	Driven fr'm homes located under homestead act	No action reported.
	Not stated	Edward Armstead, do.	Name not stated, white		
	September 28	Emerson Bently, white	Dixon, Mayo and Williams, white	Whipped	(Result of riot in St. Landry parish.)
	September 28	Two white men	Opelousas riot	Killed	Others are supposed killed in isolated places, but no positive evidence of the same.
	" 28	Nineteen freedmen	"	"	
	" 28	Two white men	"	Seriously wounded	
	" 28	Two freedmen	"	"	
	" 28	Not specified	"	Slightly wounded	
St. Mary.	Not stated	One freedwoman	Overseer Darnell Plantation	Assault and Battery	Accused under $250 bonds.
	September 13	Freed girl	Two white men	Rape attempted	One accused escaped, the other arrested, alibi proven, and discharged.
Natchitoches, Sabine, and Winn.	Not stated	One freedman	McElroy and Pearsons, white	Brutally dealt with	Lebuzan and two deputies arrested, tried by parish Court, were attempting to arrest McElroy and Pearsons at time.
	"	McElroy, white	Labazan, col., Constable, and two deputies, colored	Shooting, both seriously wounded	
	"	Pearsons, do.			
	"	John Battise, colored	Ranny McTiers	Assault	Referred to civil authorities.
	August 29	Brantley H. Allen, colored	Persons unknown	Lives attempted; several shots fired at them	Allen was teacher of colored school.
	" 29	Hull Frazier, colored	"		
	September 18	Adam Carnahan, white	"	Murdered	Supposed by reason of an old feud, designing parties endeavor to implicate the freedmen.
De Soto.	Not stated	One freedman	Not stated	Killed	On Mrs. Child's plantation.
	About August 16	James Stewart, colored	James Mosely, white	Shot through the head	No action taken.
	About Sept. 6	Bryant Offord, colored	Name not stated, white	Killed; stabbed thirty-seven times	Friends of deceased dare not complain, though perpetrators can be identified.
	September 18	Robert Stebbins, colored	James Taylor Meens	Killed	No arrest made.
	" 18	George Meens, colored	James Taylor Meens	"	No arrest made.
	" 18	One freedman	James Taylor Meens	Life attempted	No arrest made.

It is also stated that numerous other murders and outrages have been committed but the same have not been specifically reported.

List of Murders and Outrages, etc. — (Continued.)

PARISHES.	When Com'ted.	On whom Committed.	By whom Committed.	Nature of Outrage.	Remarks.
Caddo and Bossier.	September 2	Henry Jones, colored	Persons unknown	Shot; attempted murder	No action taken. *
	Rep't'd Sept. 20	**			
	Rep't'd Sept. 30	Reverdy Ogden, white	Bossier Riot.	Killed	On the 29th inst., at Shady Grove, eight miles from Shreveport.
	" 30	James Brownlee, white		"	
	" 30	Thirteen freedmen		"	
	" 30	Two freedmen		Shot and wounded	
	" 30	One freedwoman		Killed	
	September 25	William Ewell, colored	—— Frye, white	Shot and killed	About two miles from Shreveport.
Claiborne.	Rep't'd Sept. 10	***			
	Rep't'd Sept. 20	Harrison Christopher, col.	Five colored men	Shot and killed	†
	Rep't'd Sept. 30	Freedwoman	Whiteman	Assault and battery	Referred to civil authorities.
	About Sept. 26	Tom Anthony, colored	K. K. K.	Murdered	
	" 26	William Wallace, "	"	Do.	
	" 26	Moses Ferguson, "	Not stated.	Driven from parish	About the last of September.
	" 26	J. Bishof, "			
	" 26	Isaac Bradley, "			
	" 26	One freedwoman	Peter Harwell, white	Shot and wounded	††
	" 26	Nathan Hodges, colored	James Keener, white	Ill treatment	‡
	" 26	Green Hinton, colored	Not stated	Supposed murdered	‡‡
Catahoula.	September 7	Moses Neuville, colored	Four white men	Whipped and beaten	Badly cut with strap.

* Jones was taken from his home, shot, placed upon a brush pile, which was fired, and left for dead. He afterward succeeded in crawling off, though badly burned.

** That freedmen in the northern part of the parish are constantly being taken from their homes by desperadoes, and either killed, or forced to leave their homes, crops and everything they possess; that no laws of any kind are enforced.

*** States there is a spirit of brutality and terror reigning throughout the parish, and freedmen are daily driven from it, leaving their year's labor and themselves destitute; that cases are daily referred to the civil authorities, but no action is taken; that the parties complained against are by some means informed of the fact, and freed people are taken from their homes, or stopped on the highway and then taken to the depth of some wood, and whipped or shot. The freedmen are forced to leave the parish or be in constant dread of being killed.

† On the night of the 15th inst., the five colored men were arrested, tried and acquitted, and have since left the parish. It is also stated that Christopher was taken from his home by two white men and given to the colored men, with instructions for them (the colored men) to kill him; but no evidence substantiating the same was taken.

†† Harwell took a pistol and chased freedmen about town; he shot one freedwoman in the leg, snapped two caps at others, was arrested, and fined $12.00.

‡ Was compelled to leave his home and his crop; will not be permitted to return unless he submits to a punishment of one hundred lashes.

‡‡ Was taken from his home in September, head shaved, shot at, not since heard from.

List of Murders and Outrages, etc.—(Continued.)

PARISHES.	When Com'ted.	On whom Committed.	By whom Committed.	Nature of Outrage.	Remarks.
Tensas and Concordia.	Rep't'd Sept. 20	George Dyson	Calvin Humphreys	Shot and killed	Accused, arrested and released on bail to appear at next session of Court.
Ouachita and Jackson.	Rep't'd Sept. 30	William Bishop, white	Not stated	Assault and highway rob'ry	Attacked and robbed of his money and papers between Vernon and Trenton. One man arrested charged as being accessory to the act.
East Felicians.	September 26	Prince Orange, colored	Dewitt Carter	Assault and battery	Referred to civil authorities.
Madison.	September 12	One freedman	Freedman	Shot and killed	Accused arrested.
Orleans, Left Bank.	September 25	Edward Forrest, colored	Arthur Guerin, white	Shot and killed	Accused arrested; under $5000 bonds for manslaughter.

I certify that the foregoing is a correct list of murders and outrages as reported to these headquarters during the month of September, 1868.

LUCIUS H. WARREN,
Brevet Lieutenant Colonel United States Army, Captain Thirty-Ninth Infantry,
Acting Assistant Adjutant General.

SUMMARY—SEPTEMBER.

Killed		52
Wounded		11
Maltreated		18

NOTE—Numerous other murders and outrages committed which have not been specifically reported.

List of Murders and Outrages Reported to Headquarters Bureau Refugees, Freedmen and Abandoned Lands, District of Louisiana during the month of October, 1868.

PARISHES.	When Com'ted.	On whom Committed.	By whom Committed.	Nature of Outrage.	Remarks.
Orleans, Jefferson, Plaquemine, l'ft b'nk	October 25	Two Freedmen	Riot in Gretna	Killed	
	" 25	Three Freedmen		Shot and wounded	
	" 25	Two white boys		"	
Orleans, Left Bank.	October 24	Two white men	Riot October 24	Killed	Others supposed wounded, but not reported.
	" 24	Seven freedmen		"	
	" 24	Five freedmen		Wounded	
	October 27	One freedman	White men, names not stat'd	Killed	Names not reported.
	" 27	One freedman	White men, names not stat'd	Mortally wounded	
	" 27	Jack Handy and others, col.	Armed white men.	House broken open	
	" 27	Warrick King, colored	" "	Rob'ry registrat'n pap'rs etc	
	" 27	Tom Murray, colored	" "	" "	
	" 29	Charles Brown, colored	" "	House broken open, robbed	
	" 27	William Davis, colored	" "	" "	
	" 26	Stephen Strain, colored	" "	" "	
	" 28	Alexander Brown, colored	" "	Robbery, etc	
	" 25	P. M. Williams, colored	Armed mob	House sacked, etc	Estimated loss $2083, City currency.
Jefferson, Left Bank.	October	Frederick Ellis, colored	Charles C. Clayton, white	Shot, dangerously wounded	Accused arrested.
	"	Frank James, colored	Charles Wire, colored	Shot and wounded	Accused arrested.
	"	Antoine Cardenas, white girl	Sam'l Milton, colored	Rape and murder	Accused arrested.
	" 23	Dennis Frick, colored	Disguised persons	Shot and killed	These parties were confined in jail at time.
	" 23	Sam Milton, colored	"	Shot and seriously wounded	
	" 23	Freedman	Unknown	Killed, shot in the head	In hands of Grand Jury.
	" 23	John Moylan, D'pty Sheriff	Peter Blessine and Fessie	Life threatened	In hands of Grand Jury.
East Feliciana	Rep't'd Oct. 10	Freedman	Mr. Carter, white	Assault and Battery	These cases referred to civil authorities.
	" " 10	"	Do.	Shot at	
	" " 10	"	Samuel Stafford, white	Beaten	
	" " 10	Freedwoman	Do.	"	
	" " 10	"	Not stated	"	
Tensas and Concordia.	October 1	Henry Skinner, colored	Singleton Parks, colored	Murder	On Black Hawk Plantation; accused arrested.
	October 6	Wesley Gregory, colored	Joe Porter, colored	Murder	Accused acquitted on the plea of self-defense.
Ouachita and Jackson.	October 14	Mitchell Allen	Three Disguised men	Shot and killed	*

* Near Crew Lake, a few miles from Monroe, was shot six times; accused rode off shouting Ku-Klux; no clue to perpetrators.

List of Murders and Outrages, etc.—(Continued.)

PARISHES.	When Com'ted.	On whom Committed.	By whom Committed.	Nature of Outrage.	Remarks.
Catahoula.	Rep't'd Oct. 10	One white man	Not stated	Hung	Were accused of stealing.
	" " 10	Two freedmen	"	Driven from parish	
	" " 10	Bureau Agent	"	Shot at twice	*
Natchitoches, Sabine and Winn.	October 28	Dennis Lyle, colored	Armed white men	Life attempted	Came to house at night asking shelter at time of committing deed.
	" 28	Randall Lyle, colored	Armed white men	Shot and wounded	**
	" 31	Anderson West, colored	James Wiley, white	Lives threatened	For political reasons.
	" 31	James Watson			
	" 31	Joe Smith, colored	Dr. Addison, white		
	" 31	Thomas Alexander, colored	Fete Meyers, white		
		Benjamin Harrison, colored	Eugene Jordan, white	Killed	In August last. ***
Caldwell. ††	October 31	Freedboy	Frank Pain, white	Dragged about three miles with rope about his neck.	
	" 31	Norment Nobles, colored	Frank Pain, white	Whipped	†
	" 31	John Jackson, colored	Citizens of parish, white	Lives threatened	
	" 31	Davis Adams, colored		"	
	" 31	Martin Cannel, colored		"	
Rapides.	October 10	R. O. Butler, white	James Butler, colored	Assault and battery	Accused escaped.
	" 15	Office Rapides Tribune	Not stated	Broken up	Republican paper; part of press taken off, type and cases scattered in street.
St. Landry and Calcasieu.	Rep't'd Oct. 20.	†††			
St. Mary.	October 17	H. H. Pope, Sheriff	Persons unknown	Killed	Coroner's inquest.
	" 17	Valentine Chase, P'sh Judge	"	Killed	No clue to perpetrators.
	" 17	Attakapas Register	"	Destroyed	A Republican paper. ‡

* Private parties also make affidavit of receiving letters signed K. K. K. of their lives being threatened, etc.

** Supposed to be identified with case of freedman under head of Bossier and Caddo, month of November.

*** Supposed to be the same as case of Benjamin L. Vardison reported in August last.

† It is stated that in the last three cases the freedmen went with Sheriff to execute warrant in arresting Frank Pain—that they in turn were pursued and had to flee for their lives from about fifty armed men, of whom Frank Pain, Frank Stevens, Daniel Wade and Charles Legnosky were recognized.

†† Reports of colored people being killed for reason of political opinions are received, but no specific cases reported. In Vidalia, Louisiana, it is also stated that a band of desperadoes appeared in Columbia, and then dispersed over the forest and waylaid the roads, for the purpose of killing Judges T. S. Crawford, Wade H. Haugh and Mr. J. H. Crawford, and that it is impossible to execute the laws of the country.

††† One freedman found dead in road three miles from Opelousas. Others reported as found in different parts of parish. No action reported.

‡ Press and type taken out and destroyed. Editors left for New Orleans.

List of Murders and Outrage, etc.—(Continued.)

PARISHES.	When Com'ted.	On whom Committed.	By whom Committed.	Nature of Outrage.	Remarks.
Lafayette and Vermillion.	October 11	Dick Arcenaux, colored	Persons unknown	Shot and killed	No clue to murderers.
	" 16	Joseph Martin, colored and his mother, age 75, col	D. H. Corcoran, Durio, and T. Bernard, white	Killed	Accused discharged for want of evidence.
	October 16	Peter, colored	Persons unknown	"	
	" 16	Pierre, colored	"	"	
	" 16	Two freedmen		Found dead	Floating in Vermillion Bayou.
	October 30	Two freedmen	Persons unknown	Murdered	*
Caddo and Bossier.	October 14	Robert Gray, colored	Charles Wasson	Killed	** In Shreveport; no action taken.
	October 10	***			
	October 31	†			
	October 31	R. L. Faulkner,	Armed white men	Violent assault and bat'ry lives threatened, etc.	For political causes; no action taken.
	" 31	One freedman	" "		
	" 31	Alfred Hazen		Killed	
	" 27	Charles Stokes, colored	Disguised white men	Murdered	Were alleged participators in Bossier riot, were in charge of civil authorities at time of being killed.
	" 27	Henry Williams, colored	Disguised white men	Murdered	
	" 27	Frank Dupre, colored	Disguised white men	Murdered	
	" 14	Solomon Thomas, colored	Charles Wasson, white	Life attempted	At time of murder of Robt. Gray, col.
	" 17	Solomon Thomas, colored	Five white men	Life attempted	House broken open; has fled from the parish.
	" 10	Four Freedmen	Calhoun, Johnson, and about ten others, white	Murdered	Were taken from Shreveport in day time to R. White's Island and killed.
	" 11	Henry Dixon, colored	P. Ward, Mr. Cox, J. Williard, J. Arnold and others	Murdered	At Four Mile Spring, west of Shreveport.
	" 12	One freedman	Austin and others, white	Murdered	Shot; body thrown in river.
	" 12	— Forceman, colored	Wright, ex-deputy sheriff and others	Lives attempted	Forceman not killed for fear of recognition, as they were identified.
	" 12	One freed girl			
	" 14	One Freedman	White men	Murdered	In Fourth Ward, near Shreveport, was tied, taken from home; not heard from since.
Claiborne.	Rep't'd Oct. 10	††			

* In Lafayette parish, near the St. Landry line; a coroner's inquest held; no clue to the murderers. The two freedmen were leading colored Republicans.

** The body of a freedman was found floating in Red River.

*** States that probably sixty or seventry freedmen have been killed in connection with Bossier Riots, in addition to those previously reported.

† Information received that armed bodies of men have been scouring Bossier parish in search of freedmen supposed to be implicated in killing of Brownlee and Ogden in recent riots, and killing them when found—that the civil athorities take no action in bringing guilty parties to justice.

†† Much uneasiness and alarm amongst freedmen, caused by the outspoken approval by the whites of the acts of killing etc., of freedmen in Bossier parish

List of Murders and Outrages, etc.—(Continued.)

PARISHES.	When Com'ted.	On whom Committed.	By whom Committed.	Nature of Outrage.	Remarks.
Claiborne.	Rep't'd Oct. 20..	Wm. Wallace, colored.........	Parties unknown................	Murdered	Body found in woods. *
	Rep't'd Oct. 31..	Freed people.........................	Armed white men...........	Lives threatened..............	
	Rep't'd Oct. 31..	**			
	October 26.......	A. Brown, colored..............	Not stated........................	Shot and wounded..............	Wounded in hand at his own house, but made his escape.
	" 31.......	Henry Shelton, colored......	Disguised white men.......	Shot through lungs...........	Wounds considered fatal.
	" 31.......	Ben Johnson, colored.........	" "	Assault and battery..........	Nearly beaten death.
	" 31.......	Freedwoman	" "	" "	And severely beaten.
	" 31.......	One freedwoman................	" "	First ravished and then nearly beaten to death......	***

* Wallace was taken from home the night of September 26th, by four white men. Armed white men were going through the parish disarming all freedmen; much oppression and a perfect system of terror exists.

** A party of armed and disguised men visited the house of Joshua Scanlin, colored, on 20th inst., and failing to find him drew their arms on his wife and other women present, threatening them with instant death if they did not discover his, Scanlins, whereabouts. Case referred to civil authorities. No action taken.

*** The parties committing the above consisted of nine or ten men armed and disguised; they started from Haysville, about twelve miles from Homer, and travelled south in the direction of Minden, stopping at all cabins, committing violence and maltreating women. The freedpeople will not divulge anything, even of acts committed against themselves, for fear of death. No action taken by civil authorities.

I certify that the foregoing is a correct list of the murders and outrages as reported to these headquarters during the month of October, 1868.

LUCIUS H. WARREN,

Brevet Lieutenant Colonel United States Army, Captain Thirty-Ninth Infantry,

Acting Assistant Adjutant General.

SUMMARY—OCTOBER
- Killed.................... 118
- Wounded.................. 16
- Maltreated................ 45

NOTE—Armed bodies of men scour Bossier parish, capturing freedmen and killing them when found. Freedmen reported as found dead in the roads, in different parts of the parish. — Parties in Claiborne parish traverse the parish, stopping at all cabins, committing violence and maltreating women. — Freedmen will not testify from fear of death.

List of Murders and other Outrages Reported to Headquarters Bureau Refugees, Freedmen and Abandoned Lands, District of Louisiana, during the month of November, 1868.

PARISHES.	When Com'ted.	On whom Committed.	By whom Committed.	Nature of Outrage.	Remarks.
Orleans, Left Bank.	November 3	James Mason, colored	Unknown	Shop broken open; contents destroyed	Estimated loss $350; two shots fired in shop.
	" 3	James Johnson, colored			
St. Bernard and Plaquemine, Left Bank.	November 20	General Taylor, colored	Civil authorities	Long incarceration without bringing them to trial or examination	In confinement six months.
	" 20	William Brown, colored			In confinement seven months.
	" 20	John Smith, colored			In confinement one month.
	" 3	Arnold Lewis, colored	Six Spaniards	Murdered	Referred to civil authorities.
St. Helena and Livingston.	Rep't'd Nov. 15	Mumford McCoy, colored	Armed white men	Life threatened	Has fled parish.
Iberville and West Baton Rouge.	November 6	Colored Baptist Church	Unknown incendiaries	Destroyed by fire	
East Feliciana.	November	Mort, colored	Parties unknown	Assault and battery	For political reasons.
	"	Daniel, colored	"	" "	For political reasons.
	"	Henry, colored	"	" "	For political reasons.
	"	Henry Jourdan, colored		Life threatened; notified to leave parish	For political reasons.
	" 6	Louisa, colored	Dr. Felix De Lee	Assault and battery	Referred to civil authorities.
	" 6	H. E. Burton, Bureau Agent	"	Life threatened etc	
	Rep't'd Nov. 10	Smith, colored	De Witt Carter	Thr't'ng to kill, shot at twice	Referred to civil authorities.
	" 10	Freedman, name not given	" "	Thr't'ng to kill, shot at twice	
	" 10	*			
St. Mary.	Rep't'd Nov. 13	Washington Smith, colored	Names not given	Life threatened, etc	For political reasons has fled parish.
	November 10	Charles Nelson, colored	Joseph Mallon, white	Shot, wounded in left leg	Freedman instructed to make affidavit in justice court; nothing since heard regarding same.
	" 10	John Newell, colored	" "	Shot, severely wounded in leg and arm.	
	" 17	George Johnson, colored	Joseph Geary	Life threatened, etc	Referred to civil authorities.
	" 13	Mr. Mentz, Sheriff	K. K. K	" "	18th inst.; coffin with inscription, etc., placed at his door.
St. Martin.	Rep't'd Nov. 10	Eugene Jackson, colored	Don Louis Pellein	Driven from plantation by force of arms	About July 5, 1868, pay refused for labor; case referred to Parish Judge.

* In this parish freedmen complain of being ordered to leave plantations where they have been working, and it is reported that several outrages have been committed by disguised men, styling themselves Ku Klux.

List of Murders and Outrages, etc.—(Continued.)

PARIHES.	When Com'ted.	On whom Committed.	By whom Committed.	Nature of Outrage.	Remarks.
Natchitoches, Sabine and Winn.	November 10	*			
Avoyelles.	Rep't'd Nov. 10	**			
Ouachita and Jackson.	November 3	Freedmen, party of	White men	Not stated	Near Filhails plantation; accused arrested and under bonds.
	" 5	Two freedmen	Not stated	Murdered	Suspected parties arrested; in jail awaiting trial.
	" 5	One freedmen	"	Wounded	
	" 5	***			
Catahoula.	Rep't'd Nov. 10	Freedmen	Planters	Defrauding of wages and share of crops	Many complaints of this nature made.
	November 4	Emanuel Right, colored	Jones Grange and five others, whites	Over five hundred lashes and shot	Near Henry Green's plantation.
	Rep't'd Nov. 18	Freedmen, No. not stated	Not reported	Lives threatened, etc	Freedmen are fleeing from parish.
	" 18	†			
Pointe Coupee and W'st Felicians	December 1	One freedmen	A supposed white man	Killed	Warrant issued for his arrest Dec. 5, '68.
Union and Morehouse.	November 22	Green Foster, colored	William Pucker, white	Shot and badly wounded	Pucker arrested, under $2500 bonds.
	" 20	One freedman	Unknown	Killed	
	" 20	L. Hubbard, white	Freedman	Seriously stabbed	††
Bossier and Caddo.	November 5	One freedman	Unknown	Murdered	About two miles from Shreveport.
	" 5	Teacher Bureau school	Not stated	Life threatened	Has left parish.
	Rep't'd Nov. 10	†††			

* Many freedmen make complaints of being compelled to vote under compulsion; that they are threatened and fearful of personal violence and other complaints of a similar nature. No action taken.

** Freedmen complain of being discharged, etc., for voting contrary to wishes of employers, etc

*** Subsequent reports state accused parties released, under bonds, courts having adjourned to January 1st, 1869.

† The cause of these acts is the refusal to vote as the whites demand; these cases occurred in the portion of parish known as Sicily Island; no action reported.

†† Freedman killed had a difficulty with Hubbard a few days previous, in which Hubbard was stabbed. No evidence to implicate him (Hubbard) in the killing.

††† That dead bodies continue to float down the river from Bossier parish.

List of Murders and Outrages, etc.—(Continued.)

PARISHES.	When Com'ted.	On whom Committed.	By whom Committed.	Nature of Outrage.	Remarks.
Bossier and Caddo.	Rep't'd Nov. 11.	One freedman	Unknown	Murdered	*
	" 11.	One freedman	Unknown	Murdered	**
	November 11	***			
	Rep't'd Nov. 20.	Squire Jones, colored	Armed white men	Life threatened	†
	" 30.	††			
Claiborne.	November 5	Printing office of W. Jasper Blackburn	Persons unknown	Destroyed	No clue to perpetrators.
	" 20	Not stated	Not stated	Murder	Two cases reported; no definite information received.
	" 10	†††			
St. Martin.	Rep't'd Dec. 1.	Joe, colored	Arthur Barras, white	Shot and killed	‡
Lafayette.	November 21	Laura Cerina Perkins, col'd.	White men	Shot in arm	Both have fled from parish; no clue to identity of perpetrators.
	" 21	Samuel Perkins, colored	White men	Life threatened	
	Rep't'd Nov. 30.	Marcel, colored	Parties unknown	Killed	On plantation of M'me Ralph Forman; no clue as yet discovered of the murderers.
	November 21	Pierre Jean Louis, colored	Ralph Forman, Jas. Tallis Lee Smith, Durecur Smith, Frank Plaisance and others	Shot, badly wounded, supposed mortally	

* Body found 9th inst., about seven miles from Shreveport; a paper was attached to the body warning "death to any person who removes the body."

** Found dead in the woods near Lawyer Looney's place, apparently shot and dragged off the road.

*** Statements in regard to the riot in Bossier parish corroborated, resulting in the massacre of fully one hundred freedmen, and one freedwoman, on September 30th, and October 1st; states one instance where nine freedmen were taken to bank of Red River and told to swim for their lives; that they plunged in and as they arose to the surface were shot, not one escaping. Again, three freedmen, while engaged in making a coffin, for one of their friends who was killed, were brutally murdered.

† Has been in the woods since the time of the riot; has been hunted and pursued by armed white men intending to kill him.

†† That the District Court is in session; that two white men have been found guilty of murder, for the killing of two freedmen immediately after the election, at about two miles from Shreveport. Sentence has not yet been passed upon them.

††† Information has been received that the freedmen are in complete subjection to the will of the whites, by whom they were compelled to vote, subject to their dictation, under penalty of death from K. K. K., etc.

‡ About the middle of November. No coroner's inquest or examination held by civil authorities, at the time; Warrant since issued, and case to be examined, December 3d.

List of Murders and Outrages, etc.—(Continued.)

PARISHES.	When Com'ted.	On whom Committed.	By whom Committed.	Nature of Outrage.	Remarks.
Lafayette.	November 21.....	*			
East Baton Rouge.	November 30.....	Sid Rice, colored..............	Nat Magruder, white.......	Shot, wounded in head.....	No action taken.

* On the night of the 21st his gun and two horses were taken from him by a gang of armed men, of whom the above parties were recognized. The accused were arrested. Judge A. S. Moss visited Pierre and took his testimony, as he was supposed to be dying. Pierre states that Tallis snapped two caps at him; that Ralph Forman then shot him; on 25th inst., Forman escaped and went to Texas; the other four examined before Judge Moss, an alibi proven, and were discharged.

I certify that the foregoing is a correct list of murders and outrages reported to these headquarters during the time above specified.

LUCIUS H. WARREN,

Brevet Lieutenant Colonel United States Army. Captain Thirty-Ninth Infantry,

Acting Assistant Adjutant General.

SUMMARY—NOVEMBER
- Number killed....................114
- Number wounded................. 7
- Number maltreated............... 24

List of Murders and Outrages Reported to Heodquarters Bureau Refugees, Freedmen and Abandoned Lands, from the Parish of St. Bernard, Louisiana, in connection with the Riots of October 25 and 26, 1868.

When Com'ted.	On whom Committed.	By whom Committed.	Nature of Outrage.	Remarks.
October 25	Pablo Fillio, white	Andy Mayo, Thompson Morgan and others, col'd	Killed	Pablo Filio's house burnt. See recapitulation.
" 25	Mike Curtis, white	Syca John Bauef, white	Killed	Curtis was a Metropolitan Policeman; accused a member of Democratic procession.
" 25	One white man, Democratic procession	Eugene Lock, colored	Wounded	
" 25	Eugeno Locke, colored	Valery Veillon, white	Killed	
" 25	Thompson Morgan, colored,	Supposed by Pablo Fillio, white	Killed and body consumed in burning house	
" 25	Isaiah Johnson, colored	Pablo Fillio, white	Wounded	
" 25	Little Jacob, colored	" "	"	
" 25	John Proctor, colored	" "	"	
" 25	Billy Smith, colored	" "	"	
" 25	Henry Sterling, colored	Democratic procession	"	
" 25	Spencer Jones, aged fifty, colored	Vallery Veillon, white	"	
" 26	Pierre Golet, colored	Julian Cerpas, white	Killed	
" 26	Res Voltaire, colored	Treme, Lecano, Porter and party, all whites	"	
" 26	Baptist Clemir, colored		"	
" 26	Emile Agenor, colored		"	
" 26	François, colored		"	
" 26	Henry, colored		"	
" 26	Joseph Cole, colored	Vallery Veillon, white	"	
" 26	Felis Thomas, freedwoman	Alma Marshall, white	Wounded	
" 26	William Trahock, colored	Philip Goodyear, white	"	
" 26	David Jones, colored	" "	"	
" 26	—— Marshall, colored	Julien Serpas	"	
" 26	Alfred Lee, colored	Parties unknown, white	Wounded	
" 26	One freedman	" "	"	On one DeCrais' place; names not given.
" 26	"	" "	"	
" 27	Nelson, aged ninety, colored	" "	Killed	
" 27	Sophia Marshall, freedw'm'n	Julian Serpas, white	Wounded	
November 1	Eugene Joseph, colored	Sarapio Tona, white	"	
November 3	Arnold Lewis, colored	Parties unknown, white	Killed	

NOTE—In addition to the cases above specified, fifty-four minor outrages have been reported as committed on freedmen by whites on October 25, 1868, consisting of destruction of household goods, robbery of clothing, household effects, money, arms, registration papers, United States discharges, and everything of a portable nature they possessed. Twenty robberies of registration papers and four discharges from United States service are specified.

Murders and Outrages in St. Bernard Parish, of Riots of October 25 *and* 26, 1868.

	Designation.	Killed.	Wounded.	Minor Outrages.	Total.
SUMMARY	Whites........................	2	1	1	4
	Freed People..................	11	15	54	80
	Aggregate	13	16	55	84

I certify that the foregoing is a correct list of the murders and outrages reported at these headquarters in connection with the riot in the parish of St. Bernard, La., October 26, and 25, 1868.

LUCIUS H. WARREN,

Brevet Lieutenant Colonel United States Army, Captain Thirty-Ninth Infantry,

Acting Assistant Adjutant General.

RECAPITULATION.

Parishes.	Supplemental Report. Number killed positively sworn to	Supplemental Report. Number wounded by gunshot.	Supplemental Report. Number otherwise maltreated.	Supplemental. Aggregate.	Original Report. Number killed.	Original Report. Number wounded by gunshot.	Original Report. Number otherwise maltreated.	Original. Aggregate.	Total Both Repotrs. Number killed.	Total Both Repotrs. Number wounded by gunshot.	Total Both Repotrs. Number maltreated.	Both Reports. Aggregate.	Remarks.
Ascension	...	...	2	2	...	...	...	...	...	...	2	2	
Assumption	...	...	...	...	1	...	...	1	1	...	...	1	
Avoyelles	...	...	...	...	2	4	5	11	2	4	5	11	
Bienville	1	2	...	3	1	...	2	3	2	2	2	6	
Bossier	162	1	6	169	5	...	3	8	167	1	9	177	It is estimated that many more persons were killed in the Bossier *negro hunt* than the estimate given in supplemental report.
Caddo	42	...	4	46	1	1	4	6	43	1	8	52	
Caldwell	...	...	...	...	...	...	...	...	...	...	...	...	
Calcasieu	...	...	...	...	3	...	...	3	3	...	...	3	
Carroll	...	...	...	...	3	...	2	5	3	...	2	5	
Catahoula	20	...	6	26	11	...	1	12	31	...	7	38	
Claiborne	...	...	...	...	7	1	7	15	7	1	7	15	
Concordia	...	...	...	...	...	1	...	1	...	1	...	1	
De Soto	2	1	4	7	...	1	6	7	2	2	10	14	Number of Republicans illegally deprived of their right to vote, Nov 3, 1868, 2000.

www.ingramcontent.com/pod-product-compliance
Lightning Source LLC
LaVergne TN
LVHW020239110826
845151LV00003B/978
* 9 7 8 1 4 2 5 5 2 9 5 4 3 *